The Aion Lectures

Marie-Louise von Franz, Honorary Patron

**Studies in Jungian Psychology
by Jungian Analysts**

Daryl Sharp, General Editor

The Aion Lectures

Exploring the Self in
C.G. Jung's *Aion*

Edward F. Edinger

Edited by Deborah A. Wesley

Canadian Cataloguing in Publication Data

Edinger, Edward F. (Edward Ferdinand), 1922-
  The Aion lectures: exploring the self in C.G. Jung's Aion

(Studies in Jungian psychology by Jungian analysts; 71)

Based on an edited transcript of lectures delivered at the
C.G. Jung Institute of Los Angeles, 1988-89.

Includes bibliographical references and index.

ISBN 978-0-919123-72-4

1. Jung, C.G. (Carl Gustav), 1875-1961. Aion:
Beiträge zur Symbolik des Selbst. 2. Symbolism.
3. Psychology, Religious. 4. Self.
I. Wesley, Deborah A. II. Title. III. Series.

BF175.4.R44E35 1996   150.19'54   C95-931871-2

INNER CITY BOOKS
53 Alvin Avenue, Toronto, ON M4T 2A8, Canada.
Telephone 416-927-0355
Toll-free in Canada and U.S.: 1-888-927-0355
www.innercitybooks.net / **booksales@innercitybooks.net**

Honorary Patron: Marie-Louise von Franz.
Publisher and General Editor: Daryl Sharp.
Senior Editor: Victoria B. Cowan.
Office Manager: Scott Milligen.
IT Manager: Sharpconnections.com.
Editorial Assistance: David Sharp, J. Morgan, E. Jefferson.

INNER CITY BOOKS was founded in 1980 to promote the
understanding and practical application of the work of C. G. Jung.

Cover: The Mithraic god Aion (detail of illustration below, page 10).

Index by Daryl Sharp

Printed and bound in Canada by
Thistle Printing Limited

Contents

See final page for other books by Edward F. Edinger

Illustrations and Credits

Editor's Foreword

More than a few readers have picked up C.G. Jung's *Aion* and then put it down again, overwhelmed by his flood of material from classical, Christian, Gnostic and alchemical writers. It is not easy to bridge the various source materials and to follow the thread of Jung's thought, and there has been little to help readers through this rough terrain. Despite the importance of its subject—the changes in the God-image during two thousand years of the Christian era—and its relevance as this millennium comes to an end, the book has not been widely read.

Finally, in 1988-89, a guide to *Aion* appeared in the form of a series of seminar lectures by Edward Edinger. The audience was crammed into a lecture room at the C.G. Jung Institute of Los Angeles, and consisted primarily of therapists in training to be analysts, with a scattering of analysts and interested lay people.

The atmosphere was serious but with an undercurrent of excitement. There were some questions and exchanges between members of the audience and Dr. Edinger. By and large, however, those present simply listened, eager for the clarification being brought to Jung's difficult work. This book is based on an edited transcript of those lectures.*

The particular forum in which the lectures were presented gave rise to a text that actually encompasses two somewhat distinct levels. Primarily, Dr. Edinger leads the reader through *Aion* chapter by chapter, explaining difficult references, extending and discussing quotations from Jung's source material, filling in background and supplying examples.

The reader will notice a second level. Many of Dr. Edinger's examples arise from analytic practice, and at times one realizes that one is in the presence of a master analyst teaching apprentices. There are numerous seminal remarks about the nature and practice of depth analysis.

The text is supplemented by the diagrams used to illustrate the original lectures. They have been reconceived and redrawn from the author's original sketches by Thornton Ladd, for whose generous help and unfailing enthusiasm I am very grateful.

Deborah A. Wesley
Los Angeles

---

* Audio tapes are available from the C.G. Jung Bookstore in Los Angeles.

8

Author's Note

Truly it can be said that Jung's *Aion* laid the foundation for a whole new department of human knowledge, a scholarly discipline that one might call archetypal psychohistory. It is based on the application of the insights of depth psychology to the data of cultural history. The historical process can now be seen as the self-manifestation of the archetypes of the collective unconscious as they emerge and develop in time and space through the actions and fantasies of humanity.

In *Aion* Jung took the archetype of the God-image (the Self) as his subject and demonstrated how it has revealed itself progressively in the course of the Christian aeon. It is an awesome work that makes great demands on the reader. The present book is an attempt to mitigate this difficulty and to make *Aion* somewhat more accessible.

I thank Deborah Wesley warmly for her skill and devotion in editing this difficult material.

Edward F. Edinger
Los Angeles

The Mithraic god Aion (Roman, 2nd-3rd century).

Preface

Aion: Researches into the Phenomenology of the Self is volume 9, part 2, of Jung's Collected Works. It is one of Jung's last projects, published when he was seventy-six.

It must be acknowledged at the start that all Jung's late works are very difficult. After his illness in 1944 when he had a new birth, so to speak, he decided he was going to write the way he wanted to. His readers would have to meet him where he was, rather than his going to great lengths to meet them where they might be, and that has put an extra burden upon readers of these late works.

My intent is to make Jung's material more accessible to modern readers by expanding on its historical background and by showing how the Self manifests itself psychologically in everyday experience.

I suggest three guiding principles in reading *Aion*. The first is to recognize Jung's magnitude. Before starting the book, you should realize that Jung's consciousness vastly surpasses your own. If he puts something in a way that seems unnecessarily difficult, the proper procedure is to assume that he knows what he is doing and knows something you don't. If you make the assumption that you know better than he does and start out with a critical attitude—don't bother; the book isn't for you. Jung's depth and breadth are absolutely awesome. We are all Lilliputians by comparison, so when we encounter Jung we feel inferior, and we don't like it. To read Jung successfully we must begin by accepting our own littleness; then we become teachable.

Principle number two is to understand Jung's method. Especially in his later works, Jung writes about the psyche in what I call a presentational way, by which I mean he presents us with psychic facts rather than with theories about the facts. We are so used to living out of a conceptual context that we spare ourselves the encounter with the raw facts. And because we are not familiar with the psychic facts Jung presents, they seem alien and disconnected. Our task is to become familiar with the facts Jung gives us. As we gradually gain that familiarity, their inner connections and the whole presentational method become visible. This leads into a mode of thinking different from the usual; we are used to linear thinking, whereas the presentation of psychological facts by the method of amplification can be described as "cluster thinking," in which one has a central image and finds a cluster of related images connected to it.[1] It is important that we

---

[1] See below, p. 14. Other examples can be found in my *Anatomy of the Psyche: Alchemical Symbolism in Psychotherapy,* where before each chapter there is a cluster of images associated with an alchemical operation.

become familiar with cluster thinking because this is the way to amplify and assimilate dream images. If we are not thoroughly comfortable in this mode of functioning, we won't be able to penetrate the meaning of dreams.

Once past the first couple of chapters, *Aion* concerns themes and images of the objective psyche. I suggest that as you read the material presented in *Aion*, you ask yourself what theme is being presented. Jung's method is calculated to teach us to think thematically, so that when we perceive one theme or image, amplification of it leads to related images, and so on, into an increasingly larger cluster. The study of *Aion* can help the reader in learning how to perceive and extract the theme and image embedded in a body of material. Initially this is not easy to do, but it is important because when one is presented with a dream and can't recognize its thematic content, one is lost. Associations can be elicited from the patient, but without recognizing the theme one won't have anything to contribute. Locating the theme, one can then offer parallels.

Principle number three is what I would call the "fruit cake" principle. By this I mean that you must read Jung the way you eat fruit cake—very slowly. The reading is exceedingly rich, exceedingly delicious, because it is the richness of the psyche itself which is being presented. But it is very concentrated, and especially so in *Aion*. Jung just alludes to vast areas of symbolic reference because he does not want to write too long a book, and because these areas are so familiar to him that it would be boring to him to spell it all out. He just alludes, and one has these kernels, these rich pieces of nut and heavy fruit which have to be masticated and digested slowly in order to be appreciated.

Aion can be assimilated only in very small bites. This means that one must read one sentence at a time and become familiar with every term and reference in that sentence. There is a great temptation, when we encounter things with which we are not familiar, to skip over them thinking that the next sentence will explain what has been bypassed. This won't happen in *Aion*. If you skip unfamiliar matters in this text you will soon be lost, so I urge you to work with a dictionary and an encyclopedia at your side, and whenever you come to something unfamiliar, look it up. This means that you will be looking into a Latin dictionary, and you will be looking into historical matters to a considerable extent, for *Aion* is in part a book about history. It is useful to realize that Jung is discussing the cultural history of the human race as though it were the case history of a single patient. Jung has the entire record of that patient at his finger-tips, but few of us do, which means we must fill in our gaps as we go along.

The decision to present this material began with a dream of my own, in September 1987:

> Jung is speaking about his writing of *Aion*. He says that while he was writing it, he received a lot of criticism because of its content. However, he kept right on in order "to complete his escrow account with history."

Anyone who has bought a house knows what an escrow account is. An escrow is a written agreement such as a deed or a bond, put into the custody of a third party, and not in effect until certain conditions are fulfilled. My dream tells us that Jung put *Aion* in escrow with history. It means that the grantees, the receivers of this volume, have to fulfill certain conditions before it will become available to them. We are the grantees, the receivers of this account with history. I think this means that we have to work on understanding the book in order for the grant to take effect. *Aion* is just going to sit on library shelves unless or until the receivers of it fulfill the conditions necessary to understand what it means. We would all like *Aion* to become available to us, to move into that new house, but it is still in escrow, so to speak.

Jung too had a dream concerning *Aion*. In a letter to Victor White on December 19, 1947, Jung says:

> Not very long after I wrote to you, I simply had to write a new essay I did not know about what. It occurred to me I should discuss some of the finer points about anima, animus, shadow, and last but not least the self. I was against it, because I wanted to rest my head. Lately I had suffered from severe sleeplessness and I wanted to keep away from all mental exertions. In spite of everything, I felt forced to write on blindly, not seeing at all what I was driving at. Only after I had written about 25 pages in folio, it began to dawn on me that Christ—not the man but the divine being—was my secret goal. It came to me as a shock, as I felt utterly unequal to such a task. A dream told me that my small fishing boat had been sunk and that a giant (whom I knew from a dream about 30 years ago) had provided me with a new, beautiful seagoing craft about twice the size of my former boat. Then I knew—nothing doing! I had to go on. My further writing led me to the archetype of the God-man and to the phenomenon of synchronicity which adheres to the archetype. Thus I came to discuss the *ichthys* and the then new aeon of Pisces . . ., the prophecy of the Antichrist and the development of the latter from 1000 A.D. in mysticism and alchemy until the recent developments, which threaten to overthrow the Christian aeon altogether.[2]

Another comment concerning *Aion* was made to Margaret Ostrowski-Sachs in a private conversation, which she recorded. Jung said to her:

> Before my illness [in 1944] I had often asked myself if I were permitted to publish or even speak of my secret knowledge. I later set it all down in *Aion*. I realized it was my duty to communicate these thoughts, yet I doubted whether I was allowed to give expression to them. During my illness I received confirmation and I now knew that everything had meaning and that everything was perfect.[3]

---

[2] *Letters,* vol. 1, pp. 479ff.
[3] *From Conversations with C.G. Jung,* p. 68.

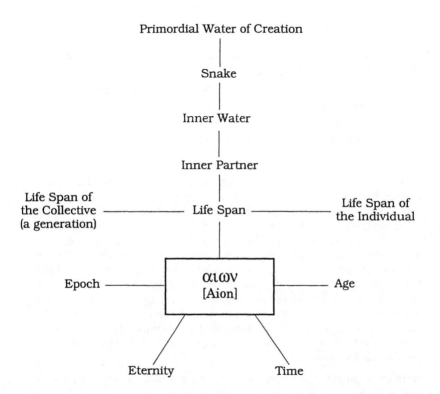

Figure 1. "Aion" Cluster.
Major ideas and images related to the Greek word *aion* (αιων)
as it has been used over the centuries.

1
Introduction

The title *Aion* refers to a very complex symbolic image which has evolved through the centuries and has a rich set of meanings. All words are psychic organisms; each has at its core some fundamental human experience and there will be an image of that experience embedded in the etymology of the word. As one traces the way its usage has evolved, a whole organism unfolds. The word *aion* is a particularly rich example.

Ancient Greek had three words for "time": *chronos, kairos* and *aion. Chronos* referred to quantitative, linear time; it would be the scientific term. *Kairos* referred to the special moment, the special content of a particular time; it would be the right moment, the time of fulfillment, for instance Christ's saying "My time *[kairos]* has not yet come." The third term, *aion,* is more diffuse and ambiguous, but has come to mean a very long period of time, something like an age, or even eternity or forever. The word *aion* is linked to other Greek words which should also be mentioned—*aionios* meaning without beginning or end, eternal or forever; and *aidios* meaning eternal. Both words have as their root the term *aion.*

The use of the word *aion* goes back to Homer, where the term *aion* is often used as parallel to psyche, to soul, or life. In Hesiod, it denotes life span; in Aeschylus, it refers to a generation, so that it can mean the time one has already lived or will live. It can relate to past as well as to future, and as the philosophers picked it up, it came to refer to the far future and to eternity.

In Homer's *Iliad,* in speaking of the death of a warrior, Hera says to Zeus, "When his psyche and *aion* have left him, then send death to bear him away."[4] Here the term means life span, a separate reality, a kind of inner partner that is practically identical to the soul. In another place Homer identifies *aion* with an inner water which is wasted away in tears. For instance, when Odysseus is weeping for his return home, Homer says, "His eyes were never dry of tears, and his sweet *[aion]* was ebbing away, as he longed mournfully for his return."[5] Here is the thought that the *aion* is a kind of inner water and there is only a limited quantity of it. When it is all used up, one dies.

In Aeschylus' *Agamemnon, aion* means quite explicitly a life partner; he is the source of the poet's inspiration. The chorus of elders exclaims, "The *aion* that has grown with me, inspireth of the gods, breatheth upon me persuasion, the strength of song."[6] The author is saying that "my inner *aion* inspired me to be a

---

4 Book 16, line 423.
5 *The Odyssey,* V, lines 151-153.
6 Line 105, modified.

15

poet and sing my song." In another place in Aeschylus, the word means a generation: "Old is the tale of sin I tell / but swift in retribution: / to the third *aion* it abides."[7] It means to the third generation; the guilt is passed on from one generation to another. In *Timaeus,* Plato says about the creation of the universe:

> Now the nature of the ideal being was everlasting, but to bestow this attribute in its fullness upon a creature was impossible. Wherefore he [the demiurge] resolved to have a moving image of *aion,* and . . . this image we call *chronos.*[8]

In other words, he resolved to have a moving image of eternity and this image we call time.

Plotinus finally refined this idea that time is the moving image of eternity, in this passage:

> If eternity, *[aion],* is life at rest, unchanging and identical and already unbounded, and time must exist as an image of eternity . . . then we must say that there is another lower life [corresponding to the higher life. The lower life has instead of a unity] without distance or separation, a . . . unity . . . by continuity; and instead of a complete unbounded whole, a continuous unbounded succession and instead of a whole all together, a whole which is and always will be going to come into being part by part.[9]

It is a psychologically profound notion that eternity, or *aion,* is an image of totality outside of time, whereas time is an image of that same totality spread out in a temporal sequence. This corresponds exactly to Jung's remark in *Mysterium Coniunctionis:* "The one-after-another is a bearable prelude to the deeper knowledge of the side-by-side."[10]

Aion was thought of as an inner water and it was also thought that after the death of the individual, that inner water was left as a snake; the snake was imagined as the soul of the departed one, inhabiting the tomb perhaps. All of these connections are included in figure 1, a cluster diagram showing the major references to *aion.*

This psychic organism called *aion* has also appeared in many Biblical passages. The Old Testament was translated into Greek in the third century B.C., and the word *aion* shows up there. Yahweh says to Abraham in Canaan, "All the land which thou seest, to thee will I give it, and to thy seed, for an *aion.*" (Gen. 13:15, ASV)[11] The usual translation is "forever." Yahweh says to Moses, concerning the celebration of the Passover, "You must keep these rules as an ordi-

---

[7] *Seven Against Thebes,* lines 742-744.
[8] 37D.
[9] *Enneads,* III, 7, 11.
[10] CW 14, par. 206. [CW refers throughout to C.G. Jung, *The Collected Works]*
[11] References to Bible editions are identified throughout by abbreviations, as follows: JB, Jerusalem Bible; AV, Authorized (King James) Version; DV, Douay Version; NEB, New English Bible; ASV, American Standard Version; RSV, Revised Standard Version.

nance for an *aion* for you and your children." (Exod. 12:24, JB) "For all time" is the way it is translated into English, but as you can see it does not mean exactly "for all time." This is what it means to late Western man, but not quite what it meant at the beginning.

There are some interesting uses of the word in the New Testament. For example: "Whosoever shall speak against the Holy Spirit, it shall not be forgiven him, neither in this *aion* nor in the *aion* to come." (Matt. 12:32, ASV) This is usually translated, "in this age or the next age." Again, "As therefore the tares are gathered and burned with fire, so shall it be in the end of this *aion.*" (Matt. 13:40, ASV)

From Hebrews 11:3: "Through faith we understand that the *aions* have been framed by the word of God [translated "worlds"]." (ASV) The Lord's Prayer ends: "For Thine is the kingdom, and the power and the glory to the *aions*" (Matt. 6:13, ASV)

To shift to another text, the inscription in Greek on Jung's Bollingen stone begins, as usually translated into English: "Time is a child—playing like a child —playing a board game—the kingdom of the child."[12] As a translation into German, Jung suggested the word *zeit* which in English is "time," but the Greek word which starts that inscription on the stone is the word *aion.* So it reads *"Aion* is a child playing a board game." "Time" is not exactly right; it would probably be better to say, "The age, the *aion,* is a child, playing a board game."

In late syncretism, *aion* became the name of the deity, as shown in the frontispiece of Jung's *Aion* (and above, page 10). This is the so-called Mithraic god, Aion, whom Franz Cumont describes in these words:

At the pinnacle of the divine hierarchy . . . [in Mithraic theology was] boundless Time. Sometimes they would call it aion. . . . He was represented in the likeness of a human monster with the head of a lion and his body enveloped by a serpent. The multiplicity of attributes with which his statues are loaded is in keeping with the kaleidoscopic nature of his character. He bears the scepter and the bolts of divine sovereignty[13] and holds in each hand a key as the monarch of the heavens whose portals he opens. His wings are symbolic of the rapidity of his flight. The reptile whose sinuous folds enwrap him, typifies the tortuous course of the Sun on the ecliptic; the signs of the zodiac engraved on his body and the emblems of the seasons that accompany them, are meant to represent the celestial and terrestrial phenomena that signalize the eternal flight of the years. He creates and destroys all things; he is the Lord and master of the four elements. . . . Sometimes he is identified with Destiny.[14]

---

12 Jung, *Memories, Dreams, Reflections,* p. 227.
13 In the statue used as the frontispiece of *Aion* the bolts are broken, but in other representations they can be seen.
14 *The Mysteries of Mithra,* pp. 107f.

"Destiny" would be a word for life span here, another term that belongs in this same symbolic cluster. So *aion* also means destiny. Including all these meanings, Aion becomes the total deity.

This idea of the *aion* is picked up in Gnosis, in which the initial boundless deity emanates from himself a series of thirty *aions*. The Gnostic emanation of the *aions* is another amplification or elaboration of this rich, complex psychic organism that Jung writes about. Hans Jonas describes the role of the term *aion* in Gnosticism:

> In invisible and nameless heights there was a perfect Aeon pre-existent. His name is Fore-Beginning, Fore-Father, and Abyss. [This is the original, primordial deity, named Aion.] No thing can comprehend him. Through immeasurable eternities he remained in profoundest repose. With him was . . . Thought, also called Grace and Silence. And once this Abyss took thought to project out of himself the beginning of all things, and he sank this project like a seed into the womb of the Silence that was with him, and she conceived and brought forth the Mind *(nous:* male) who is like and equal to his begetter and alone comprehends the greatness of the Father. He is also called Only-Begotten, Father, and Beginning of all beings. Together with him Truth *(Aletheia:* female) was produced, and this is the first Tetrad: Abyss and Silence, then Mind and Truth.[15]

This first tetrad is a pair of two syzygies (syzygy means pair). Further *aions* were generated out of this second pair. From them came forth Man and Church (which is again a male/female pair), and Word and Life. This then gave a total of four syzygies, and that was called the ogdoad, the first eight.

> These Aeons, produced to the glory of the Father, wished to glorify the Father by their own creations, and produced further emanations. From Word and Life issued ten additional Aeons, from Man and Church twelve, so that out of Eight and Ten and Twelve is constituted . . . thirty Aeons in fifteen pairs [and that totality was called the Pleroma].[16]

This basic image was something quite fundamental to Jung. He used some of this terminology, such as the word "pleroma." The second chapter of *Aion* is called "The Syzygy." One is not apt to know what that means unless one is familiar with this grand Gnostic conception of the origin of things.

---

[15] *The Gnostic Religion,* pp. 179f.
[16] Ibid., p. 180.

2
Jung's Foreword to *Aion*

In the Foreword to *Aion* Jung tells us that the theme of this book is the change of the psychic situation in the Christian aeon, which coincides with the astrological conception of the Platonic month of the fishes, in other words, Pisces.

The notion of the Platonic month is based on the astronomical fact of the precession of the equinoxes. Figure 2 (page 20) pictures the way the earth, the sun and the circle of the zodiac line up at various times. The largest circle represents the circle of the zodiac in the heavens. One can think of it as representing the background of the fixed stars. At the center of the figure is the sun, with the planet earth orbiting around it once a year. It can be seen that at any given time of year the sun, as viewed from the earth, will have in its background one of the zodiacal signs.

A long time ago, at the date of the spring equinox the sun appeared to be in the sign of Aries the ram. Due to the precession of the equinoxes there is a very tiny loosening, or play, of the celestial mechanism. It is not absolutely tight, so that over a long period of time the sun shifts its position relative to the background of the zodiacal signs. At the spring equinox in about 1 A.D., at the beginning of the Christian aeon, it appeared to have left the sign of Aries and started into the sign of Pisces. Now, 2,000 years later, it is about to leave the sign of Pisces and enter that of Aquarius.

Similarly, if you go back to 2,000 B.C., you find that the sun was just leaving the sign of the bull, Taurus. This movement of the sun through each zodiacal sign is called the Platonic month, and each takes approximately 2,000 years. For a complete circuit to take place, to make a Platonic year, 26,000 earth years are required. It is that astronomical fact to which astrologers have attached certain meaning, and to which Jung attaches a synchronistic meaning. The Christian aeon, which corresponds synchronistically to the 2,000-year period in which the sun occupies Pisces, is the Platonic month that is now coming to an end. That is what Jung refers to when he speaks in his Foreword of the change of psychic situation in the Christian aeon (which coincides with the astrological conception of the Platonic month of the fishes).

There are two other important statements in the Foreword which can use some elaboration. In one, Jung says, "I write as a physician, with a physician's sense of responsibility, and not as a proselyte." (page x) That word "proselyte" is *bekenner* in the German text, and perhaps could be better translated as "one confessing a faith." So Jung announces that he writes as a physician and not as one confessing a faith. I take this to mean that he is speaking out of an objective,

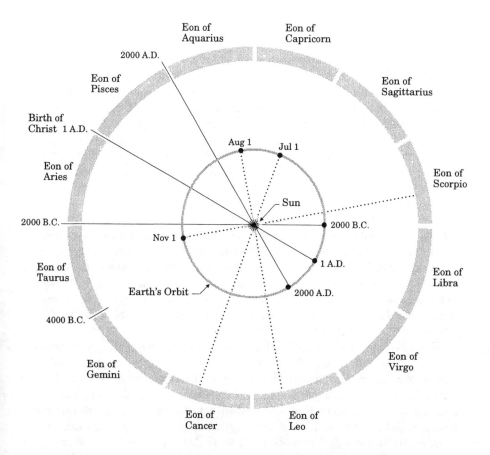

Figure 2. Precession of the Equinoxes.

The astronomical precession of the equinoxes, with the sun at the center, the orbiting earth, and, in the outer circle, the surrounding background of the fixed stars, seen from the earth as the constellations. The dotted lines indicate how the sun is seen from earth in relationship to the constellations at various times of the year. The solid lines show how the apparent position of the sun at the spring equinox has shifted over the millennia until it now appears to be leaving Pisces and entering Aquarius.

empirical point of view corresponding to the medical attitude, and also that he feels constrained by the medical ethics which dictate that one be primarily concerned for the health and well-being of the patient, that one do no harm. Jung is trying to be helpful in attempting to heal what he calls "the utopian mass psychoses of our time." (page x)

This remark about the physician's sense of responsibility raises an important issue which Jung was keenly aware of, the problem of writing for a mixed audience. Anybody who wishes to can pick up Jung's books, which means that what Jung has to say is being directed simultaneously to people of many different levels of psychological development. Jung was particularly aware of this issue because what he had to talk about could be healing panacea—saving knowledge—for some people, while it could be absolute poison for others, depending upon the reader's ability to understand what was presented. This is a grave issue and it goes a long way to explain Jung's particular mode of expression in his later work. In "Answer to Job,"[17] for instance, he speaks largely at a mythological level. Those who can make the translation get the message; those who can't won't be harmed. This is how I understand Jung's statement, "I write as a physician with a physician's sense of responsibility."

The other comment that needs elaboration is:

> Nor do I write as a scholar, otherwise I would wisely barricade myself behind the safe walls of my specialism and not, on account of my inadequate knowledge of history, expose myself to critical attack. (pages x-xi)

This is an allusion to the fact that Jungian analysts, just by the nature of their task of working with the psyche, are necessarily poachers on the posted domains of other disciplines. They are constantly venturing into scholarly realms of history and anthropology and mythology and all the arts, pursuing their prey, whose tracks are to be found in these various places. What they are tracking, of course, is the objective psyche, whose trail can be seen in all these old documents, so they have to go after it there. This makes them vulnerable to criticism from scholars who "barricade" themselves behind the "safe walls" of a specialty.

---

[17] See *Psychology and Religion: West and East,* CW 11.

3
Paragraphs 1-12

The Ego

Aion begins with a chapter on the ego. This book is built in the same way the psyche is, so naturally it starts with the ego, which we encounter first when we start to deal with the psyche in ourselves or in someone else. Jung begins the first paragraph with a good definition:

> We understand the ego as the complex factor to which all conscious contents are related. It forms, as it were, the centre of the field of consciousness; and, in so far as this comprises the empirical personality, the ego is the subject of all personal acts of consciousness. The relation of a psychic content to the ego forms the criterion of its consciousness, for no content can be conscious unless it is represented to a subject.

Jung then goes on to describe how the ego rests on two different bases, the somatic and the psychic. In paragraph 6 he says,

> It [the ego] seems to arise in the first place from the collision between the somatic factor and the environment, and, once established as a subject, it goes on developing from further collisions with the outer world and the inner.

We use the term "ego" very freely, indeed glibly, but we shouldn't, because as we reflect on the ego, on what it is and on its very existence, we see that it is a profound mystery. We can only define it as the center of consciousness. All consciousness must be registered by an ego in order to exist.

We have not been aware of the ego's existence for very long. So far as the history of Western culture is concerned, full consciousness of the ego was discovered by René Descartes. Of course, there had been some sense of individual conscious identity before then, but full awareness of the ego was discovered by him and described in his "Discourse on Method," published in 1637.

Descartes started out his philosophical reflections by doubting the existence of everything. He said that for all we know, some malevolent deity put us into a dream state so that everything we see is no more than an illusion or a fantasy, and that we can't really be sure that anything exists except for one thing that is absolutely certain: we can't doubt the existence of our own ego. His expression of that was *Cogito ergo sum,* commonly translated as "I think, therefore I am," which is not quite accurate. A better translation would be "I am conscious, therefore I am." This is the bedrock foundation of every individual's existence; we can't deny that the ego exists, because it is the seat of consciousness. Anything else can be denied.

A person who was well educated and had some knowledge of Latin had a dream related to this. The dream was a Latin sentence that started out with Descartes' statement *Cogito ergo sum* and continued with *ergo scivio deo gratias, deus est,* which means "I am conscious, therefore I am; therefore I know by God's grace, that God is." That is an interesting addition which the modern unconscious has made to Descartes's discovery of the ego.

The Cartesian discovery of the ego reoccurs in the childhood of the individual. The young child at first refers to itself in the third person, and then perhaps at about the age of three, starts to use the pronoun "I." But that does not mean that the child has conscious awareness of the ego; that only comes later, if it comes at all. For Jung it came at about the age of eleven. Here is his account:

> I was taking the long road to school from Klein-Hüningen, where we lived, to Basel, when suddenly for a single moment I had the overwhelming impression of having just emerged from a dense cloud. I knew all at once: now I am *myself!* It was as if a wall of mist were at my back, and behind that wall there was not yet an "I." But at this moment *I came upon myself.* Previously I had existed, too, but everything had merely happened to me. Now I happened to myself. Now I knew: I am myself now, now I exist. Previously I had been willed to do this and that; now *I* willed. This experience seemed to me tremendously important and new: there was "authority" in me.[18]

What Jung describes here with particular clarity happens only dimly to some people, and to many it does not happen at all. For myself, I had no clear-cut single experience that would correspond to the one Jung describes. I do remember around the age of eleven or twelve becoming fascinated with the word "I" and its meaning. I would repeat the word again and again until dark, mysterious vistas would open up. The whole notion of being a separate, conscious individual, a carrier of unique consciousness set apart from the world, took on a profound mystery for me, which was revealed just by the repetition of this word "I."

The next philosophical elaboration on this subject was by Schopenhauer (following Kant). He was an important author for Jung. This is how Schopenhauer starts his masterpiece *The World As Will and Representation:*

> "The world is my representation": this is a truth valid with reference to every living and knowing being, although man alone can bring it into reflective, abstract consciousness. If he really does so, philosophical discernment has dawned on him. It then becomes clear and certain to him that he does not know a sun and an earth, but only an eye that sees a sun, a hand that feels an earth; that the world around him is there only as representation, in other words, only in reference to another thing, namely that which represents, and this is himself. If any truth can be expressed *a priori,* it is this; for it is the statement of that form of all possible and conceivable experience, a form that is more general than all others, than time,

---

18 *Memories, Dreams, Reflections,* p. 32.

space, and causality, for all these presuppose it. . . . The division into subject and object . . . is the common form of all those classes. . . . Everything that in any way belongs and can belong to the world is inevitably associated with this being-conditioned by the subject, and it exists only for the subject. The world is representation.[19]

This theme that Schopenhauer elaborates so vividly is the distinction between subject and object. It is a critical theme for Jungian psychology, an idea at the core of Jung's typology of extraversion and introversion. The extravert is the one who naturally and spontaneously relates to the object; the introvert naturally and innately relates primarily to the subject. It has been my experience that this distinction is easier for an introvert to perceive than for an extravert; in fact, I often have the feeling that extraverts really don't get it at all. But it is absolutely necessary to be able to differentiate between subject and object if one is to distinguish oneself consciously from the collective soup, from the state of *participation mystique* with the world and all the objects that are in it. Keenness of distinction between subject and object is an aspect of the well-developed ego.

As Jung tells us in this chapter, the ego as the subject of consciousness has two aspects. The ego is the seat of perception (or consciousness) and it is also the agent of the will. This brings up the whole problem of free will, to which Jung refers in paragraph 9:

The ego is, by definition, subordinate to the self and is related to it like a part to the whole. Inside the field of consciousness it has, as we say, free will. By this I do not mean anything philosophical, only the well-known psychological fact of "free choice," or rather the subjective feeling of freedom. But, just as our free will clashes with necessity in the outside world, so also it finds its limits outside the field of consciousness in the subjective inner world, where it comes into conflict with the facts of the self. And just as circumstances or outside events "happen" to us and limit our freedom, so the self acts upon the ego like an *objective occurrence* which free will can do very little to alter.[20]

Another way of describing free will is to define it as the libido disposable by the ego. This is of considerable importance both for self-understanding and in work with patients. One needs to have an estimate, at least an approximation, of the extent of one's own free will, and the extent of the patient's free will. No one can be expected to take responsibility for something that is clearly outside the range of his or her free will.

In paragraph 11 Jung tells us that the ego's freedom is limited by its dependence on the unconscious:

---

[19] *The World As Will and Representation,* p. 3.
[20] [Readers will note that the translators of *Aion* did not capitalize the word "self" when it refers to the archetype. In this book, as in most current Jungian writing, it is capitalized throughout in order to avoid confusion with the mundane ego-self.—Ed.]

[With the discovery of the Self] the position of the ego, till then absolute, became relativized; that is to say, though it retains its quality as the centre of the field of consciousness, it is questionable whether it is the centre of the personality. It is part of the personality but not the whole of it. As I have said, it is simply impossible to estimate how large or how small its share is; how free or how dependent it is on the qualities of this "extra-conscious" psyche. We can only say that its freedom is limited and its dependence proved in ways that are often decisive. In my experience one would do well not to underestimate its dependence on the unconscious. Naturally there is no need to say this to persons who already overestimate the latter's importance. Some criterion for the right measure is afforded by the psychic consequences of a wrong estimate, a point to which we shall return later on.

That last sentence deserves emphasis. I think it is an important one for analytic work: "Some criterion for the right measure is afforded by the psychic consequences of a wrong estimate."

Now what does that mean? I think it is calling for an experimental approach. If I don't know for sure the extent of a patient's free will, I can put it to the test. I can try out a certain attitude and then observe the psychic consequences. If my estimate has been wrong, then I can correct it. It is most important to keep an empirical attitude in the matter; then one is free to experiment. As long as one is conscious, what one does is always correctable.

First we must ask ourselves, "How much free will does the ego we are talking to have?" Then, at any given time, we must also ask ourselves the related question: "To whom are we speaking?" The fact that the person is in front of us, and looking at us, and may even be smiling, does not necessarily mean we are speaking to the ego. We may be speaking to a complex; we may be speaking to the shadow, to the anima or animus, or even to the Self or some combination. Even in the course of an interchange the energy to which we are speaking, the "who," can fluctuate.

This is something always to be kept in mind, so we can change our manner of speaking accordingly.

4
Paragraphs 13-42[21]

The Shadow

In discussing the shadow, we are likely to constellate this subject in ourselves and in the surroundings. "Speak of the devil and he shows up." If that can be remembered, the devil may be less likely to sneak up from behind. The material about the ego in the last chapter stayed on a superficial level. That is the nature of the ego: it is a surface phenomenon. In order to get below the ego you have to crack that ice; then the next thing to be encountered in the individual psyche is the shadow.

This brief chapter in *Aion* is Jung's most extensive account of the shadow, which he refers to throughout his work but not in any lengthy or systematic way. In *Two Essays on Analytical Psychology* he speaks of the shadow as corresponding to the personal unconscious, and he also defines it as "the 'negative' side of the personality, the sum of all those unpleasant qualities we like to hide, together with the insufficiently developed functions."[22] What he calls the "insufficiently developed functions" I consider to be a reference to the infantile psyche; the undeveloped aspect is the residual infantility.

In paragraph 17 of *Aion,* Jung writes of shadow projection and observes that the effect of projecting the shadow is to isolate the subject from the environment, turning a real relationship into an illusory one. This theme comes up repeatedly in the course of practical analysis. Again and again a patient will bring into the analytic hour relationship problems which have shadow projections at their root. When that happens, especially when dreams bring up shadow figures associated with persons in the dreamer's environment, the shadow figure has to be referred back to the patient's own psyche. An image for such a procedure is that of the reflux flask, pictured in figure 3. The contents of the flask are heated and vapor rises; it condenses in the upper portions and then is fed back into the belly of the flask. This is what we do when we analyze shadow projections. Rather than let the projection leak out onto the environment, we feed it back into the psyche of the projector.

This can be done successfully only if the patient is an authentic candidate for analysis, and we must not be too optimistic in our evaluation of how many of our patients are. If there is violent resistance to this reflux procedure, it means that analysis is not appropriate for the individual. One is dealing with a weak

---

21 A correction to par. 40 of the English translation of *Aion* can be found below, p. 194, together with other text corrections and additions.
22 *Two Essays,* CW 7, par. 103, n. 5.

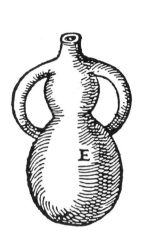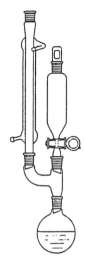

Figure 3. The Reflux Flask.
The reflux flask in two versions—one from a seventeenth-century alchemical text
and one from a modern chemical laboratory. In each case, material heated in the
bottom of the flask vaporizes and rises to the top, where it condenses and so is fed
back into the belly of the flask whence it originated, a parallel to psychological
work on shadow projection.

ego, or a young ego, that does not at present have the capacity to assimilate
shadow. It is as if such a person is out in a little rowboat and can't take in any
very sizable fish or the rowboat will sink. Therefore resistance to the analysis of
shadow projections must be respected. The young ego, in order to develop, has
to start out by separating itself from the shadow and establishing that it is good
and worthy. Such an ego is in the "negative confession" phase of ancient Egyptian religion. According to the Egyptian Book of the Dead, the deceased comes
into the judgment hall to meet the Goddess of Truth, Maat, and is then obliged to
make the following confession.[23] The deceased is talking to the Goddess:

> Verily I have come unto thee, and I bring before thee Right and Truth. For thy sake
> I have rejected wickedness. I have done no hurt unto man, nor have I wrought
> harm unto beasts. I have committed no crime in the place of Right and Truth. I
> have had no knowledge of evil; nor have I acted wickedly. Each day have I labored
> more than is required of me. My name hath not come forth to the boat of the
> Prince. I have not despised God. I have not caused misery . . . . I have done not that
> which God doth abominate. I have caused no wrong to be done to the servant by
> his master. I have caused none to feel pain. I have made [no man] to weep. I have
> not committed murder. . . . I have not wronged the people. I have not filched that

---

[23] E.A. Wallis Budge, *The Book of the Dead,* p. 346.

which hath been offered in the temples; nor have I purloined the cakes of the gods. . . . I have not committed fornication. . . . I have not added unto nor have I diminished the offerings which are due. I have not stolen from the orchards. . . . I have not added to the weight of the balance. . . . I have not snatched the milk from the mouth of the babe. I have not driven the cattle from their pastures. . . . I have not caught fishes with bait of their own bodies. . . . I have not broken the channel of running water. I have not quenched the flame in its fullness. . . . I have not thwarted the processions of the god. I am pure. I am pure. I am pure. I am pure.

In such a case, the ego needs to be supported and strengthened before any shadow analysis is possible. Therefore, the analyst will heartily agree with the patient that those are bastards he has to deal with out there; they are nasty people. There will be some truth in this, too; there can be sizable hooks for these projections. Which way one's analytic weight should be thrown depends on the evaluation of the patient's stage of ego development.

The Syzygy: Anima and Animus

Jung's chapter on the syzygy begins with paragraph 20. Let us first examine the term itself. It means pair or couple. The pairs of aions that the Gnostic god emanated were called syzygies, but the original meaning of the word was "to yoke together." It is derived from two different stems: "syn" meaning with, and "zygon" meaning yoke or the cross-bar of a harness. The longitudinal bar of the harness is connected to the wagon as illustrated opposite in figure 4, and the cross bar is called the zygon. The necks of the horses slip into the two loops of the zygon. The zygon or the syzygy literally means the pair of horses that are yoked together in a single harness.

As Jung uses this term, it refers to the masculine and feminine principles that are yoked together in the human psyche. Figure 5 (page 31) can be thought of as an abstract representation of the psyche. It is also a representation of this book, *Aion*. Working our way down from above, we start with the ego at the top. Next comes the shadow, drawn in a way to indicate that the shadow is cast because of the light of the ego, so to speak. It could also be drawn as just another layer. As one goes deeper there is the syzygy, the masculine and feminine principles represented by the anima in the man and animus in the woman. Deeper still comes the Self, first in its personal manifestations, then in its more collective ones as history, world, and then as the total space-time continuum. All these levels will be explored exhaustively later.

Figure 5 also illustrates how the masculine and feminine egos approach the Self through their contrasexual components. In the middle of the diagram there is a kind of neutral ego that sneaks right between the masculine and feminine principles, which is an ideal situation that does not really exist. On the left hand side is the feminine ego which, in order to get to the Self, must go through the animus. Contrariwise, the masculine ego has to go through the anima.

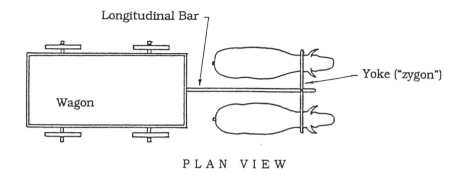

PLAN VIEW

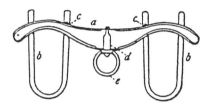

FRONT VIEW OF YOKE

Figure 4. Syzygy.

Jung tells us that the anima and animus in the psyche are composed of three factors: the contrasexual qualities of the individual, the archetypal image, and the person's life experience of the opposite sex. (par. 41, note 5) The first two factors are innate. The third, one's life experience of the opposite sex, is acquired, and of course in actual living experience those innate and acquired factors are not neatly discriminated, but are overlapping and intermixing. In the third factor, the experience of the mother and father is overwhelmingly important, but the parents are not the only ones to contribute the acquired characteristics. The major contributors to the anima experience in the man, in addition to the mother, are the sister, the daughter, the lover, the wife and companion. Those are all on the acquired level. Behind those personal experiences will be archetypal factors which will be met as divine guide and source of inspiration, or evil seductress, or a personification of fate or destiny or life itself, and finally the principle of eros.

In the woman's animus experience there will be similar factors: first of all the father, then brother, son, lover, husband and companion, all on the personal, acquired level. At the archetypal level may be found the divine guide and source of inspiration, or the evil rapist, or the personification of spiritual meaning, and finally the principle of Logos.

Also important in this context are the different states of the ego's relation to anima or animus, which is of some importance in evaluating analytic patients. I distinguish four different states: the infantile state, the projected state, the possessed state, and the conscious state. The infantile state is the original one of symbolic mother-son or father-daughter incest. Jung describes this condition in a man in a lengthy passage which is profoundly relevant to daily analytic work. This is the man's infantile relation to the anima:

> His Eros is passive like a child's; he hopes to be caught, sucked in, enveloped, and devoured. He seeks, as it were, the protecting, nourishing, charmed circle of the mother, the condition of the infant released from every care, in which the outside world bends over him and even forces happiness upon him. No wonder the real world vanishes from sight!
>
> . . . Often a mother appears beside him who apparently shows not the slightest concern that her little son should become a man, but who, with tireless and self-immolating effort, neglects nothing that might hinder him from growing up and marrying. You behold the secret conspiracy between mother and son, and how each helps the other to betray life.
>
> . . . There is in him a desire to touch reality, to embrace the earth and fructify the field of the world. But he makes no more than a series of fitful starts, for his initiative as well as his staying power are crippled by the secret memory that the world and happiness may be had as a gift—from the mother. The fragment of world which he, like every man, must encounter again and again is never quite the right one, since it does not fall into his lap, does not meet him half way, but remains resistant, has to be conquered, and submits only to force. It makes demands on the masculinity of a man, on his ardour, above all on his courage and resolution when it comes to throwing his whole being into the scales. For this he would need a faithless Eros, one capable of forgetting his mother and undergoing the pain of relinquishing the first love of his life. (pars. 20-22)

The quality described so baldly here is a significant feature of almost all analyses of men, especially of young men. Naturally, they are not going to express themselves that directly, but the basic unconscious attitude will be there if you have eyes to see it.

In this chapter Jung does not give a similar description of the woman's relation to the father, but in *Mysterium Coniunctionis* he alludes to it, saying:

> The dark sun of feminine psychology is connected with the father-imago, since the father is the first carrier of the animus-image. He endows this virtual image with substance and form, for on account of his Logos he is the source of "spirit" for the daughter. Unfortunately this source is often sullied just where we would expect clean water. For the spirit that benefits a woman is not mere intellect, it is far more: it is an attitude, the spirit by which a man lives. Even a so-called "ideal" spirit is

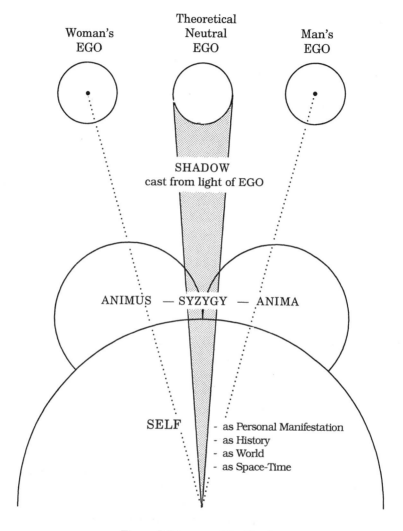

Figure 5. Diagram of the Psyche.

At the top is the ego, with the shadow appended; feminine and masculine egos are indicated separately, showing how each must move through its contrasexual aspect (animus or anima) to approach the Self. At the bottom, the Self appears first in personal manifestation, then, at deeper levels, in collective aspects such as history, world and space-time.

not always the best if it does not understand how to deal adequately with nature, that is, with the animal man. This really would be ideal. Hence every father is given the opportunity to corrupt, in one way or another, his daughter's nature, and the educator, husband, or psychiatrist then has to face the music. For "what has been spoiled by the father" can only be made good by a father.[24]

These passages tell us that the danger for the son, in the mother complex, is that it will poison his masculine urge to engage life; and that for the daughter, the danger of the father complex is that it will corrupt her relation to spirit or to meaning. These are the perils of the infantile relation to the anima or animus.

In the second or projected state, the anima and the animus are experienced in projection upon a member of the opposite sex. Further distinction can be made between remote and nearby projections. By remote projections I mean such things as the adulation of movie stars and rock singers, and other "groupie" phenomena; a collective projection is usually participated in by a whole group, and the projection carrier is not available to provide any corrective response, so the projection has a sizable infantile component. Nearby projections get closer to home, and these lead one into actual life encounters in which the projected image is contrasted with the reality of the person carrying the projection. That results in greater consciousness.

The third stage of relation to anima/animus I call the possessed state: the anima-possessed man and the animus-possessed woman. When a man is anima-possessed, a condition that usually comes and goes with moods, he is sensitive and resentful, and his feelings are very easily hurt. I would say that the key word for the anima-possessed man is resentment—a sour, disappointed attitude. Another way of putting it would be that the anima-possessed man is inappropriately soft. The animus-possessed woman is quite the reverse. She is opinionated, argumentative, brittle. When the animus state is uppermost, she is inappropriately hard.

Finally, the fourth state would be conscious relation to anima or animus. At this stage of things, as Jung puts it in paragraph 40, anima and animus "represent *functions* which filter the contents of the collective unconscious through to the conscious mind." When the ego has a conscious relation to animus or anima, it is no longer subject to possession, and the contrasexual element becomes a conduit by which the contents of the collective unconscious can move from the unconscious to the ego. This conscious relation to the anima or animus leads to an attitude that gives regular attention to the unconscious. Jung refers to this:

> Though the effects of anima and animus can be made conscious, they themselves are factors transcending consciousness and beyond the reach of perception and volition. Hence they remain autonomous despite the integration of their contents, and

---

24 CW 14, par. 232.

for this reason they should be borne constantly in mind. This is extremely important from the therapeutic standpoint, because constant observation pays the unconscious a tribute that more or less guarantees its co-operation. The unconscious as we know can never be "done with" once and for all. It is, in fact, one of the most important tasks of psychic hygiene to pay continual attention to the symptomatology of unconscious contents. (par. 40)

The ultimate goal of these masculine and feminine principles which make up the syzygy is the *coniunctio,* their union. This dynamic, the urge of the syzygy to achieve the *coniunctio,* lives itself out in external life in a fairly typical way. This is what I would call the concrete or exteriorized *coniunctio* sequence: a man and woman fall in love; in other words, they fall into mutual anima and animus projections. That stage of things is really delicious. Each is convinced that he or she has found a soul-mate in the other, and there is a blissful feeling of wholeness whenever they are together. On the other hand, there is a very painful sense of loss when they are apart. This initial state of things, because it is largely unconscious, usually cannot last long. It generally evolves in one of three ways.

One possibility is that the concrete *coniunctio* proceeds in life, so that there is marriage, family and a joint life, and the libido that had been flowing between the anima and animus projections is progressively led into the effort of developing a concrete existence together.

The second possibility is that instead of a concrete *coniunctio* there will be a concrete *separatio;* in other words, the projection drops off for one or the other. It drops off for one person, and then the other is abandoned. When that happens, the rejected one is exposed to grief and despair, and sometimes resorts to violence. This is the Dido phenomenon, the Medea phenomenon, the Don Jose phenomenon in *Carmen.* Extremes of despair or violence are activated because one has lost one's soul-mate and this is experienced as a total defeat, a failure of the possibility of *coniunctio;* the despair leads to destruction. The alternative is the realization that the other person was not the essential thing; then one starts to make connection with the anima or animus internally. This has been expressed as "When half-gods go, the gods arrive," which was Ariadne's experience when Theseus abandoned her and then Dionysus arrived on the scene.

The third possibility is that progressive development occurs in the midst of the mutual projection: the individuals gradually discover that their in-loveness is based on a projection of the anima or animus. But, as a consequence of having been the carriers of that projection, they are also led to the discovery of and the capacity for conscious object love. Then it becomes possible to love the partner as he or she actually is, simultaneously developing and maintaining a living connection to the inner image of the animus or the anima.

5
Paragraphs 43-67

The Self

We have now worked our way down the psyche through the ego, the shadow, and anima and animus to arrive at the Self. Defining the term Self is difficult. The word ego is also problematical, but it is nothing when compared with the term Self as it is used psychologically. Self does refer to an empirical reality, but its exact nature is impossible for the ego to delineate. All that can be done is to approach it from various angles and get little pieces of its meaning.

One definition of the Self is that it is the totality of the psyche which manifests itself as a unitary entity. It can also be said that the Self is the psyche in its wholeness, which includes both the ego and the totality of the unconscious. A third formulation is that the Self is both the center and circumference of the psyche, corresponding to the old definition of God as a circle whose center is everywhere and whose circumference is nowhere.

There is a logical problem in all of this, because when the Self is defined as the totality of the psyche, the totality includes the ego. How can the ego, a mere part of the whole, stand separate and speak of the totality as though it were something separate from itself? This paradox is built into the human psyche and into the phenomenon of consciousness. It is as though the ego as the son takes over some of the qualities of the Self as the father, and presumes to be a separate entity even while it is still part of the whole.

Empirically, the psyche has two centers: the ego, the subjective center, and the Self, the objective center. Considerable psychological development is necessary before a person experiences that, although it is easy enough to grasp the idea that there are two centers. Jung, a psychological genius, had a clear awareness of the two centers in his youth, as a passage from his autobiography demonstrates. Jung is talking here about personalities number one and number two:

> No. 2 regarded No. 1 as a difficult and thankless moral task, a lesson that had to be got through somehow, complicated by a variety of faults such as spells of laziness, despondency, depression, inept enthusiasm for ideas and things that nobody valued, liable to imaginary friendships, limited, prejudiced, stupid (mathematics!). . . neither an honest Christian nor anything else. No. 2 had no definable character at all; he was a *vita peracta* [a completed life], born, living, dead, everything in one; a total vision of life. Though pitilessly clear about himself, he was unable to express himself through the dense, dark medium of No. 1, though he longed to do so. When No. 2 predominated, No. 1 was contained and obliterated in him, just as, conversely, No. 1 regarded No. 2 as a region of inner darkness. No. 2 felt that any

conceivable expression of himself would be like a stone thrown over the edge of the world, dropping soundlessly into infinite night. But in him (No. 2) light reigned, as in the spacious halls of a royal palace whose high casements open upon a landscape flooded with sunlight. Here were meaning and historical continuity, in strong contrast to the incoherent fortuitousness of No. 1's life. which had no real points of contact with its environment. No. 2, on the other hand, felt himself in secret accord with the Middle Ages, as personified by *Faust,* with the legacy of a past which had obviously stirred Goethe to the depths. For Goethe too, therefore— and this was my great consolation—No. 2 was a reality.[25]

Jung's youthful experience is astonishing; he is talking about an episode at the age of twelve or thirteen. Of course, he is describing this occurrence from the greatly enlarged consciousness of old age, and it is probably safe to say that he could not have formulated it this way in his youth, but the experience was there and he then became able to formulate it retrospectively. This is relevant to this chapter on the Self, because what Jung has to say about the Self here presupposes a very well-developed ego in the second half of life. That kind of ego is not encountered very often.[26]

Figure 6 (page 36) shows how the relation between the ego and the Self develops in the course of unfolding consciousness. It refers to four different stages of ego development, four ways the ego might relate to the Self.

In the first stage, the ego is still contained in the original unconscious Self. It has not been born yet, so to speak. In the second stage, it starts to peep out; nevertheless, in spite of the fact that it has some separate existence, the ego's center still remains in the Self, so there is still a predominant state of ego-Self identity, which means that there can be no experience such as that which Jung describes as personality No. 1 and No. 2. Ego and Self would be felt as identical.

In the third stage, the center of the ego has emerged from its containment in the Self, and the ego is now in a position to experience itself as a separate center; the connection between the ego and the Self becomes conscious. What I call the ego-Self axis becomes a connecting link of which one is aware. Of course there would be no awareness of such a link until there is awareness of a duality rather than a unity. The fourth stage is a hypothetical ideal, an imaginary state with no residual ego-Self identity at all.

To the extent that the ego is identified with the Self, which is the state of the vast majority of humanity, unconscious assumptions prevail that the ego carries the qualities of the Self, that the ego is immortal, that it is the center of the world, and that its desires have the imperative of deity. This is not thought con-

---

[25] *Memories, Dreams, Reflections,* pp. 86f.
[26] For a fuller discussion of the relation between the ego and the Self at different stages of development, see my *Ego and Archetype: Individuation and the Religious Function of the Psyche,* pp. 5ff. and 62ff.

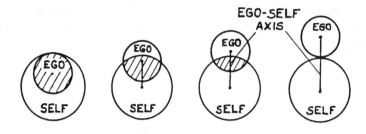

Figure 6. Stages of the Ego-Self Relationship.
The diagram shows relationships between ego and Self, the two centers of the
personality, as the ego becomes differentiated from the Self in the process of
psychological development.

sciously of course; consciously, one can be quite civilized and apparently hum-
ble, yet still have quite different underlying unconscious assumptions which
come into view under special circumstances.

Figure 7 presents a schema for the way development proceeds from stages
one to four. This figure represents a sequence of events which occur when one
acts out the unconscious ego-Self identity. As long as the identity is not acted
upon, nothing happens, but if it is expressed in action it meets a rebuff from
reality. That rebuff causes a wounding and reflection, then a *metanoia* or change
of mind, which heals the wound and reconnects the ego with the Self, returning
it to its state of ego-Self identity until the next episode. Each time that circle is
made, a little bit of ego-Self identity is dissolved, so to speak, and a little more
consciousness is born.[27]

One other point preparatory to Jung's discussion of the Self concerns the
breakdown of religious projections, illustrated in figures 8a and 8b (pages 38
and 39).[28] As long as one is contained in a particular set of religious beliefs, the
dogma carries the projection of the Self. The Self is equivalent to the inner God-
image, and in such a situation the Self, or the God-image, is found in a metaphysical projection. This serves a certain protective function. While the projection remains intact, there will not be any direct encounter between ego and Self.

If that projection breaks down, various things can happen: one can lose one's
connection to the Self and fall into a state of alienation and despair because life
becomes meaningless. Or one can fall into an inflation, which very often leads to
alienation, its opposite. Or the Self may be reprojected—for instance onto a political system, a common phenomenon. The meanings that used to be carried by
religious contents are now often carried by political movements.

---

[27] See ibid., pp. 41f. for further discussion.
[28] These are also diagrammed and discussed on pp. 65ff. of my *Ego and Archetype.*

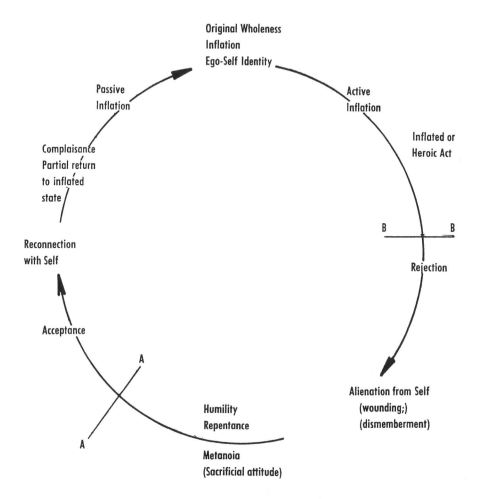

Figure 7. The Psychic Life Cycle.
The typical cycle in a person's early development is shown, starting at the top with
the original state of ego-Self identity. The subsequent typical events lead to a return to the original state, but with some increase in consciousness. The cycle may
be interrupted at two points (A and B).

A fourth possibility following the breakdown of the religious projection is
that individuation can occur, in which case the ego has a living encounter with
the Self as a psychological entity. Jung's discussion of the experience of the Self
in this chapter pertains to individuals who have lost their religious projection. It
will not have any meaning for people whose religious projection is still intact.

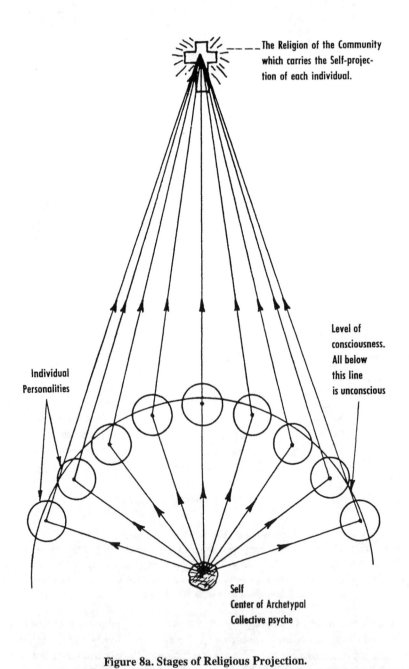

The Religion of the Community which carries the Self-projection of each individual.

Level of consciousness. All below this line is unconscious

Individual Personalities

Self
Center of Archetypal
Collective psyche

Figure 8a. Stages of Religious Projection.
The diagram pictures a community of individuals in whom the Self is projected
onto a religious system.

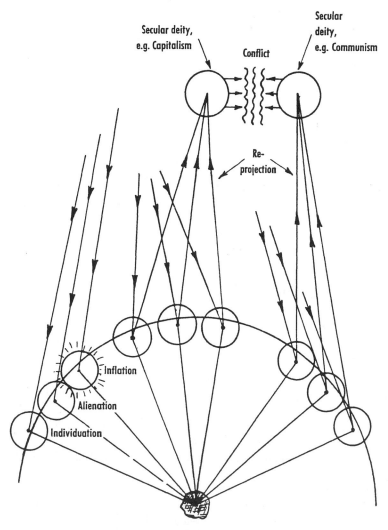

Figure 8b. Stages of Religious Projection.
The diagram indicates possible outcomes for different individuals when the religious projection of the Self breaks down.

Inflation is one of the problems Jung speaks of in the ego's encounter with the Self. In paragraph 44 he says:

The more numerous and the more significant the unconscious contents which are assimilated to the ego, the closer the approximation of the ego to the self, even though this approximation must be a never-ending process. This inevitably produces an inflation of the ego, unless a critical line of demarcation is drawn between it and the unconscious figures. But this act of discrimination yields practical results only if it succeeds in fixing reasonable boundaries to the ego and in granting the figures of the unconscious—the self, anima, animus, and shadow—relative autonomy and reality (of a psychic nature).

Fixing reasonable boundaries to the ego is an important feature of practical analysis. For instance, it is commonplace to hear such remarks as, "I made this mistake, I had that reaction," when in fact these events are products of the unconscious. Jung gives an example of this in his Houston interviews. The young interviewer asks him why a patient selects a particular symptom and Jung jumps on him with a vengeance: "He doesn't select; they happen to him. You could ask just as well when you are eaten by a crocodile, how you happened to select that crocodile; he has selected you!"[29]

The ego does not choose its symptoms; it is a victim of the particular symptom that the unconscious throws up. The symptom is like a crocodile that grips and possesses one. This is most important to realize. This is how we fix reasonable boundaries to the ego: we don't grant to the ego power and responsibility that don't properly belong to it. That would be inflation.

Jung's discussion of inflation continues with its perils:

No more than a flight of steps or a smooth floor is needed to precipitate a fatal fall . . . . This condition [inflation] should not be interpreted as one of conscious self-aggrandizement. Such is far from being the rule. (par. 44)

Inflation is far more subtle than that. It is a completely unconscious, unscrutinized presupposition almost universally held, that there is no such thing as an autonomous psyche beyond the ego; anyone who talks in public about the autonomous psyche is suspected of being a little crazy. Although this state of unconscious inflation is practically universal, one generally does not get into trouble with it. It is astonishing that the vast majority of people can live quite happily in a state of inflation. It is a natural condition unless the individuation process is activated; then one is held to account.

Another important point in this same paragraph is that one symptom of inflation is a growing disinclination to take note of the reactions of the environment and pay heed to them. It is good to remember that the unconscious comes to us from the outside as well as the inside, so that the reactions people have to us, the

---

29 Richard Evans, *Jung on Elementary Psychology,* p. 216.

events that happen around us, are all expressions of the unconscious just as much as a dream is.

Jung then goes on to speak of two alternative psychic catastrophes, one in which the ego is assimilated by the Self, and the other where the Self is assimilated by the ego. Now, "assimilation" is a euphemism for being eaten. Throughout nature, the basic question is who eats whom. If the Self eats the ego, at the worst there is an overt psychosis. If the ego eats the Self—which seems like an impossible thing to do since the smaller should not be able to swallow the larger; still Jung does speak of such conditions—then *"the self. . . becomes assimilated to the ego . . . .* [in which case] the world of consciousness must now be levelled down in favour of the reality of the unconscious." (par. 47)

If the ego devours the Self, then we have the rationalistic inflation that is so predominant in which the ego assumes itself to be the totality. In such a case, the antidote must be that the powers of the ego be levelled down in favor of the reality of the unconscious. In the previous situation, in which the Self assimilates the ego, the contrary is called for: all the conscious virtues—attention, conscientiousness, patience, adaptation—must be mobilized to the maximum degree. Jung continues in paragraph 48:

> The real moral problems spring from *conflicts of duty.* Anyone who is sufficiently humble, or easy-going, can always reach a decision with the help of some outside authority. But one who trusts others as little as himself can never reach a decision at all, unless it is brought about in the manner which Common Law calls an "Act of God" . . . In all such cases there is an unconscious authority which puts an end to doubt by creating a *fait accompli.*

Jung goes on in paragraph 49 to say that such a *fait accompli,* an action of uncontrollable natural forces, is from a psychological standpoint much better thought of as the will of God than as the result of natural or instinctual forces, because, he says:

> If . . . the inner authority is conceived as the "will of God" . . . our self-esteem is benefited because the decision then appears to be an act of obedience and the result a divine intention.

Jung does admit that this point of view can be used as a convenient way of escaping ego responsibility, but this criticism is justified only when one is "knowingly hiding one's own egoistic opinion."

This idea of the conflict of duty is quite important practically. When one encounters a major conflict of duty, the opportunity arises to discover the reality of the second center of the psyche, to move from stage two to stage three, because in such a conflict one is obliged to choose between two evils. One would like to have a choice simply between what is good and what is bad, but when there is a real conflict of duty, the choice is between two evils, which means one cannot avoid experiencing the opposites. Whatever choice one makes, it is apparent that goodness and badness are being carried simultaneously. An example of such a decision might be whether to have an abortion. Abortion is a crime against nature and one pays a heavy psychological price for it. On the other hand, it can also be a real crime to bring a child into the world in circumstances that are gravely unsuitable for its well-being. In such a case, the choice is between evils and there is no way of avoiding it.

Jung makes the point that the unconscious authority puts an end to such a conflict of duty by creating a *fait accompli.* All our unconscious, unwilled actions, all our so-called mistakes, are such *faits accomplis.* Such mistakes may have two different interpretations: for the young, the appropriate interpretation is that the mistake results from a failure of the will, because the young must have ego consolidation, and the emphasis must be on ego responsibility. If a mistake is made by the young, it is proper that they take responsibility for it. For someone in the second half of life, a mistake is properly understood as an act of God, and this is how I think one should understand so-called mistakes in analytic work with patients. They are meaningful acts of God, and in that sense they are not quite mistakes at all; they are interventions from the unconscious that have a purposefulness still to be discovered.

Jung continues in paragraph 59 with an important statement:

> Although "wholeness" seems at first sight to be nothing but an abstract idea (like anima and animus), it is nevertheless empirical in so far as it is anticipated by the psyche in the form of spontaneous or autonomous symbols . . . . Wholeness is thus an objective factor that confronts the subject independently of him.

As Jung points out here, the factor of wholeness is at the top of the hierarchy of psychic entities. This is something we should have constantly in mind as we work with patient material, because images of wholeness, of the Self, show up in dreams all the time. They can go unrecognized, so it is important to be thoroughly versed in the autonomous images of wholeness such as quaternites, mandalas, the Axiom of Maria,[30] the interplay of opposites, the union of opposites. All such images are expressions of that objective factor that confronts the subject independently of himself.

In paragraph 60, Jung says that "individual mandalas are symbols of *order,* and . . . occur in patients principally during times of psychic disorientation or reorientation." Images of order do not show up from the unconscious unless consciousness is in a state of disorder. Every now and then someone will say, "Oh, I wish I could have such nice mandala dreams as such-and-such in that book."

---

[30] "One becomes two, two becomes three, and out of the third comes the one as the fourth." See *Psychology and Alchemy,* CW 12, par. 26, and my *Mysterium Lectures: A Journey Through C.G. Jung's Mysterium Coniunctionis,* pp. 276ff.

That person doesn't know what he or she is asking for! Such dreams come at a heavy price.

Finally, I should mention paragraph 65 in which Jung speaks of metaphysical concepts that have lost their root connection with natural experience. Such concepts were once the containers for the collective projection of the Self-image. When that projection is withdrawn from the metaphysical ideas, the individual loses the sense that there is any meaning in them. Jung thought that one of his tasks in his later years was the redemption of metaphysics. He wanted to preserve the meaning that previously had been embedded in theological and metaphysical concepts, by uncovering the psychic realities which had formerly been projected into them.

6

Paragraphs 68-80

Christ, A Symbol of the Self

Chapter five of *Aion* deals with the expression of the Self in the Christian myth, the prevailing myth of Western civilization. The rest of the book is about various aspects of the Self, deeper and more profound ones, and as we go deeper the viewpoint broadens out until it reaches a kind of infinite extent.

Early in this chapter, in paragraph 70, Jung makes a revolutionary statement which amounts to the announcement of a whole new world view. The statement is that *Christ exemplifies the archetype of the self.*

That is a simple sentence, but it is a blockbuster once it is understood in its full reality, not just as an intellectual token. It is the first clear announcement that Western man's experience of the Self has shifted from religious projection, into the human psyche, and that man, at least one man, Jung, is conscious of that fact. Human consciousness has discovered the religion-creating archetype, of which the figure of Christ is just one expression, though the relevant one for our particular culture. We can now see what is prior to, or behind, the metaphysical projection which is personified by Christ. What is prior to it is what goes by the name of the Self.

Let us consider some of the evidence that Christ exemplifies the archetype of the Self. The characteristics that have gathered around the Christ image correspond in many respects to the phenomenology of the Self as it is observed empirically. For example, Christ is identified as the central source in such phrases as "I am the vine, you are the branches." (John 15:5, JB) This is a symbolic feature of the Self. Christ is also described as a union of opposites. He says, "I am Alpha and Omega." (Rev. 1:8, AV)

The symbolism of four and twelve, commonly occurring in association with the Self, is also associated with Christ who is surrounded by the disciples corresponding to the twelve signs of the Zodiac; there is the fourfold symbolism of the cross, and the image of Christ as the center of Christian mandalas, surrounded by symbols of the four evangelists. Various images symbolizing the kingdom of heaven are practically identical with the image of Christ, such as the pearl of great price, or the treasure buried in the field, or the mustard seed that grows to be the great tree, or the heavenly city.

Jung goes into the analogies between the Christ figure and the phenomenology of the Self in more detail in his essay "A Psychological Approach to the Dogma of the Trinity":

The most important of the symbolical statements about Christ are those which reveal the attributes of the hero's life: improbable origin, divine father, hazardous birth, rescue in the nick of time, precocious development, conquest of the mother and of death, miraculous deeds, a tragic, early end . . . post-mortem effects (reappearances, signs and marvels, etc.). . . . Christ is himself God, an all-embracing totality. . . . representation of the *Rex gloriae* in a mandala . . . . [He] symbolizes the integration of the kings and prophets of the Old Testament. . . . His body is bread to be eaten, and his blood wine to be drunk . . . .

These mythological statements, coming from within the Christian sphere as well as from outside it, adumbrate an archetype that expresses itself in essentially the same symbolism and also occurs in individual dreams or in fantasy-like projections upon living people . . . . The content of all such symbolic products is the idea of an overpowering, all-embracing, complete or perfect being, represented either by a man of heroic proportions, or by an animal with magical attributes, or by a magical vessel . . . or, geometrically, by a mandala. This archetypal idea is a reflection of the individual's wholeness, i.e., of the self, which is present in him as an unconscious image. . . .

It was this archetype of the self in the soul of every man that responded to the Christian message [Jung is talking about the beginning of the Christian era], with the result that the concrete Rabbi Jesus was rapidly assimilated by the constellated archetype.[31]

This is why we know practically nothing about the historical Jesus. He was hidden behind projections of the Self.

The archetype of the Self can also be spoken of as the image of God in the human psyche, the *imago dei.* With certain ideas such as this, it is helpful to follow Jung and use the Latin terminology. This emphasizes that we are dealing with a technical term in Jungian psychology, and fixes it in mind by baptizing the term in Latin, so to speak. Jung writes about Christ as being equated with the *imago dei,* psychologically speaking, with the Self. He quotes several texts related to Christ as the *imago dei,* starting with the first chapter of Genesis. God says, "Let us make man in our own image." (Gen. 1:26, JB) This passage at the beginning of the Bible establishes that man contains an *imago dei,* and this basic mythological fact has undergone immense reflection, theological scrutiny, and elaboration. It is this original *imago dei* which is considered to have been damaged by the Fall of man.

Jung refers to the idea here in paragraph 72:

The God-image in man was not destroyed by the Fall but was only damaged and corrupted ("deformed"), and can be restored through God's grace. [Jung is describing the mythological understanding, and speaking in terms of the Christian myth.] The scope of the integration is suggested by the *descensus ad inferos,* the descent of Christ's soul to hell, its work of redemption embracing even the dead. The psy-

---

31 *Psychology and Religion,* CW 11, pars. 229ff.

chological equivalent of this is the integration of the collective unconscious which forms an essential part of the individuation process.

Jung assumes that his readers are thoroughly familiar with this reference, though it is not even a Biblical reference—it is legendary. According to the legends which became quite widespread in the pictorial material of the Middle Ages, between the time of Christ's death on the cross and his resurrection, he descended into hell, or more specifically, into limbo. He broke the brass gates of hell and rescued the ancient worthies, leading them back to the upper realm. Jung refers to this image as symbolizing the integration of the collective unconscious. In other words, one aspect of individuation involves the descent to hell and the rescuing of the lost worthies, their redemption and restoration to consciousness.[32]

Jung continues his discussion of the God-image in paragraph 73:

> The God-image in man that was damaged by the first sin can be "reformed" with the help of God . . . . The totality images which the unconscious produces in the course of an individuation process are similar "reformations" of an *a priori* archetype. . . . This is in exact agreement with the empirical findings of psychology, that there is an ever-present archetype of wholeness which may easily disappear from the purview of consciousness or may never be perceived at all until a consciousness illuminated by conversion recognizes it . . . . As a result of this "anamnesis" the original state of oneness with the God-image is restored.

Jung mentions four different words for this restoration, which relate to the return of the state of wholeness. They all have very rich associative connections. The words are reformation, renewal, anamnesis, and apocatastasis. Apocatastasis is a term Jung was fond of; he uses it quite a few times in his works. It is important to understand the word, as it leads to an understanding of the essential nature of Jungian analysis. This word shows up only once in the New Testament, in Acts 3:19ff. Peter is speaking to a crowd of people:

> Now you must repent and turn to God, so that your sins may be wiped out, and so that the Lord may send the time of comfort. Then he will send you the Christ he has predestined, that is Jesus, whom heaven must keep till the universal apocatastasis comes which God proclaimed, speaking through his holy prophets. (JB)

This is not the word that is usually used in English translations; the usual word is restoration—till the universal restoration comes—but we will use the original word apocatastasis. Jung refers to the use of the term by the prophets for the return of the Jews to their homeland from the Babylonian exile; the restoration of the temple was referred to as the apocatastasis. In another place,[33] Jung

---

[32] Further discussion of this theme can be found in my *Christian Archetype: A Jungian Commentary on the Life of Christ*, pp. 109ff.
[33] *Nietzsche's Zarathustra*, vol. 2, p. 1341.

suggests that Paul may have acquired the idea of the apocatastasis from his Hebrew teacher, Rabbi Gamaliel the Elder. Jung describes the Rabbi as a Jewish Gnostic, and suspects that Gamaliel may have taught Paul the old tradition about Paradise—that after Adam and Eve were expelled from the garden, the garden was no longer any good, having been damaged in the same way that the *imago dei* in man had been damaged, and for that reason God moved Paradise into the future. In the future there will be a Messianic age and a return to Paradise; that will be an apocatastasis, a return to the original ordering of things.

The term apocatastasis corresponds to the Platonic idea of anamnesis, or what is called recollection. Jung uses the term anamnesis in the Platonic sense that as we acquire consciousness, knowledge, all our learning is only a remembering of prenatal knowledge. All our cognition is no more than re-cognition, a remembering of what we once knew and had forgotten. We find this same archetypal idea in T.S. Eliot's poem "Little Gidding":

> We shall not cease from exploration
> And the end of all our exploring
> Will be to arrive where we started
> And know the place for the first time.[34]

This archetypal theme is important to Jungian analysts because analysis is just that: a deliberate, orderly process of anamnesis which starts with a recollection of the personal life and then keeps going deeper.

The term apocatastasis was also used in early Christian doctrine, in the first two or three centuries. The doctrine stated that all free moral creatures—angels, men and devils—would ultimately be saved. Origen, one of the Christian Fathers, subscribed to this doctrine, which in its complete form stated that even the devil would be saved. The doctrine was formally branded a heresy at the Council of Constantinople in 543.

Origen was a favorite of Jung, who quotes him many times in *Aion,* starting with this chapter. His dates are approximately 185-254. He was born in Alexandria, a Greek-Egyptian city, of Christian parents. His father, Leonides, was a teacher of Greek rhetoric and grammar, and supervised his son's education. Origen was a precocious, brilliant pupil of both Greek culture and the Hebrew scriptures. When he was seventeen years old, his father was martyred in a persecution; this was when he began his career as a teacher of grammar. He quickly gained a sizable reputation. The Bishop of Alexandria appointed him master in the catechetical school when he was only eighteen. Origen combined this work with study and interpretation of the scriptures. He, along with Plotinus, was a pupil of Ammonius Saccas, the great neo-Platonic philosopher. So Origen was saturated with the whole of Greek philosophical wisdom and also the Hebrew

---

34 "Little Gidding," V, lines 26-29, in *Four Quartets,* p. 39.

scriptures and the recent Christian material. He was a voluminous writer; his most important work was called *Peri Archon*—archon: the same word that "archetype" comes from. The title is generally translated as *The First Principles.* Origen should be especially honored by Jungians because he first put forth the heretical idea of the ultimate salvation of the devil. That means that Origen already foresaw the potential healing of the Christian split that was just then happening. Now we are in a position to understand his prescient wisdom.

In paragraphs 74-76, Jung tells us that although the figure of Christ has gathered symbols of wholeness around itself, still, in regard to the opposites good and evil, it remains one-sided:

> If we see the traditional figure of Christ as a parallel to the psychic manifestation of the self, then the Antichrist would correspond to the shadow of the self, namely the dark half of the human totality, which ought not to be judged too optimistically. So far as we can judge from experience, light and shadow are so evenly distributed in man's nature that his psychic totality appears, to say the least of it, in a somewhat murky light. The psychological concept of the self, in part derived from our knowledge of the whole man, but for the rest depicting itself spontaneously in the products of the unconscious as an archetypal quaternity bound together by inner antinomies, cannot omit the shadow that belongs to the light figure, for without it this figure lacks body and humanity. In the empirical self, light and shadow form a paradoxical unity. In the Christian concept, on the other hand, the archetype is hopelessly split into two irreconcilable halves, leading ultimately to a metaphysical dualism—the final separation of the kingdom of heaven from the fiery world of the damned. (par. 76)

Examples of this irrevocable split in the Christian psyche are seen in medieval pictures of the Last Judgment.[35] They are all essentially the same. The upper half of the picture is a scene of heaven where the choirs of the blessed surround the heavenly throne. There is light and joy and order. Then about halfway down the picture there is a line, an absolutely schizoid line, and below it the chaos of hell, where the damned are. It is a picture of the Christian psyche, and this is why Origen's notion of the possible salvation of the devil is so significant: he held out the idea that the split need not be perpetual, that there might be a reconciliation sometime. As long as that split exists, everyone is going to do his best to identify with heaven, but as we know psychologically, whenever such a one-sided identification exists, it generates its opposite in the unconscious. Sooner or later, a swing over to the opposite takes place. That leads Jung to say, "The coming of the Antichrist is not just a prophetic prediction—it is an inexorable psychological law." (par. 77)

Jung continues with an important summarizing statement:

---

[35] For example, see my *Anatomy of the Psyche,* p. 205.

A factor that no one has reckoned with, however, is the fatality inherent in the Christian disposition itself, which leads inevitably to a reversal of its spirit—not through the obscure workings of chance but in accordance with psychological law. The ideal of spirituality striving for the heights was doomed to clash with the materialistic earth-bound passion to conquer matter and master the world. This change became visible at the time of the "Renaissance." The word means "rebirth," and it referred to the renewal of the antique spirit. We know today that this spirit was chiefly a mask; it was not the spirit of antiquity that was reborn, but the spirit of medieval Christianity that underwent strange pagan transformations, exchanging the heavenly goal for an earthly one, and the vertical of the Gothic style for a horizontal perspective (voyages of discovery, exploration of the world and of nature). The subsequent developments that led to the Enlightenment and the French Revolution have produced a world-wide situation today which can only be called "antichristian" in a sense that confirms the early Christian anticipation of the "end of time." It is as if, with the coming of Christ, opposites that were latent till then had become manifest, or as if a pendulum had swung violently to one side and were now carrying out the complementary movement in the opposite direction . . . . The double meaning of this movement lies in the nature of the pendulum. Christ is without spot, but right at the beginning of his career there occurs the encounter with Satan, the Adversary, who represents the counterpole of that tremendous tension in the world psyche which Christ's advent signified . . . . Both strive for a kingdom: one for the kingdom of heaven, the other for the *principatus huius mundi* [the rule of this world]. We hear of a reign of a "thousand years" and of a "coming of the Antichrist," just as if a partition of worlds and epochs had taken place between two royal brothers. The meeting with Satan was therefore more than a mere chance; it was a link in the chain. (par. 78)

To underscore what Jung says here, the advent of Christ represented psychologically the split of the opposites in the God-image into two irreconcilable halves, Christ and Satan. This was a necessary step in the development of consciousness, but it has led to a profound one-sidedness and to a dissociated condition that now has to be corrected.

The first stage in that correction, if one has been identified with the image of Christ, is an encounter with the opposite of Christ, namely, Antichrist. Jung says that the same idea is alluded to in the symbol of the Savior crucified between two thieves. According to legendary material, one thief blessed Christ and went to heaven, and the thief on his other side, who cursed him, went to hell. The twofold movement can be seen taking place within that Crucifixion scene, so that simultaneously there is a movement up and a movement down, and a containing of the conflict between those opposite movements. It presaged what William Blake finally described as "the marriage of heaven and hell," in which the up and down movements become reconciled or united in a third image.

7

Paragraphs 81-104

Christ, A Symbol of the Self (cont.)

A major theme of Jung's chapter on Christ as a symbol of the Self, and of his overall thought as well, is the *privatio boni*. This is a fundamental doctrine of the Christian aeon. It is a corollary of the tenet that God is good only, and that God can be defined as the *summum bonum,* the highest good.

The basic idea of the *privatio boni* principle is that evil has no existence of its own; it is merely a privation or an absence of the good. A corollary of the doctrine is that all good comes from God and all bad from man. Jung points out very explicitly that the *privatio boni* precept is based on a *petitio principii,* a begging of the question, which means philosophically that one slips an assumption (the assumption of what one is trying to prove) into an argument at the beginning, and so the answer is assumed in advance. In this case, it is done by defining God as good and defining all existing things as necessarily good because they are created by a good God. A good God, by this definition, is not capable of creating evil. Thus, a metaphysical assumption is smuggled into the discussion at the beginning.

As Jung notes in paragraph 83, Basil the Great settled this question this way:

> It is equally impious to say that evil has its origin from God, because the contrary cannot proceed from the contrary. Life does not engender death, darkness is not the origin of light, sickness is not the maker of health. . . . Now if evil is neither uncreated nor created by God, whence comes its nature? That evil exists no one living in the world will deny. What shall we say, then? That evil is not a living and animated entity, but a condition . . . of the soul opposed to virtue, proceeding from light-minded *[rathumous]* persons on account of their falling away from good. . . . Each of us should acknowledge that he is the first author of the wickedness in him.

The operative word in this passage is "light-minded" *(rathumous).* What this word means literally is easy-souled, loose, careless. Jung makes a great point of this term in paragraph 85:

> When therefore Basil asserts on the one hand that evil has no substance of its own but arises from a "mutilation of the soul," and if on the other hand he is convinced that evil really exists, then the relative reality of evil is grounded on a real "mutilation" of the soul which must have an equally real cause. If the soul was originally created good, then it has really been corrupted and by something that is real, even if this is nothing more than carelessness, indifference, and frivolity, which are the meaning of the Greek word *rathumia.* When something—I must stress this with all possible emphasis—is traced back to a psychic condition or fact,

it is very definitely not reduced to nothing and thereby nullified, but is shifted on to the plane of *psychic reality,* which is very much easier to establish empirically than, say, the reality of the devil in dogma.

What makes Basil's formulation (the origin of evil as this *rathumia,* this carelessness or indifference) so interesting, is that it is an early expression of the psyche as the source of something substantial. Even though Basil tries to say *rathumia* isn't anything, if it produces something substantial it must indeed have some considerable substance of its own.

Jung makes a great deal of this issue of the *privatio boni,* and he tells us why:

> Psychology does not know what good and evil are in themselves; it knows them only as judgments about relationships. "Good" is what seems suitable, acceptable, or valuable from a certain point of view; evil is its opposite. If the things we call good are "really" good, then there must be evil things that are "real" too. It is evident that psychology is concerned with a more or less subjective judgment, i.e., with a psychic antithesis that cannot be avoided in naming value relationships . . . . There are things which from a certain point of view are extremely evil, that is to say dangerous. There are also things in human nature which are very dangerous and which therefore seem proportionately evil to anyone standing in their line of fire. It is pointless to gloss over these evil things, because that only lulls one into a sense of false security. Human nature is capable of an infinite amount of evil, and the evil deeds are as real as the good ones so far as human experience goes and so far as the psyche judges and differentiates between them. Only unconsciousness makes no difference between good and evil. (par. 97)

This tells us that the clear and unambiguous distinction between good and evil is an attribute of egohood. Jung goes on to say:

> Today as never before it is important that human beings should not overlook the danger of the evil lurking within them. It is unfortunately only too real, which is why psychology must insist on the reality of evil and must reject any definition that regards it as insignificant or actually non-existent. Psychology is an empirical science and deals with realities. (par. 98)

You will notice that Jung uses the terms "experience" and "empirical" again and again and this is in contrast to the *privatio boni* doctrine which has a metaphysical basis; it is not experiential. Jung's basic point is that the reality of good and evil is based on the judgment of the conscious ego. Only unconsciousness makes no distinction. We could say that *privatio boni* is a kind of unconscious trick of the Christian psyche which pulls the wool over the eyes of the ego regarding the reality of evil. Jung is doing his very best to analyze this collective complex in the Christian psyche. His efforts in this regard include not only his criticism of *privatio boni,* but his criticism of the definition of God as the *summum bonum.* His whole approach has encountered massive resistance, which indicates that a deeply rooted, entrenched complex is being touched.

A letter written by Jung to Victor White is instructive. Father White had read something of what Jung had written about the *privatio boni* and the *summum bonum,* and in a published paper had criticized Jung for his "misunderstandings" of the doctrine of the *privatio boni* and for his "quasi-Manichaean dualism," and had commented on Jung's "somewhat confused and confusing pages . . . another infelicitous excursion of a great scientist outside his orbit."[36]

Jung responded to this criticism in a way that illuminates his thinking on the whole theme of the *privatio boni:*

> You have kept me busy for a while with your *correctio fatuorum* [correction of fools] in *Dominican Studies* . . . .It has forced me to go as far back as *Basilius Magnus.* . . . This *privatio boni* business is odious to me on account of its dangerous consequences: it causes a negative inflation of man, who can't help imagining himself if not as a source of the good,[37] at least as a great destroyer, capable of devastating God's beautiful creation. This doctrine produces Luciferian vanity and it is also greatly responsible for the fatal underrating of the human soul being the original abode of Evil. . . .
>
> As long as Evil is a non-entity *[meon] nobody will take his own shadow seriously.* Hitler and Stalin go on representing a mere "accidental lack of perfection." *The future of mankind very much depends upon the recognition of the shadow.* Evil is—psychologically speaking—*terribly real.* It is a fatal mistake to diminish its power and reality even merely metaphysically. I am sorry, this goes to the very roots of Christianity. Evil verily does not decrease by being hushed up as a non-reality or as mere negligence of man.[38]

These thoughts have generated massive resistances; books have been written to refute them. It is a basic Jungian principle to honor resistance and not to ride roughshod over it; whenever we meet a resistance, particularly a severe resistance to an interpretation, we must ask the reasons for it. What does this resistance mean? Jung raises that question in paragraph 98:

> My criticism of the *privatio boni* holds only so far as psychological experience goes. From the scientific point of view the *privatio boni,* as must be apparent to everyone, is founded on a *petitio principii,* where what invariably comes out at the end is what you put in at the beginning. Arguments of this kind have no power of conviction. But the fact that such arguments are not only used but are undoubtedly believed is something that cannot be disposed of so easily. It proves that there is a tendency, existing right from the start, to give priority to "good," and to do so with all the means in our power, whether suitable or unsuitable. So if Christian metaphysics clings to the *privatio boni,* it is giving expression to the tendency always to

---

36 Quoted in Jung, *Letters,* vol. 1, p. 539, note.
37 I have restored Jung's original word "good" in place of an incorrect editorial change by the editors of the *Letters,* who in note 40 refer to the use of the word "good" as a slip and substitute the word "evil." It is not a slip.
38 *Letters,* vol. 1, pp. 539f.

increase the good and diminish the bad. The *privatio boni* may therefore be a metaphysical truth. I presume to no judgment on this matter. I must only insist that in our field of experience, white and black, light and dark, good and bad, are equivalent opposites which always predicate one another.

It can be seen here what Jung does to accommodate the intense resistance. The resistance indicates that the reality Jung is pointing out is so horrible that it has to be denied. Certainly this matter is not something to be argued about with one who vigorously holds to the *privatio boni* doctrine. Jung therefore offers a way out of the impasse by saying, "The *privatio boni* may therefore be a metaphysical truth. I presume to no judgment on this matter."

The word "metaphysical," rather than "psychological," fits the situation because Jung does presume judgment in psychological matters; it is in metaphysical matters that he does not. I see this statement as an instance in which Jung fulfills the promise he made in the Foreword, when he said he was going to write as a physician, with a physician's sense of responsibility. Anyone who cannot stomach Jung's interpretation of the reality of evil is free to demur on the grounds that one is acquainted with a metaphysical fact which is beyond empirical experience. Jung will not argue with such a person; he opens that door quite specifically.

It is my view that in addition to the reasons he gives, a further reason Jung makes such an issue of the *privatio boni* is that he realizes he is writing for posterity, that he is establishing the agenda for the new aeon, and in order to be true to his task he has to spell out that new doctrine and how it differs from the old one. One's basic reaction to the *privatio boni* question is a kind of touchstone that indicates to what extent one belongs to the Christian aeon and to what extent to the new aeon. If one believes with Victor White that Jung shouldn't dabble in metaphysics beyond his depth, then the whole idea of a new age is ridiculous, and the current aeon is the only living, real one.

I would not offer any argument to that at all because I can perceive a similar divided reaction within myself. The Jungian standpoint meets my complete intellectual agreement. It is flawless so far as its logic is concerned, but emotionally it is a horror and I don't like it at all. If I can find some way to say that I think Jung is a little too hard, that the universe really is stacked ultimately in the favor of good, I am going to do that. We are in a transition between the two aeons, and each person has to ask what fits his or her own individual experience.

Next in this consideration of the relationship of good and evil is the Pseudo-Clementine text which Jung quotes. The so-called Pseudo-Clementine literature is apocryphal material that circulated under the name of St. Clement of Rome, probably starting at the end of the second century.[39] Jung quotes the homilies of

---

[39] A. Roberts and J. Donaldson, eds., *The Ante-Nicene Fathers,* vol. 8.

Pseudo-Clement because they picture a deity not yet split into irreconcilable opposites of good and evil. As Christian doctrine underwent further development, the split became greater, but it had not yet happened in Pseudo-Clement. Jung writes:

> The unknown author [Pseudo-Clement] understands good and evil as the right and left hand of God, and views the whole of creation in terms of syzygies, or pairs of opposites. . . . There is no denying that Clement's theology helps us to get over this contradiction [arrived at when the God of Christianity is defined as only good] in a way that fits the psychological facts. (par. 99)

It provides a bridge from Christian symbolism to Jungian psychology, which is what Jung is looking for. Jung quotes Pseudo-Clement's description of the nature of creation, in which man is a compound of two mixtures, two "pastes." Later in paragraph 100 we read from Clement:

> These two principles have not their substance outside of God, for there is no other primal source [archon]. Nor have they been sent forth from God as animals, for they were of the same mind . . . with him . . . . But from God were sent forth the four first elements—hot and cold, moist and dry. In consequence of this, he is the Father of every substance [ousias] . . . but not of the knowledge which arises from the mixing of the elements. For when these were combined from without, choice [proairesis] . . . was begotten in them as a child.

Jung only alludes to the idea in Pseudo-Clement that in the act of creation God sent forth the four elements, and when they were combined, knowledge and choice were begotten in them as a child. Now the Greek word translated as "choice" means purpose, and the verb derived from that noun means to have purpose, to decide. So what we are dealing with here is a phenomenon of consciousness. Without distorting the meaning, we could actually translate the Clementine passage to say that "when the four elements were combined from without, consciousness was begotten in them, as a child." This is a subtle reference to the idea that the creator God is unconscious and what he created generates consciousness out of itself, after God's creation, so to speak, and that with consciousness comes choice, comes good and evil. Jung says: "It seems as if, without God's intending it (and possibly without his knowing it) the mixture of the four elements took a wrong turning." (par. 102)

Well, it took a wrong turning insofar as it created evil, but it took a right turning insofar as it created consciousness. Those two go together. Consciousness generates knowledge of good and evil.

Another amplification of the separation of good and evil in the Christian psyche is the vision in the *Ascension of Isaiah,* an apocryphal Christian work of the second century. It uses the figure of Isaiah, the prophet of the Old Testament, but it puts Christian material into his experience. This work has two sections: one describes a magnificent vision of Isaiah's in which he is given a guided tour of the seven heavens; the other part describes his martyrdom, in which he is sawn in two with a saw like that used to cut down trees. There is a shocking disparity between the two parts, but as is stated in the work, the reason he was martyred was that he had the vision. That gives us an indication of the psychological cost of certain kinds of revelatory experience. Several Christian martyrs experienced the same image of being sawn apart. Such images express symbolically what was happening to the Christian psyche as the Church was being established and the dogma laid down: the psyche was being torn into separate parts.

Jung refers to the *Ascension of Isaiah* in paragraph 104.[40] In his vision Isaiah, guided by an angel, goes upward through a series of heavens. The characteristics of the heavens change as he ascends. In the first heaven, praise was going on; in the second heaven, more praise. When Isaiah arrived at the third heaven, nobody had ever heard of the world, though in the lower heavens they were familiar with it and with what was going on there. In the lower heavens, there were angels divided into different groups—right hand angels and left hand angels. Higher, there weren't any left hand angels anymore, just right hand ones.

When Isaiah arrived at the seventh heaven, he liked it so much that he didn't want to go back. This is how Jung also reacted in his experience of almost dying.[41] But the angel told Isaiah, just as Jung was told, "I am sorry, but your days are not yet fulfilled. You must go back." And so Isaiah had to return, but as he did so he witnessed Christ descending with him. When Christ got down to earth he went into the womb of the Virgin Mary where his whole destiny started to unfold. There are a lot of implications in this tale; it is as if Isaiah's trip helped bring Christ down.

The same phenomenon took place in the passion of Perpetua which was the subject of a companion essay to the German version of *Aion*.[42] Saint Perpetua was martyred, but in the midst of that experience she had a vision of ascending a great ladder, the same theme as that in the story of Isaiah. So far as the vision of Isaiah is concerned, Jung emphasizes that the upper realm and the lower realm were not then completely split apart. There was an interpenetration between them corresponding to the right and left hands of God that Clement also speaks about, and only later in the development of the doctrine did the split become total and irrevocable, such as we find in medieval pictures of the Last Judgment.

---

[40] A somewhat enlarged version of the text can be found in Edgar Hennecke, *New Testament Apocrypha,* book 2.
[41] See *Memories, Dreams, Reflections,* pp. 292f.
[42] This essay, by Marie-Louise von Franz, was translated into English and published as *The Passion of Perpetua.*

Christ, A Symbol of the Self (cont.)

In Jung's chapter on Christ as a symbol of the Self, he makes reference to Hippolytus and his book *Elenchos* or *The Refutation of All Heresies.* This work is also sometimes referred to as *Philosophumena.* Hippolytus was one of the early Christian fathers and lived from approximately 170 to 236. He was a Presbyter at Rome and he wrote a very comprehensive treatise refuting the Gnostic heresies. In the course of attacking them, he described them all in considerable detail. As a result, his work is one of our best sources for the understanding of Gnosticism, which was not his intention. There may be a psychological lesson to be learned from this.

The early Christian fathers hated the Gnostics with a passion, and they searched out and destroyed all the Gnostic writings. Until the discovery of the Nag Hammadi library in 1945, we had practically no original writings of the Gnostics at all. What was known of them came from what the Christian heresy hunters said about them, and even Hippolytus's *Refutation* was lost; it was only rediscovered in 1842, when a manuscript of it was found in the library of a monastery on Mt. Athos, an island off Greece. I think it is very significant that the discovery of the Nag Hammadi library occurred in the twentieth century, and the discovery of Hippolytus's work on the heresies only took place in the nineteenth century.[43] There is an historical synchronicity in these phenomena.

To turn to Jung's material in the last part of this chapter, let us first take up the subject of the paradoxical Yahwistic God-image. In his previous discussion, Jung quoted the *Pseudo-Clementine Homilies,* which described a God-image incorporating good and evil as the "right and left hands of God." Jung noted that this text was linked to Jewish Christians. He then turns to the Yahwistic God-image which was being elaborated in Judaism at about that same time. A few of Jung's examples, an accumulation from various Jewish sources belonging to the first two or three centuries A.D., illustrate the idea of the paradoxical Yahwistic God-image. Referring to the occasion of the Exodus: "Once permission has been granted to the destroyer, he does not distinguish between the righteous and the wicked. Indeed, he even begins with the righteous." (par. 106)

This refers to the avenging angel that executed the Egyptian first-born. The destroyer does not distinguish between the righteous and the wicked, indeed he

---

[43] Available in English in Roberts and Donaldson, *The Ante-Nicene Fathers,* vol. 5.

even begins with the righteous, so you had better stay out of sight on that particular night. Another text says that you should hide yourselves at the moment of Yahweh's wrath, because we are warned by Him that at the moment of His unbridled irascibility, if a curse is uttered it will indeed be effective. In other words, you had better be very careful what you say, and what is said to you, at the particular moment when God's wrath is kindled. Another text says, "God's left hand dashes to pieces; his right hand is glorious to save." (par. 107)

These quotations illustrate forcefully just what is meant by the paradoxical Yahwistic God-image, and these images have direct psychological application. For instance, the remark that "a curse uttered at the moment of divine wrath will be effective" would refer to the psychological fact that if there has been a serious offense committed such that the Yahweh level of the psyche is activated, what takes place at that moment has extraordinary power and consequences.

The statement that the destroyer does not distinguish between the righteous and the wicked corresponds to the psychological fact that the wrath of the Self is an unconscious phenomenon; it is a force of nature. A tornado does not distinguish between the righteous and the wicked; it might even hit the righteous first. The same applies to the activated Self.

Pursuing the idea of the existence of opposites within the God-image or the Self, we come next to Jung's theme of the Self as a quaternion of opposites. (pars. 115-117) Figure 9 shows Jung's diagrams of two different crossed pairs of opposites which are specifically related to the image of Christ. The first relates to the Christ-image as a union of God and man, having both human and divine, and both eternal and historical aspects.

Figure 9. Opposites Related to the Christ-Image.
The set on the left describes the Christ of Christian dogma. The set on the right involves the opposites of good and evil, represented by Christ and Satan.

According to the doctrine, Christ was a pre-existent entity; he existed prior to creation on the one hand, and on the other hand he was born into space and time, into an historical setting, and was therefore a specific historical being. Jung pictures that state of affairs—a figure that has an historical, individual existence and yet is also eternal; and that is unique while being universal. His universality is represented symbolically as his being an inner figure that is contained in all humanity—"he is the vine, you are the branches."

Jung then spells out a second quaternity. This quaternity would apply if one considers that Christ and Satan go to make up a whole. In that case, good and evil constitute one polarity. Spiritual and material constitute the other polarity, because Christ is a spirit but also becomes embodied by incarnation, and so he unites that pair of opposites. Although these diagrams may seem to be only interesting abstractions, they are more than that because they correspond to occasional dream images. One should be alert for dream images that combine opposites in such a fashion; they indicate a Self-image.

Further material on the theme of the contradictory God-image appears in Jung's discussion of Basilides' threefold sonship. This subject is taken up in paragraph 118, a paragraph so highly condensed that, like much of this book, it needs elaboration to be really comprehensible. Basilides is one of the Gnostics whom Hippolytus discusses. He was of particular importance to Jung, who even attributed to Basilides his own "Seven Sermons to the Dead."[44]

We know nothing about Basilides personally except that he was a brilliant Christian Gnostic teacher and a prolific author who flourished and taught in the first half of the second century. He wrote a great number of commentaries on the Gospels and applied the Christian material to Gnostic formulations. One of his ideas was the so-called threefold sonship. Jung was particularly interested in this image, referring to it in several places.[45]

Figure 10 shows the image graphically. The idea of the threefold sonship is that initially there is a non-existent God, a deity that only exists latently and has not come into manifest being yet. This God emanates from himself, a kind of creative "word" which generates a cosmic seed that emits or gives birth to three sonships—that is what they are called, sonships. Emanations would be another term, but sonships is a little more personalized.

The first of these is very refined and pure, and immediately reverts to its origin, the non-existent God. The second sonship is grosser and heavier than the first, but it is winged and can fly and so it gets part of the way back to the source. It is in an intermediate position between the cosmic seed and the original source, the non-existent God. The third sonship, which is the most interesting one from our standpoint, is described as formless and unpurified, and intermixed with the undiscriminated seeds of all things. It is what is called a *pan-spermia,* a jumbled mixture of seeds, the seed bed of the world that hasn't sprouted yet, or hasn't manifested. It is a matrix of all possibilities.

---

[44] See *Memories, Dreams, Reflections* (paperback edition), appendix 5.
[45] See, for example, *Mysterium Coniunctionis,* CW 14, par. 124.

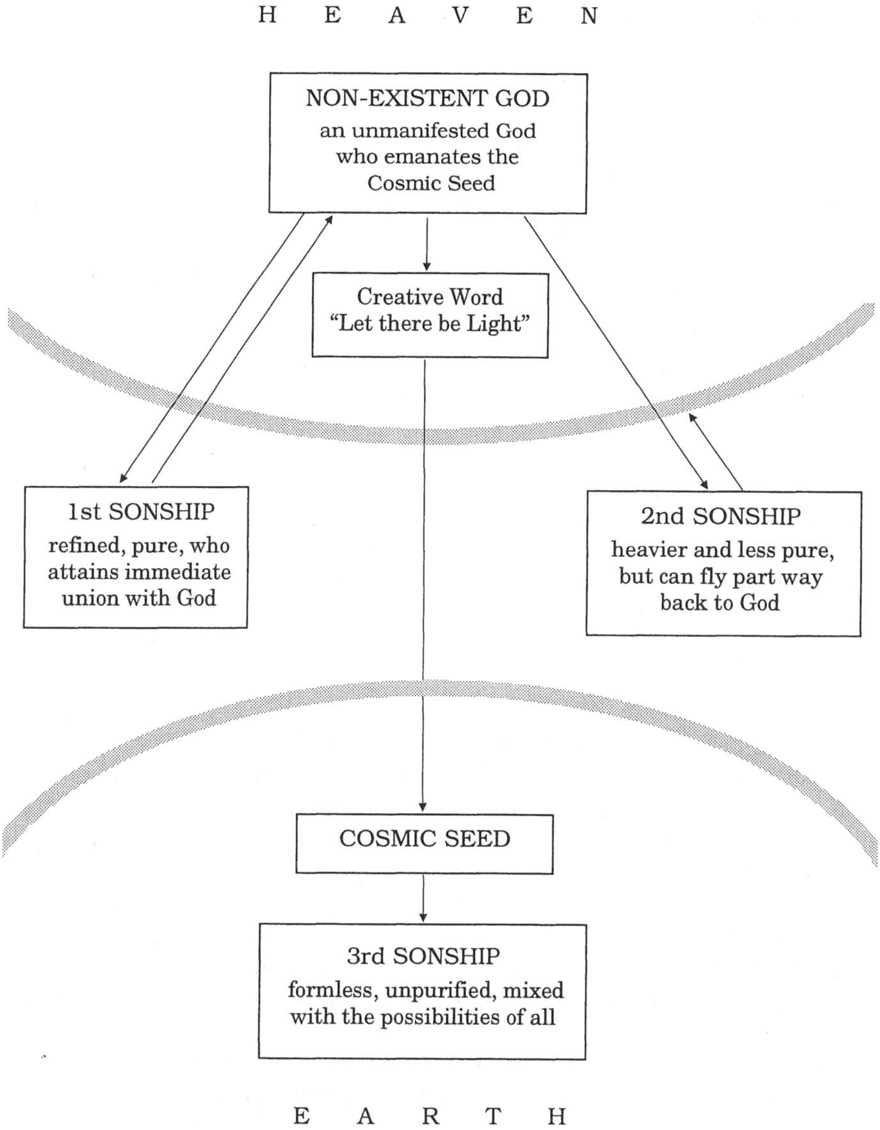

H E A V E N

NON-EXISTENT GOD
an unmanifested God
who emanates the
Cosmic Seed

Creative Word
"Let there be Light"

1st SONSHIP
refined, pure, who
attains immediate
union with God

2nd SONSHIP
heavier and less pure,
but can fly part way
back to God

COSMIC SEED

3rd SONSHIP
formless, unpurified, mixed
with the possibilities of all

E A R T H

Figure 10. The Threefold Sonship of Basilides.
Basilides' idea of the creation of the world by the unmanifested
("non-existent") God also provides an image of the creation of the
individual psyche out of the unconscious.

Jung talks briefly about this threefold sonship in paragraph 118, and he obviously considers it very suggestive concerning the nature of certain aspects of the psyche. It can be thought of as an image of ego development. The ego, as we know, is the son or daughter of the unconscious. This creation myth of Basilides tells us that the emergence of the individual psyche out of the general unconscious is a threefold process; one part of it (the first sonship) never separates from original wholeness; it clings to that original unborn state of things, the non-existent God. Part two achieves a kind of intermediate position. Part three falls totally into matter. Part two would be the only really conscious part. Part one would be completely identified with original wholeness. Part three, which is described as falling into matter or into formlessness, might be seen in several ways; it might be seen as that aspect of the psyche that resides in the body. Jung speaks of another way to understand it in paragraph 120:

> This picture of the third sonship has certain analogies with the medieval *filius philosophorum* and the *filius macrocosmi,* who also symbolize the world-soul slumbering in matter. Even with Basilides the body acquires a special and unexpected significance, since in it and its materiality is lodged a third of the revealed Godhead. This means nothing less than that matter is predicated as having considerable numinosity in itself, and I see this as an anticipation of the "mystic" significance which matter subsequently assumed in alchemy and—later on—in natural science.

This is an important aspect of Jungian thinking, the idea that a certain aspect of the Self falls into matter and thus brings about the numinosity of matter, which is reflected in the phenomena of both alchemy and natural science. It was very obvious in alchemy, because the alchemists were gripped by the mystery of the transformation of matter in the alchemical retort. But when you stop to think of it, the same thing is true of the whole scientific development that followed alchemy, the development of chemistry and physics and the biological sciences as well. The fascination that grips scientific investigators, that leads them to pour their energy into the task of discovering the secrets of matter, also reflects the numinosity of matter. This is how one can see the whole scientific revolution. The three sonships of Basilides illuminate that particular phenomenon as well as many others.

Another image appears in the last part of paragraph 118 in a manner that can't possibly be understood without going back to the original material. What Jung does here is to bring in another idea from Basilides, the image of the three Christs. This image derives from Basilides' conception of the universe, which is illustrated in figure 11.

At the top is the realm of the non-existent God, the realm of super-mundane space, and the celestial vault is the ceiling. Just below this realm is the dwelling place of the archon of the ogdoad (the ruler of the eight). The archon resides in

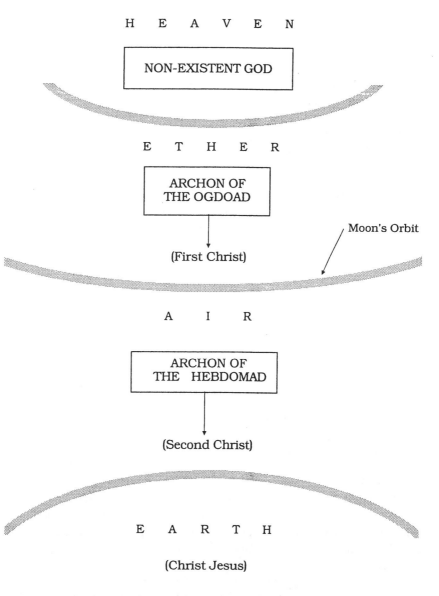

Figure 11. Basilides' Conception of the Universe.
Wisdom filters down from the "non-existent" God to the three Christs.
Through this, Christ Jesus becomes the means for bringing consciousness
to the original chaos of the third sonship on earth.

the ether, and the floor of that realm is the orbit of the moon; below that is the realm of another archon, that of the hebdomad (ruler of the seven) and he occupies the realm of air. Below that is the earth.

In the context of this model of the universe, Basilides describes the image of the three Christs, which Jung outlines at the end of paragraph 118. The idea is that the archon of the ogdoad had a son, a Christ, and the archon of the hebdomad had a son too, a second Christ. Some wisdom filtered down from the nonexistent God and was picked up by the first Christ; it informed him that there was a higher God than the archon of the ogdoad, so he proceeded to tell his father who was very upset to learn that there was a higher God, because he thought he was the highest one. The wisdom filtered on down farther to the second Christ (son of the archon of the hebdomad) who then also learned that there was a higher God, and he also told his father. The son knew more than the father because he had received this information before his father. The archon of the hebdomad was very upset also. When the archons learned about this higher God, they fell into a terror, the text says. But the wisdom didn't stop there because a third Christ had been created on earth, and that Christ was Jesus, son of Mary. The wisdom percolated on down to him, and he then informed the world about the higher God.

This is Basilides' image of the three Christs. Jesus the son of Mary, the third Christ, is an example that this impure third sonship lost in matter here on earth is supposed to follow, in order to be recovered from its formless state. The purification of this third sonship is described in paragraph 118:

> It was known, and stated, very early that the man Jesus, the son of Mary, was the *principium individuationis.* Thus Basilides is reported by Hippolytus as saying: "Now Jesus became the first sacrifice in the discriminations of the natures *[phulokrinesis],* and the Passion came to pass for no other reason than the discrimination of composite things. For in this manner, he says, the sonship that had been left behind in a formless state *[amorphia]* . . . needed separating into its components *[phulokrinethenai]* . . . in the same way that Jesus was separated."

We know that this passage was very important to Jung because he used it as the motto for the book *Aion.* On the title page Hippolytus is quoted: "These things came to pass, they say, that Jesus might be made the first sacrifice in the discrimination of composite natures." Now all one has to do is figure out what this means.

We have here a profound image concerning the nature of individuation and the way consciousness emerges. What is meant by composite things? It refers to the *prima materia,* the chaos, the undifferentiated condition of the third sonship which is in the same state as the cosmic seed bed—a confused mixture of seeds of all things. The third sonship, which is amorphous, without any form or structure, learns how to take on form, to purify itself; it learns from the example of the third Christ, Jesus, son of Mary. As Jung says in various places,[46] this is achieved through the Crucifixion image, by imposing the experience of the cross on the original amorphous condition.

The cross has the effect of separating the opposites, bringing about a discrimination, but at the same time ordering them and unifying them. In footnote 86, Jung speaks of the *horos* doctrine of the Valentinians in which the cross was equated with *horos,* which means boundary, limit or fence. This gives us an idea of how it is that this third sonship undergoes differentiation. It is through an encounter with the activated image of totality, which has the conscious power to discriminate the opposites, while at the same time containing them; the image of the cross does that.

The Christ image contrasted with the idea of the Self leads us to Jung's theme of completeness as opposed to perfection. In paragraph 123 he talks about teleiosis. To strive after teleiosis in the sense of perfection is quite natural, but there is another meaning of teleiosis, which is completion. Jung refers to the scripture which enjoins the believer, "Be you therefore perfect . . . as also your heavenly Father is perfect." (Matt. 5:48, DV) This is the Christian injunction to perfection, to one-sided goodness, but it is based on a translation of the word teleiosis as "perfect," which isn't quite correct. Telos means goal, end or fulfillment; it is the root of our word teleology. Teleios means that which has reached its goal, is mature, is complete, fulfilled or fully grown. Teleiosis, then, would be a state of completion or wholeness. This scripture could perhaps better be translated, "Be you therefore whole and complete, as also your heavenly Father is whole and complete." The third Christ makes this remark to the third sonship, informing it of how to get out of its state of amorphousness and back into relation to its source.

A final related idea arising in this chapter of *Aion* is that of involuntary or repressed individuation. Jung alludes to this in paragraph 125, where he talks about the task of individuation imposed on us by nature, saying we should take it as a binding personal commitment to realize our wholeness or completeness:

> If he does this consciously and intentionally, he avoids all the unhappy consequences of repressed individuation. In other words, if he voluntarily takes the burden of completeness on himself, he need not find it "happening" to him against his will in a negative form. This is as much as to say that anyone who is destined to descend into a deep pit had better set about it with all the necessary precautions rather than risk falling into the hole backwards.

Jung once said that whoever came to see him took his life in his hands. I understand this to mean that since individuation was operating so powerfully in Jung, whenever a patient worked with him, individuation was inevitably constel-

---

[46] For example, *Aion,* par. 79, and *Psychology and Religion,* CW 11, par. 433.

lated in the patient. One can't get close to such an archetypal force field without its having an effect. If the patient does not consciously accept the task constellated in him or her, that person is caught in a situation of repressed, involuntary individuation. That repressed urge to individuate can become dangerously destructive. I think this dynamism may lie behind certain chronically "unlucky" people who are perpetually accident prone; in extreme cases repressed individuation can kill you. A variation of involuntary individuation is what might be called "exteriorized" individuation. Jung also alludes to this in paragraph 126:

> The psychological rule says that when an inner situation is not made conscious, it happens outside, as fate. That is to say, when the individual remains undivided and does not become conscious of his inner opposite, the world must perforce act out the conflict and be torn into opposite halves.

Jung is referring there to the political division of East and West, but lesser versions of this phenomenon also occur. The idea is that if the opposites have been activated in the process of individuation, and if one remains unconscious of that fact, and of a conflict, the unconscious opposite manifests itself in one's environment. Then the conflict hits one from the outside rather than from the inside. I always try to consider any such external events that come my way as "external dreams"; I assume they are carrying a psychological meaning in the same way a dream does, and I interpret them in the same way.

The Sign of the Fishes

Christ symbolized as a fish is a major theme that runs throughout the rest of *Aion.* As will be recalled from the discussion of the precession of the equinoxes,[47] approximately 2,000 years ago the sun at the spring equinox moved from the zodiacal sign of Aries the ram into the sign of Pisces the fishes. That transition corresponds to the beginning of the Christian aeon. The aeon is now about to end as the sun moves out of Pisces into Aquarius.

One of Jung's basic ideas here is that the fish symbolism that gathered around the figure of Christ was synchronistically parallel to the new astrological age of the fishes which was then dawning. Christ became a kind of personification of his aeon. His representation as a fish was not caused by any general knowledge that the sun had moved into Pisces—rather, it was a synchronistic parallel. We know from a wealth of data that the early Christians explicitly identified Christ with the fish. The sign of the fish was used as a secret talisman to identify one Christian to another. (That sign is still around; you still find it on bumper stickers.) One of Christ's names was *Ichthys,* the Greek word for fish, and a kind of anagram was devised to account for that. The first letters of the phrase "Jesus Christ, son of God, Savior," in Greek, go to make up the word *Ichthys.* Augustine refers to this anagram in *The City of God:*

> "Fish" [is the word in which] Christ is mystically understood, because He was able to live, that is, to exist, without sin in the abyss of this mortality as in the depth of waters.[48]

The New Testament alludes to fish symbolism in several places, which also helps to account for the connection of Christ with the fish. Christ chose fishermen to be his disciples, saying, "Follow me and I will make you fishers of men." (Matt. 4:19, JB) The miracle of the five loaves and two fishes which multiplied miraculously and fed the multitude (Matt. 14:15-21) is another example, and this is very likely the source for the use of the fish in the eucharistic meal of early Christianity. The miraculous draught of fishes (Luke 5:4-6) is still another example. This symbolic image of the fish appears again and again in *Aion.*

Another major theme continued throughout *Aion* is the double aspect of Christ; this chapter begins this second theme also. The zodiacal sign of Pisces is

---

47 See above, pp. 19-20.
48 Book 18, chap. 23.

a double sign; it represents two fishes, one vertically and one horizontally oriented. This doubleness parallels the fact that the image of Christ took on doubleness very early in its manifestation. As Jung points out in paragraph 130, the double aspect of Christ is prefigured in the ancient Egyptian image of the pair of hostile brothers, Horus and Set, the good brother and the evil brother. They parallel the pair Christ and Satan.

Elaborating on the parallel, Jung says in paragraph 130: "One thinks involuntarily of the ancient Egyptian pair of hostile brothers, Horus and Set, the sacrificer and the sacrificed." Jung is writing of an image to which he has referred earlier, in which Set appears as a sacrificed one, tied to a slave's post. Horus is standing before him with a knife in his hand. Jung points out that in the Egyptian myth it is the evil one who is sacrificed. In the Christian version this is reversed; the good one is sacrificed. In note 40, following this remark, Jung states:

> Crucifixion was a well-known punishment for slaves. The Cross with a snake on it, instead of the Crucified, is often found in medieval works of art, and also in the dreams and fantasy-images of modern people who know nothing of this tradition. A characteristic dream of this sort is the following: *The dreamer was watching a Passion play in the theatre. On the way to Golgotha, the actor taking the part of the Saviour suddenly changed into a snake or crocodile.*

This image of the snake on the cross shows up in dreams occasionally. It is a symbolic image of a psychological transformation process in which the cold-blooded primordial psyche represented by a snake, fish, lizard or something of this order, is sacrificed. This is a very prominent feature of Christian symbolism, but it originates autochthonously from within the psyche, the same place from which the Christian symbolism originated. Tertullian said, "The soul [is] by nature Christian,"[49] and we can understand this statement today in a psychological sense, as suggesting that images of this type are spontaneously produced from the psyche.

In classical mythology a different kind of pairing is expressed in the image of the two brothers, Castor and Pollux (or Polydeuces): one is mortal and the other is immortal; the good/evil dichotomy is not present. Those two brothers are said to have become the astrological constellation of Gemini, the twins. A similar image of doubling or twinship is applied to Christ in the Gnostic work *Pistis Sophia,* from which Jung quotes a story about the childhood of Christ. Mary is talking to Jesus:

> When thou wert a child, before the spirit had descended upon thee, when thou wert in the vineyard with Joseph, the spirit came down from the height, and came unto me in the house, like unto thee, and I knew him not, but thought that he was thou. And he said unto me, "Where is Jesus, my brother, that I may go to meet him?"

---

[49] *Apology,* chap. 17.

And when he had said this unto me, I was in doubt, and thought it was a phantom tempting me. I seized him and bound him to the foot of the bed which was in my house, until I had gone to find you in the field, thee and Joseph; and I found you in the vineyard, where Joseph was putting up the vine-poles. And it came to pass, when thou didst hear me saying this thing unto Joseph, that thou didst understand, and thou wert joyful, and didst say, "Where is he, that I may see him?" And it came to pass, when Joseph heard thee say these words, that he was disturbed. We went up together, entered into the house and found the spirit bound to the bed, and we gazed upon thee and him, and found that thou wert like unto him. And he that was bound to the bed was unloosed, he embraced thee and kissed thee, and thou also didst kiss him, and you became one. (par. 131)

This particular image is part of what was called Docetism, an early Christian heresy. According to this doctrine, the Christ nature, the divine nature of Jesus, descended on the ordinary human being at a certain time, usually thought to be at his baptism. It entered him and performed its work through him, and when its work was done and Jesus was on the cross, it abandoned him. He had to suffer the consequences of the work which the spirit had done through him. I consider this a very important image for understanding the nature of individuation. The Self does behave somewhat like this in relation to the ego: it descends on the ego, imposes assignments on the ego which the ego would much rather not do— they are usually onerous—and then the spirit leaves the ego to pay the bill.

Jung comments on this quotation from *Pistis Sophia:*

It appears from the context of this fragment that Jesus is the "truth sprouting from the earth," whereas the spirit that resembled him is "justice *[dikaiosune]* looking down from heaven." (par. 132)

Jung refers here to a passage prior to the fragment just quoted, in which Mary had repeated a passage from Psalm 85:11, and then went on to tell about the event of the phantom Christ coming down. Psalm 85:11 reads, "Truth shall spring [or sprout] out of the earth; and righteousness [or justice] shall look down from heaven." (AV) Jung goes on to say that Jesus accordingly is conceived as a double personality, part of which rises up from the Chaos or *hyle,* sprouts from the earth, while the other part descends as pneuma from heaven: truth sprouting up from the earth and justice looking down from heaven: a fruitful image.

These two terms, justice and truth, have interesting usages in the Old Testament. The basic idea is that truth concerns sincerity, authenticity, fidelity to one's reality. Psychologically, truth means being genuine, being what one truly is. This is what sprouts up from below. Justice or righteousness, on the other hand, is defined as submission to principles, to laws of proper conduct, to spiritual standards that have been previously established. What we have here is something very close to a pair of opposites in which genuine "truthful being" grows from the earthy concrete reality of one's Self, whereas one's spiritual rightness comes from above. So the passage describing the coming together of Christ's heavenly brother with himself corresponds to the coming together of truth with justice or righteousness.

This same image—it probably came to him spontaneously—was used by Milton in the final line of his masque called *Comus,* in which he talks about a feminine personification of virtue, of fidelity, of honest, truthful living. Milton ends with this beautiful line, expecting that Virtue will be successful, but if not, he says, "Or if Virtue feeble were, / Heaven itself would stoop to her." It is the same image; that which is sprouting up from below in its authentic being generates a response from above and they come together.

When two planets appear to come very close to one another, as seen from the earth, they are said to be in conjunction. This is an unusual event; it is very striking and therefore it regularly evokes collective projections. Jung refers to several examples of planetary conjunctions and to the collective psychic projections which arose following them.

For instance, the conjunction of Saturn and Jupiter that occurred in the thirteenth century B.C. is considered to have presaged the birth of Moses. In the twelfth century A.D., it was predicted that the Messiah would come at the time of a conjunction of Jupiter and Saturn in Pisces. The conjunction of Jupiter and Saturn in Pisces in seven B.C. is considered to have signaled the birth of Christ. Jung says about the conjunction of Jupiter and Saturn that since the latter is considered the evil planet, and Jupiter is the planet of justice, the supreme being, the conjunction of these two planets is one of extreme opposites—good and evil, life and death. In this respect they correspond to the symbolism of the two fishes in the zodiacal sign of Pisces. Jung also mentions the fact that a conjunction of Jupiter and Pisces in Gemini occurred in 531 A.D., and he finds this synchronistically connected to the founding of the first monastery by St. Benedict, in 529 A.D. The underlying idea is that whenever opposites come together the *coniunctio* takes place, and one can expect something important to happen.

This is illustrated by a medieval tradition according to which the great religions originated from planetary conjunctions. Jung refers to this:

> The religion of the Jews originated in a conjunction of Jupiter with Saturn, Islam in [Jupiter with Venus], Christianity in [Jupiter with Mercury], and the Antichrist in [Jupiter with the moon]. (par. 130)

I think there are psychological implications in all four of these conjunctions. The most obvious ideas that arise from this symbolism are that Judaism contains and is the result of the greatest possible condition of oppositeness, Jupiter with Saturn, and that Islam's derivation from the conjunction of Jupiter with Venus suggests that it contains the greatest eros content, and I think this is the case. Arabic Islam is an eros religion, and that helps to account for the crescent present in so many flags of Islamic nations. Christianity's derivation from Jupiter's conjunction with Mercury suggests that it emphasizes spirituality to the greatest extent, which I think is true. It has the greatest denial of the body. The Antichrist coming as a result of the conjunction of Jupiter with the moon suggests that the Antichrist will incorporate all that is most ambiguous about moon symbolism.[50] The moon is a very dubious entity.

Throughout *Aion,* Jung gives us a great number of references to significant events in the Christian aeon, and a pattern of the aeon gradually starts to emerge. Figure 12 (page 70) roughly outlines this pattern, as an orienting aide in the flood of raw data that Jung supplies in the coming chapters. The diagram represents approximately a 2,000-year span of history. Events of major psychological importance tend to cluster at certain nodal points in the course of these 2,000 years. They cluster around points approximately one-quarter of the way through, about 500 A.D.; one-half the way through, 1000 A.D.; three-quarters of the way through, 1500 A.D.; and again at the very end, at 2000 A.D.

It is a cluster phenomenon; there is nothing precise, but the greatest intensity of clustering tends to occur around these four nodal points. One thousand A.D. is particularly important because it is then that the age of the first fish is coming to an end and the age of the second fish is dawning. At about 500, the first half of the aeon has reached its high point. At about 1500, the anti-Christian aspect of the aeon comes very much into its own. Jung considers quite significant the beginning of monasticism, with St. Benedict's founding of the first monastery in 529, and also Joachim of Flora, who will be discussed below, who came a little after 1000 A.D. Also around 1000 A.D. there was a great flowering of cults and heresies. Around 1500 came events with which we are particularly familiar—the Renaissance, the Reformation and the emergence of science. One other significant item is that the historical Doctor Faustus is supposed to have lived from 1450 to 1540. That is when the Faust legend begins.

In this context, there should be some additional discussion of St. Benedict of Nursia, who lived from about 480 to 547. Jung noted that there was a conjunction of Jupiter and Saturn in Gemini in 531, which he connects with the founding of the first monastery by Benedict in 529. Benedict was the father of Western monasticism. He was shocked by the licentiousness of Rome, where he lived initially, and he retired as a young man to a hermit's life in a cave. He acquired a reputation of sanctity and gathered a great many disciples around him, and finally founded his monastery at Monte Cassino, where he established the famous Benedictine rule. That rule became the guiding code for Western monasticism and has been so ever since. The rule tells just about everything one needs to know about how to set up and run a monastery. An idea of what is in the rule

---

[50] See Jung's extensive material on moon symbolism in *Mysterium Coniunctionis,* CW 14, espec. pars. 154-233; also my *Mysterium Lectures,* pp. 105-129.

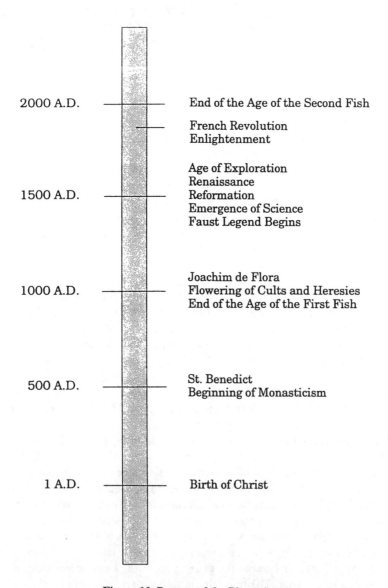

Figure 12. Pattern of the Pisces Aeon.
A time line of the age of Pisces, relating nodal points of the period
to historical events.

can be grasped just by reading from its table of contents:

> The kinds of monks; What kind of man the Abbot should be; . . . The tools of good
> works; Of obedience; Of silence; Of humility; . . . How many Psalms to be said at
> the night office; . . . At what seasons the alleluia is to be said; How the work of
> God is to be performed in the day-time; . . . Of reverence in prayer; . . . How the
> monks are to sleep; Of excommunication for faults; . . . Of those who though often
> corrected will not amend; . . . The tools and property of the monastery; . . . Of sick
> brethren; . . . Of the weekly reader; The measure of food; . . . The hours of meals;
> . . . Of the daily manual labor; . . . Whether a monk should receive letters or any-
> thing else; The clothes and shoes of the brethren; . . . How pilgrim monks are to be
> received; . . . If a brother is commanded to do impossible things; Let the brethren
> be obedient to one another.[51]

This is instruction on learning humility:

> The second degree of humility is that a man love not his own will, nor delight in
> fulfilling his desires, but carry out in deed the saying of the Lord: *I came not to do
> my own will but the will of him who sent me. . . .*
>
> The third degree of humility is that a man for the love of God submit himself to
> his superior in all obedience, imitating the Lord, of whom the apostle says, *He was
> made obedient even unto death.*
>
> The fourth degree of humility is that, meeting in this obedience with difficulties
> and contradictions and even injustice, he should with a quiet mind hold fast to pa-
> tience, and enduring neither tire nor run away; for the Scripture saith, *He that shall
> persevere to the end shall be saved,* and again: *Let thy heart take courage, and
> wait thou for the Lord.*[52]

The basic principles of monasticism were poverty, chastity and obedience. Monasticism became an immense collective process that extended over many centuries. Millions of people participated in the monastic life in the course of those centuries. From our position, we are particularly aware of the shadow side of monasticism, seeing how it could be an escape from life, but I think it had a different meaning during the time when it was thriving, because it generated a massive collective operation that was involved in taming the instinctual psyche, taming concupiscence and subjecting it to a spiritual counterpole.

The insistence on poverty, chastity and obedience is a radical frustration of everything that one desires. It pretty well covers it all—one's greed, one's lust, one's desire for power. To be obedient, one must subordinate the desire for power. It is my view that the monastic phenomenon performed a profound service in the transformation of the collective psyche through the centuries, and this is why Jung gives it such importance that he refers to it as being actually pre-saged by a major conjunction between Jupiter and Saturn.

---

[51] *The Rule of St. Benedict,* pp. 1ff.
[52] Ibid., p. 43.

10
Paragraphs 139-149

The Sign of the Fishes (cont.)

The second nodal point in the pattern of the Christian aeon comes around 1000 A.D., a time characterized by the emergence of a number of heretical sects and cults and also the prominent spokesman for the Holy Ghost, Joachim of Flora, also called Fiore, from the town in the southern part of Italy.

Joachim of Flora lived from approximately 1132 to 1202. He founded an order of monks and attained considerable renown in his lifetime. His ideas left a deep imprint on the spiritual movements of the times and also historically. Not much is known about him personally. He was born and lived most of his life in southern Italy. He went on a pilgrimage to the Holy Land. He became a Cistercian monk and at one time he broke away from the monastery and retired into the mountains to follow a contemplative life of solitude.

He had a rich inner life, but not much is known of the details except that according to the legends he had three very significant illuminations. One apparently occurred on his pilgrimage. The second one took place on Easter eve after a frustrated period of studying the Book of Revelation. At this time, after an interval of feeling imprisoned, his mind was suddenly flooded with clarity. The third occasion, the one for which he is most known, was an experience at Pentecost, when after a time of agonizing doubt concerning the doctrine of the Trinity (something he was obsessed with throughout his lifetime), he had a vision of a psalter, a kind of primitive harp. The Psalms are also called the psalter because their singing was often accompanied by the playing of this stringed instrument. Joachim's vision was of a psalter with ten strings on it; the instrument was in a triangular form, signifying the Trinity. The vision brought a resolution of his doubts about the Trinity, which was ultimately the subject of his major doctrine.

His novel idea was to see that the Trinity, which had been thought of as a static entity expressing the Christian deity, could be conceived of as an historical process. He thought that the Age of the Father manifested itself in history during the Old Testament period, approximately the thousand years before Christ. Joachim characterized that period as the time of law and fear. The Age of the Son, considered to be the New Testament Age, occurred during the first thousand years of the Christian aeon, and was described as the period of grace and faith. The Age of the Holy Ghost was considered by Joachim to begin about 1000 A.D., and that period was to be characterized by the qualities of love and spirit, the manifestation and indwelling of the Holy Ghost in individuals.

There has been a whole series of creeds which define the Trinity; Jung cites this particular description from the Creed of the Lateran Council which took place in 1215, and which characterizes the Trinity in these words:

> We firmly believe and wholeheartedly confess that there is only one true God, eternal, infinite and unchanging; incomprehensible, almighty and ineffable; Father and Son and Holy Ghost; three Persons, but one essence; entirely simple in substance and nature. The Father is of none, the Son is of the Father alone, and the Holy Ghost is of both equally; for ever without beginning and without end; the Father begetting, the Son being born, and the Holy Ghost proceeding; consubstantial and coequal and coalmighty and coeternal.[53]

This is the dogmatic formulation of the doctrine of the Trinity in its most elementary form. Joachim's great contribution was to translate this symbolism into a temporal sequence. Joachim was a forerunner of Jung in the sense that Jung has also translated the symbolism of the Trinity into a temporal process—a process of psychological development. In his Trinity essay, Jung discusses the symbolism of the Father, Son and Holy Ghost as three stages of a developmental process: "The world of the Father typifies an age which is characterized by a pristine oneness with the whole of Nature,"[54] an age far removed from critical judgment and moral conflict. It is man in his childhood state. It corresponds to the psychological condition of original oneness. About the world of the Son, Jung writes:

> [The world of the Son is] a world filled with longing for redemption and for that state of perfection in which man was still one with the Father. Longingly he looked back to the world of the Father, but it was lost forever, because an irreversible increase in man's consciousness had taken place in the meantime and made it independent. . . .
>
> The stage of the "Son" is therefore a conflict situation *par excellence* . . . . "Freedom from the law" brings a sharpening of opposites.[55]

This state of affairs corresponds to the meaning of the number two, which symbolizes the conflict of the opposites. The Holy Ghost takes us to the symbolism of the number three, and concerning the world of the Holy Ghost, Jung writes:

> The advance to the third stage means something like a recognition of the unconscious, if not actual subordination to it. . . . Just as the transition from the first stage to the second demands the sacrifice of childish dependence, so, at the transition to the third stage, an exclusive independence has to be relinquished. . . .

---

[53] "A Psychological Approach to the Dogma of the Trinity," *Psychology and Religion,* CW 11, par. 219.
[54] Ibid., par. 201.
[55] Ibid., pars. 203, 272.

This third stage . . . means articulating one's ego-consciousness with a supraordinate totality, of which one cannot say that it is "I," but which is best visualized as a more comprehensive being.[56]

So there are considerable analogies between Joachim's threefold historical process and Jung's threefold developmental sequence. One striking similarity is that Joachim thought of the final age of the Holy Ghost as ushering in what he called the *ecclesia spiritualis,* the church of the spirit. Jung makes use of this term; it shows up in alchemy; it corresponds to that church in which each individual has a unique relation to the Holy Ghost. Joachim's ideas are a prelude to psychological thinking. Jung tells us in *Aion* that in Joachim's day,

> Everyone felt the rushing wind of the pneuma [the Holy Ghost manifesting itself; this was a time when cults and heresies were springing up everywhere] . . . Cathari, Patarenes, Concorricci, Waldenses, Poor Men of Lyons, Beghards, Brethren of the Free Spirit, "Bread through God," and whatever else these movements were called. (par. 139)

Typical of these heretical cults were the Cathars who in some areas were also called the Albigenses. They originated in the eleventh century, around the turn of the millennium, and spread throughout Europe. Theirs was a neo-Manichean sect of radical dualism, which believed that all matter was evil, and some sections of this sect believed Satan to be an independent deity.

The Cathars had a Docetist doctrine of Christ; that is, they believed that Christ was an angel with only a phantom body, so he did not really suffer. Their radical dualism could not allow the son of God to enter concretely into that evil stuff, matter; it had to be only a semblance, only a "seeming." They had an extremely rigorous moral doctrine; they forbade the use of all animal products. They called themselves "the pure ones" which is the meaning of the word "cathars." They considered that man was an alien in an evil world, just a sojourner here, and that he shouldn't soil himself with the matter of this world.

They practiced extreme asceticism and condemned marriage, but they did apply different standards to their different groups. The faithful were divided into two groups, the perfect and the believers. The perfect were set apart from the others by an initiation ceremony called the *consolamentum,* and they then devoted themselves to contemplation and maintained the very highest moral standards. Of course by following their ascetic practice, the human race would die out in a generation, but the second group, the believers, were allowed more liberties. This term *consolamentum,* which was part of the initiation ceremony for the perfect ones, means the consoling or comforting function of the Holy Ghost, considered to be the Paraclete promised by Christ, the one who was to come after Christ had gone. The initiation ceremony was thought to amount to a baptism

---

[56] Ibid., pars. 273, 276.

in the Holy Ghost, a baptism which brought with it a *consolamentum.*

The word *consolamentum* appears in one of Jung's letters in which he talks about Joachim's vision of a new age and new gospel.[57] Jung says Joachim had that vision "when the great tearing apart had just begun," and such a vision, says Jung, seems to be granted as divine grace, as a sort of "consolamentum" so that man is not left in a completely hopeless state in the time of darkness. It is not too hard to read into this some analogy of Jung's own experience of *consolamentum,* which functioned as a comfort in the face of perhaps more consciousness than an individual should be asked to carry.

The Cathars and all the other heretical sects of that age had certain characteristics in common. Jung summarizes them in paragraph 139, using a quote from another scholar:

> [These various heretics] believe themselves to be God by nature without distinction . . . and that they are eternal . . . that they have no need of God or the Godhead . . . that they constitute the kingdom of heaven . . . that they are immutable in the new rock, that they rejoice in naught and are troubled by naught . . . that a man is bound to follow his inner instinct rather than the truth of the Gospel which is preached every day . . . that they believe the Gospel to contain poetical matters which are not true.

Then Jung comments:

> These few examples may suffice to show what kind of spirit animated these movements. They were made up of people who identified themselves (or were identified) with God, who deemed themselves supermen, had a critical approach to the gospels, followed the promptings of the inner man, and understood the kingdom of heaven to be within. In a sense, therefore, they were modern in their outlook, but they had a religious inflation instead of the rationalistic and political psychosis that is the affliction of our day.

Jung understood the phenomenon of Joachim and the stirrings of the Holy Ghost as it manifested in these sects as the first stirrings of the second fish, the first fish being Christ, the second Antichrist. Jung draws attention in paragraph 143 to the phrase in which the heretics were described as believing "they are immutable in the new rock." He then goes on to talk about this new rock as being analogous to the Philosophers' Stone, saying that it refers to the symbolic equation of Christ with the rock. Jung also alludes to the water from the rock which was struck by Moses in the Sinai desert. (Exod. 17:5-6, Num. 20:7-13) That sacred rock was equated with Christ from whom living water flowed when his side was pierced at his Crucifixion. Jung also speaks of the water from the rock as equivalent to the alchemical *aqua permanens.* He then summarizes:

> The new rock, then, takes the place of Christ, just as the everlasting gospel was

---

[57] *Letters,* vol. 2, p. 136.

meant to take the place of Christ's message. Through the descent and indwelling of the Holy Ghost, the . . . sonship is infused into every individual, so that everybody who possesses the Holy Ghost will be a new rock, in accordance with I Peter 2:5: "Be you also as living stones built up." This is a logical development of the teaching about the Paraclete and the filiation [which means the becoming a son], as stated in Luke 6:35: "You shall be sons of the Highest." (par. 144)

This is all individuation symbolism, in which the individual discovers the inner rock which then grants a certain immutability. The rock is found within as a consequence of connection to the Holy Ghost, as opposed to its being projected or collectively exteriorized.

Jung alludes to another feature of this symbolism of the new rock, suggesting a comparison with "the building of the seamless tower (church) with 'living stones' in the 'Shepherd' of Hermas."(par. 144, note 70)

The "Shepherd" vision took place at the beginning of the Christian aeon. Hermas saw before him a great tower being built on the water with shining square stones. It was being built foursquare by six young men. Tens of thousands of other men were bringing stones, some from the depths of the sea, some from the land. The stones which had been dragged from the deep they then placed without exception, as they were, into the building, for they had all been shaped and fitted into the joints with the other stones. And they so fastened one to the other that the joints could not be seen, but the tower appeared as if it had been built of a single stone.

The image is of stones coming from all sides, joining to make a single building which became a single rock without seams. Then Hermas asks the woman who is showing him this vision "What is this?" and she replies that the tower he sees being built is the Church. So the Church took over the rocklike image of Christ.

A modern dream concerning this imagery is an interesting contrast to the Hermas vision which came at the beginning of the Christian aeon. This is a dream occurring at the end of the Christian aeon:

> I see a large aggregate of stones, nearly vertical, in my view, shaped in some circular pattern. The stones were alive and angry, screaming like magpies. They became angry when anyone attempted to remove one of the stones, but someone explained to me that each person has to remove his own stone from the aggregate if he is to be an individual. Then I do remove my own stone. The person who had been talking to me points out a tiny dark spot in the center of my stone, and explains that each stone has that center, and that in some way that center is identical to the total aggregate.

This is a beautiful example of what the new aeon calls for. The Hermas vision was appropriate for the beginning of our aeon because the Church was just in the process of being constructed 2,000 years ago. Individuals had to hand over their inner stone, so to speak, in order for it to be realized in collective form. But now that aggregate must be disassembled so that one can leave containment in that collective rock and discover one's own individual stone, thus becoming a member of the *ecclesia spiritualis.*

This issue is also alluded to in terms of Christian fish symbolism. Jung says:

> The Christian fish symbol first appeared in Alexandria around A.D. 200 . . . the baptismal bath was described as a *piscina* (fish-pond) quite early. This presupposes that the believers were fishes, as is in fact suggested by the gospels. (par. 145)

This is a very significant symbolic image, that of the religious believers as fishes swimming in an ecclesiastical fish pond. Tertullian in his essay on baptism says specifically: "We, little fishes, after the example of our *Ichthys,* Jesus Christ, are born in water, nor have we safety in any other way than by permanently abiding in water."[58]

The same idea was also applied in Judaism: "The Israelites, especially those faithful to the Law, are little fishes swimming in the Torah where alone they can live."[59] This is exactly the same as Tertullian's image of Christians swimming in their Christian fish pond. In this context, Jung says in paragraph 147:

> The symbolism shows Christ and those who believe in him as fishes, fish as the food eaten at the Agape [the religious meal], baptism as immersion in a fish pond, etc. At first sight, all this points to no more than the fact that the fish symbols and mythologems which have always existed had assimilated the figure of the Redeemer; in other words, it was a symptom of Christ's assimilation into the world of ideas prevailing at that time. But, to the extent that Christ was regarded as the new aeon, it would be clear to anyone acquainted with astrology that he was born as the first fish of the Pisces era, and was doomed to die as the last ram (*[arnion]* lamb) of the declining Aries era.

We can say something analogous about Jung. We are about to enter the aeon of Aquarius the water carrier, and leave the aeon of Pisces, so in a sense Jung is the last fish and the first water carrier. There is very significant symbolism in those two images of transition. Fish live within the medium of water and are contained by it. Aquarius carries water, indicating a totally different relation to the psyche. This is reminiscent of a funny little anecdote which at the same time is quite profound. It is the riddle "Who discovered water?" The answer is, "I don't know, but I know who didn't discover it—the fish."

There is another interesting item, with echoes of twinship and doubling, further along in paragraph 147: "Matthew 27:15ff. hands down this mythologem in the form of the old sacrifice of the seasonal god." This scripture refers to the custom of releasing a prisoner at Passover; Pilate brought out a criminal, Barab-

58 Roberts and Donaldson, *The Ante-Nicene Fathers,* vol. 3, p. 669.
59 E.R. Goodenough, *Jewish Symbols in the Greco-Roman Period,* vol. 5, p. 33.

bas, and asked the mob, "Whom do you want me to release? Shall it be Jesus or Barabbas?" In other words, this was a twofold event, and how completely twofold is revealed by the literal translation of this passage. The only Bible I know which translates it literally is the New English Bible. The other translations obscure this very significant psychological fact. The New English Bible translates Pilate's question in these words: "Which would you like me to release to you—Jesus Bar-Abbas or Jesus called Messiah?" (Matt. 27:17f.) In other words, they were two individuals with the same name. What the first name means literally is Jesus, son of the father; the second is Jesus the messiah. Those were the alternatives.

Turning back now to the imagery of the Christian aeon as the age of the fishes, figure 13 is a crude representation of the way the two fishes are outlined in conventional astronomical representations in relationship to the ecliptic, the path the sun takes through the heavens. We are dealing with the precession of the equinoxes, so that the ecliptic represents the movement of the point of the rising sun at the vernal equinox through the centuries. Jung speaks of star Alpha, also called number 113. When the sun reached that point it was 146 B.C. (par. 149, note 83) When the sun reached about the midpoint of the horizontal fish, it was approximately 1500 A.D.

An absolute psychological explosion in the collective psyche took place then, as though the Holy Ghost descended with a vengeance. We had the Reformation, the Renaissance, the age of exploration, the birth of science and art, and critical examination of all the sacred scriptures that up until then could not be touched, just as one had not, until then, dared examine the human body. In 1543, Vesalius, having robbed the gallows for corpses for dissection, brought out his first major work on human anatomy. Nothing was sacred anymore. The Holy Ghost had descended and everything was up for grabs.

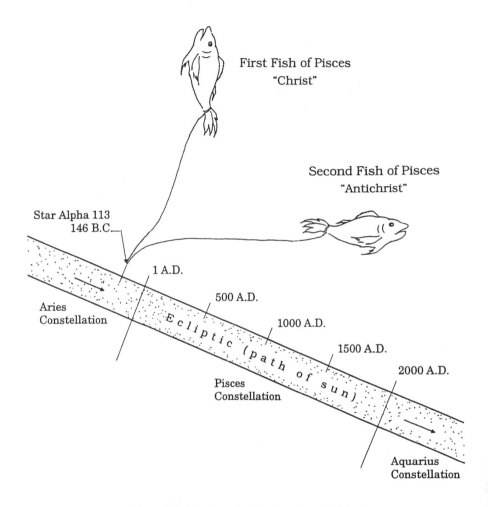

Figure 13. Movement of the Sun through Pisces.
The diagram shows how the position of the sun at the time of the spring
equinox has shifted over the centuries of the Christian era in relationship to the
background stars of the constellation Pisces. The ecliptic represents the
movement of the sun's position at the spring equinox, over the centuries.

11
Paragraphs 150-161

The Prophecies of Nostradamus

Jung sets the scene for his discussion of Nostradamus with the first paragraph of chapter seven, a concise summarizing statement:

> The course of our religious history as well as an essential part of our psychic de- velopment could have been predicted more or less accurately, both as regards time and content, from the precession of the equinoxes through the constellation of Pisces. The prediction, as we saw, was actually made and coincides with the fact that the Church suffered a schism in the sixteenth century. [In other words, our nodal point of 1500.] After that an enantiodromian process set in which, in contrast to the "Gothic" striving *upwards* to the heights, could be described as a horizontal movement *outwards,* namely the voyages of discovery and the conquest of Nature. The vertical was cut across by the horizontal, and man's spiritual and moral devel- opment moved in a direction that grew more and more obviously antichristian [corresponding to the movement of the equinoctial point through the two fishes: first through the vertical fish and then, starting about 1500, through the horizontal fish], so that today we are confronted with a crisis of Western civilization whose outcome appears to be exceedingly dubious.

Jung then turns to the astrological prophecies of Nostradamus. As is evident to the readers of *Aion,* Jung casts his net very widely. Who would have thought Nostradamus would come into the picture! But here he is.

This man whom Jung thought was worth a chapter in *Aion* lived from 1503 to 1566, so he was born right on the nodal point of 1500. His parents were French Jews who were forced to convert to Christianity on the threat of exile. Nos- tradamus lived a very dramatic life. Both his grandfathers were famous physi- cians and astrologers, a combination very common in those days, and they were in the service of the Dukedom, which was equivalent to French royalty.

Nostradamus was a precocious child, and his education was supervised by his grandfather, who saw that he had the best. He went to medical school at Mont- pelier, and did brilliantly. He spent several years as a successful wandering physician, which was usual in those days. He developed quite a reputation for his courageous treatment of plague victims. In his early thirties he settled down with a wife and two children. After a few years the plague struck home and his whole family was wiped out except for himself. He then had ten years of wan- dering as a physician, and at forty-four he married again, to a rich widow. He became a court favorite and turned more and more to the writing of prophecies in verse—at first, about the coming year, then gradually he ranged farther and farther afield. His published prophecies were very popular although they were quite obscure and not very specific. Nostradamus tells us that he only began writing, or at least publishing them, at the age of fifty-one. He said that he found "an unaccountable and new enthusiasm springing up uncontrollably in his mind, which at last amounted almost to a maddening fever, till he sat down to write [the prophecies]."[60]

Nostradamus was really gripped by the activation of the unconscious. In his preface to the prophecies, written as a letter to his son, he says that he refrained from writing down his prophecies for a long time because people would be offended by what they heard. He quotes Christ's saying, "Give not that which is holy unto dogs, nor cast your pearls before swine." But he changed his mind, and evidently the reason he did so was that maddening fever he experienced internally. He makes an interesting remark: "Later, because of the vulgar advent, I decided to give way, and by dark and cryptic sentences tell you of the causes of the future mutation of mankind."[61]

The term "vulgar advent" is usually assumed by Nostradamus scholars to refer to the French Revolution, but I think the use of the term "advent" suggests that it might rather refer to his vision of the coming of the Antichrist. In another place he confesses: "Many times in the week I am overtaken by an ecstasy."[62] Again he says that his calculations "have been determined by the celestial movements combined with the emotion handed down to me by my forbears, which come over me at certain hours."[63] In other words, Nostradamus would be meditating on astrological images and patterns, and in the midst of that meditation he would be gripped by intense emotions which he identified with residues of his ancestors within his own makeup.

In another place, Nostradamus says,

> Hidden prophecies come to me by the subtle spirit of fire, sometimes through the understanding being disturbed in contemplating the remotest of stars while remaining alert. The pronouncements are taken down in writing without fear, without a taint of excess verbiage . . . because all these things proceeded from the divine power of the great eternal God.[64]

So he was absolutely convinced that his prophecies were divinely inspired. Now with this background, let us look at the one particular prophecy Jung chose to quote:

> After detailing a year characterized, among other things, by [various astrological

---

60 Charles A. Ward, *Oracles of Nostradamus,* p. 8.
61 Edgar Leoni, *Nostradamus and His Prophecies,* p. 123.
62 Ibid., p. 127.
63 Ibid., p. 329.
64 Ibid., p. 123.

conjunctions], he says: "Then the beginning of that year shall see a greater persecution against the Christian Church than ever was in Africa, and it shall be in the year 1792, at which time everyone will think it a renovation of the age. . . . And at that time and in those countries the infernal power shall rise against the Church of Jesus Christ. This shall be the second Antichrist, which shall persecute the said Church and its true vicar by means of the power of temporal kings, who through their ignorance shall be seduced by tongues more sharp than any sword in the hands of a madman. . . . The persecution of the clergy shall have its beginning in the power of the Northern Kings joined by the Eastern ones. And that persecution shall last eleven years, or a little less, at which time the chief Northern king shall fail." (par. 151)

This reference to 1792 is generally understood as referring to the French Revolution. Concerning this, Jung says, after reviewing some other facts which led to the date of 1789:

Both dates are suggestive, and a knowledge of subsequent events confirms that the things that happened around that time were significant forerunners of developments in our own day. The enthronement of the "Déesse Raison" [the "Goddess Reason"] was, in fact, an anticipation of the antichristian trend that was pursued from then onwards. (par. 155)

Jung alludes to the enthronement of the Goddess Reason several times and gives considerable historical importance to it as a symbolic event. The closest thing I find to this event is in Will Durant's *The Age of Napoleon,* in which he writes:

A crowd of sansculottes [rebels] invaded the Abbey of St. Denis on October 16, 1793, emptied the coffins of French royalty there entombed, and melted the metal for use in the war. . . . On November 10 men and women from the working-class quarters and the ideological haunts of Paris paraded through the streets in mock religious dress and procession; they entered the hall of the Convention and prevailed upon the deputies to pledge attendance at that evening's fête in the Cathedral of Notre-Dame—renamed the Temple of Reason. There a new sanctuary had been arranged, in which Mademoiselle Candeille of the Opera, robed in a tricolor flag and crowned with a red cap, stood as the Goddess of Liberty [I guess that would be the equivalent of the Goddess of Reason], attended by persuasive ladies who sang a "Hymn to Liberty." . . . The worshippers danced and sang in the naves, while in the side chapels, said hostile reporters, profiteers of freedom, celebrated the rites of love. [In other words they copulated.] On November 17 . . . the bishop of Paris, yielding to popular demand, appeared before the Convention, abjured his office, handed over to the president his episcopal crozier and ring, and donned the red cap of freedom. On November 23 the Commune ordered all Christian churches in Paris closed.[65]

That shows you what was going on in the cathedral of Notre Dame, renamed

---

[65] *The Age of Napoleon,* p. 73.

the temple of the Goddess of Reason. Jung expands on this issue in his essay "The Spiritual Problem of Modern Man":

> There can be no doubt that from the beginning of the nineteenth century—ever since the time of the French Revolution—the psyche has moved more and more into the foreground of man's interest . . . . The enthronement of the Goddess of Reason in Notre Dame seems to have been a symbolic gesture of great significance for the Western world—rather like the hewing down of Wotan's oak by Christian missionaries. . . .
>
> It is certainly more than an amusing freak of history that just at the time of the Revolution, a Frenchman, Anquetil du Perron, should be living in India and, at the beginning of the nineteenth century, brought back with him a translation of the *Oupnek'hat,* a collection of fifty Upanishads [simultaneously with this enthronement of the Goddess of Reason], which gave the West its first deep insight into the baffling mind of the East. To the historian this is a mere coincidence independent of the historical nexus of cause and effect. My medical bias prevents me from seeing it simply as an accident. Everything happened in accordance with a psychological law which is unfailingly valid in personal affairs. If anything of importance is devalued in our conscious life, and perishes—so runs the law—there arises a compensation in the unconscious. We may see in this an analogy to the conservation of energy in the physical world, for our psychic processes also have a quantitative, energic aspect. No psychic value can disappear without being replaced by another of equivalent intensity. This is a fundamental rule which is repeatedly verified in the daily practice of the psychotherapist and never fails. The doctor in me refuses point blank to consider the life of a people as something that does not conform to psychological law.[66]

Here we have a glimpse of how Jung perceives the history of humanity as the history of one more patient. He says that as the spiritual value that had been carried in the vessel of Christianity was in the process of being so severely depreciated, the new version of that psychic value was being brought from the East. It is even significant that a Frenchman had to do it, since it was the French who were enthroning the Goddess of Reason.

This historical archetypal event, the enthronement of the Goddess Reason, is something that we see relived in the life of the young individual again and again. We don't see it as much now as in earlier times because there are not so many people who have been exposed to a religious childhood, but there are still some. We see friends or patients who have gone through a religious childhood and at adolescence go through the "French Revolution," in effect enthroning the Goddess Reason in Notre Dame. This is an archetypal event which takes place individually as well as historically.

Jung continues his consideration of Nostradamus's prophecy regarding the

---

66 *Civilization in Transition,* CW 10, pars. 174f.

emergence of the Antichrist and his reference to the northern kings, and enlarges it to include both the idea of the power from the north and the concept of the lower or chthonic triad:

> That a usurper from the North would seize power is easily understood when we consider that the Antichrist is something infernal, the devil or the devil's son, and is therefore Typhon or Set, who has his fiery abode in the North. Typhon's power is triadic, possessing two confederates, one in the East and one in the South. This power corresponds to the "lower triad." (par. 156)

> Adam Scotus imagined there was a frightful dragon's head in the north from which all evil comes. From its mouth and snout it emitted smoke of a triple nature. (par. 158)

And then there is a reference to footnote 24, in which Jung says, "Allusion to the lower triad."

What is this "lower triad"? Concerning the alchemical image of the lower triad, we find in *Alchemical Studies* a picture of a hermaphrodite standing on a three-headed serpent which is identified as the lower triad.[67] This image is particularly important in dream interpretation. The Christian aeon has been characterized by the creation of an upper triad represented by the Christian Trinity, the trinity that so fascinated Joachim of Flora. But as Jung tells us, the creation of an upper trinity generates its opposite, a lower trinity. We have a striking image of this in Dante's *Inferno*. At the very beginning of the work there is an image of the lower triad, as Dante is faced with three animals—a leopardess, a lion and a she-wolf. This encounter is followed by his descent into hell. At the lowest part of hell, he finds Satan embedded in a rock of ice:

> How frozen and how faint I now became,
> Ask me not, reader, for all language here
> Would not make words enough for me to tell.
> I did not die, nor yet remain alive:
> If genius flowers in you, now imagine
> What I became, deprived of life and death!
> The emperor of all the realms of woe
> From his midbreast emerged above the ice.
> Better with giants I myself compare
> Than do the giants with his mighty arms.
> Now mark how vast must be the whole of him
> To be in scale with parts of such proportions!
> If he was once as fair as now he's foul,
> Yet lifted up his brows against his Maker,
> Well should all tribulation come from him:
> And what a monster he appeared to me

---

[67] CW 13, plate B2 (following p. 160).

When I perceived three faces on his head!
The one in front was of a crimson hue,
And to it were the other two attached
Above the very middle of each shoulder; . . .
The right-hand one was of a yellowish white,
While that upon the left was just as black
As any Ethiopian's on the Nile.
Beneath each face there sprang forth two great wings . . .
Like wings of bats; and he was flapping them
To make three separate blasts of icy wind,
Enough to freeze the confines of Cocytus.
With all six eyes he wept, and from three chins
The tears and bloody foam were trickling down.[68]

A terrible image of an infernal trinity—horrible. That is what, in neutral psychological terminology, Jung calls the lower triad. He goes into this image in very nice detail in another essay, "The Phenomenology of the Spirit in Fairy-tales," where he interprets a fairy tale that involves a three-legged horse.[69] This horse had been acquired by a magician from a witch who had owned it, but as the magician rode away on the horse, which originally was four-legged when owned by the witch, and crossed the border of the witch's realm, twelve wolves attacked him and tore off one of the horse's hooves, so the magician was left with a three-legged horse. There is more to the tale, but this is the part that concerns the lower triad. Jung tells us that this three-legged horse represents the lower or chthonic triad. He then says:

[Threeness] denotes polarity, since one triad always presupposes another, just as high presupposes low, lightness darkness, good evil. In terms of energy, polarity means a potential, and wherever a potential exists there is the possibility of a current, a flow of events, for the tension of opposites strives for balance. If one imagines the quaternity as a square divided into two halves by a diagonal, one gets two triangles whose apices point in opposite directions. One could therefore say metaphorically that if the wholeness symbolized by the quaternity is divided into equal halves, it produces two opposing triads. This . . . shows how three can be derived from four, and in the same way the hunter of the captured princess explains how his horse, from being four-legged, became three-legged, through having one hoof torn off by the twelve wolves. The three-leggedness is due to an accident, therefore, which occurred at the very moment when the horse was leaving the territory of the dark mother. In psychological language we should say that when the unconscious wholeness becomes manifest, i.e., leaves the unconscious and crosses over into the sphere of consciousness, one of the four remains behind, held fast by the *horror vacui* of the unconscious. There thus arises a triad, which as we

---

[68] Canto 34, lines 22-54.
[69] *The Archetypes and the Collective Unconscious,* CW 9i, par. 423.

know—not from the fairytale but from the history of symbolism—constellates a corresponding triad in opposition to it—in other words, a conflict ensues.[70]

Jung continues, saying that the fourth leg missing from the horse corresponds to the inferior function which remains connected to the matrix in the unconscious. Here is a very finely presented formulation:

> The lost component which is in the possession of the wolves belonging to the Great Mother is indeed only a quarter, but, together with the three [that got away], it makes a whole which does away with division and conflict.
>
> But how is it that a quarter, on the evidence of symbolism, is at the same time a triad? . . . I have said previously that three functions can become differentiated, and only one remains under the spell of the unconscious. This statement must be defined more closely. It is an empirical fact that only *one* function becomes more or less successfully differentiated, which on that account is known as the superior or main function . . . . This function has associated with it one or two partially differentiated auxiliary functions which hardly ever attain the same degree of differentiation as the main function, that is, the same degree of applicability by the will. Accordingly they possess a higher degree of spontaneity than the main function, which displays a large measure of reliability and is amenable to our intentions. The fourth, inferior function proves on the other hand to be inaccessible to our will. . . . It always comes and goes of its own volition. From this it is clear that even the differentiated functions have only partially freed themselves from the unconscious; for the rest they are still rooted in it and to that extent they operate under its rule. Hence the three "differentiated" functions at the disposal of the ego have three corresponding unconscious components that have not yet broken loose from the unconscious. And just as the three conscious and differentiated parts of these functions are confronted by a fourth, undifferentiated function which acts as a painfully disturbing factor, so also the superior function seems to have its worst enemy in the unconscious.[71]

What this means is that when the auxiliary functions, the second and third functions, undergo their differentiation, they in effect split, and part of them goes with the superior function and the other part goes with the inferior function. The result is a pair of triads. This is the simple psychology that lies behind the massive images of the heavenly Trinity of Christianity and the Luciferian trinity in the depths of hell. But encountering those symbolic images, one starts to feel the impact of what it means for the two triads to have undergone such a separation. We do well to keep these ideas in mind whenever we encounter in a dream a threesome of a lowly nature, especially of an animal nature; it can be thought of as the lower triad.

To turn to the symbolic image of the north, Jung takes the idea from Nos-

---

[70] Ibid., par. 426.
[71] Ibid., pars. 430f.

tradamus's prophecy in which he says the Antichrist shall have its beginning in the power of the northern kings. Starting with the image of the northern kings, Jung discusses the symbolism of the north. A number of Biblical passages emerge as Jung starts circumambulating the idea of the Antichrist coming from the north:

A second time the word of Yahweh was spoken to me, asking,"What do you see?" "I see a cooking pot on the boil," I answered, "with its contents tilting from the North." Then Yahweh said: "The North is where disaster is boiling over for all who live in this land; since I am now going to summon all the kingdoms of the North [to come down and attack Jerusalem]." (Jer. 1:13ff., JB)

This is a prototype of the Antichrist coming from the north. There are other Biblical examples of evil arising in the north:

How did you come to fall from the heavens,
Daystar, son of Dawn?[Lucifer]
How did you come to be thrown to the ground,
you who enslaved the nations?
You who used to think to yourself,
"I will climb up to the heavens;
and higher than the stars of God
I will set my throne.
I will sit on the Mount of Assembly
in the recesses of the north." (Isa. 14:12ff., JB)

So there is Lucifer coming from the north. Ezekiel is another very important reference. The beginning of Ezekiel's vision reads as follows: "There the hand of Yahweh came on me. I looked; a stormy wind blew from the north, a great cloud with light around it, a fire from which flashes of lightning darted." (Ezek. 1:4ff., JB) So Ezekiel's grand vision of the nature of God also came from the north. There is another reference in Job 26:7.

In paragraph 158 Jung speaks of a Christian writer who quotes Ezekiel and his vision of God coming from the north; the writer relates that to the coming of the Antichrist. Jung comments:

The pious author never stops to think how remarkable it is that the prophet's [Ezekiel's] vision of God should be blown along on the wings of the north wind, wrapped in this devilish smoke of threefold ignorance.

This material which Jung lays out indicates that the unconscious of these pious authors is pointing out the fact that both devilish and divine attributes come from the same source. They are the positive and negative manifestations of the Self. Those realizations are slipped into religious discourse by the unconscious of those who do not realize what they are revealing. So the north is both the abode of Set, Typhon, Lucifer, the devil, and the source of the most magnificent revelation of deity that the whole Old Testament offers us.

The Historical Significance of the Fish

Jung begins his chapter on the historical importance of the fish with a discussion of the birth of the Messiah. He writes:

> Like every hero, Christ had a childhood that was threatened (massacre of the innocents, flight into Egypt). The astrological "interpretation" of this can be found in Revelation 12:1: "A woman clothed with the sun, with the moon under her feet, and on her head a crown of twelve stars." (par. 163)

This image of the woman clothed with the sun is part of a grand apocalyptic vision experienced by St. John the Divine on the island of Patmos:

> Now a great sign appeared in heaven: a woman, adorned with the sun, standing on the moon, and with the twelve stars on her head for a crown. She was pregnant, and in labor, crying aloud in the pangs of childbirth. Then a second sign appeared in the sky, a huge red dragon which had seven heads and ten horns, and each of the seven heads crowned with a coronet. Its tail dragged a third of the stars from the sky and dropped them to the earth, and the dragon stopped in front of the woman as she was having the child, so that he could eat it as soon as it was born from its mother. The woman brought a male child into the world, the son who was to rule all the nations with an iron scepter, and the child was taken straight up to God and to his throne, while the woman escaped into the desert, where God had made a place of safety ready, for her to be looked after in the twelve hundred and sixty days. (Rev. 12:1-6, JB)

Jung refers to this account in Revelation as a variation of Christ's nativity. He attaches considerable importance to the image, as indicated by his lengthy discussion of it in "Answer to Job."[72] He observes there that the image also corresponds to the myth of Leto's giving birth to Apollo. Leto was pregnant with the twins Artemis and Apollo, but Hera in the form of a python pursued her and allowed her no rest, nor was any place on earth permitted to aid at the birth, which finally came to pass on Delos, a floating island. The passage in Revelation gives us a parallel image of a pregnant woman with a serpent or dragon waiting to devour the child as soon as it comes forth. In his commentary in "Answer to Job," Jung notes that in the Revelation text she is "a woman clothed with the sun," emphasizing that she is simply " 'a woman' —an ordinary woman, not a goddess and not an eternal virgin immaculately conceived."[73]

---

[72] *Psychology and Religion,* CW 11, pars. 710ff.
[73] Ibid., par. 711.

Jung puts forth the idea that the next incarnation of the Self is symbolized by the birth of this child, and that as it appears in the individuation process, it will be born out of the ordinary human being and not the special purified one represented by the Virgin Mary. He points out that the child is born out of the union of opposites. Since the woman is clothed in the sun and has the moon at her feet; she personifies the *coniunctio* of Sol and Luna. Jung continues:

> The man-child is "caught up" to God, who is manifestly his father, and the mother is hidden in the wilderness. This would seem to indicate that the child-figure will remain latent for an indefinite time and that its activity is reserved for the future. The story of Hagar may be a prefiguration of this. The similarity between this story and the birth of Christ obviously means no more than that the birth of the man-child is an analogous event . . . . This strange repetition or duplication of the characteristic events in Christ's life gave rise to the conjecture that a second Messiah is to be expected at the end of the world. What is meant here cannot be the return of Christ himself, for we are told that he would come "in the clouds of heaven," but not be *born* a second time, and certainly not from a sun-moon conjunction. . . . The fact that John uses the myth of Leto and Apollo in describing the birth may be an indication that the vision, in contrast to the Christian tradition, is a product of the unconscious.[74]

This image is particularly relevant to the individuation process, and it has been discovered and made explicit at the present time. The man-child who is caught up to God is an image of the Self which is to be realized through the efforts of the ordinary person at the end of the Christian aeon. The image is a prefiguration of the discovery of the individuation process, which is why Jung paid so much attention to it.

In *Aion* Jung gives us another account of the birth of the Messiah from a Jewish legend. This is a parallel to the vision in Revelation. It reads as follows:

> Elias [Elijah] found in Bethlehem a young woman sitting before her door with a newborn child lying on the ground beside her, flecked with blood. She explained that her son had been born at an evil hour, just when the temple was destroyed. Elias admonished her to look after the child. When he came back again five weeks later, he asked about her son. "He neither walks, nor sees, nor speaks, nor hears, but lies there like a stone," said the woman. Suddenly a wind blew from the four corners of the earth, bore the child away, and plunged him into the sea. Elias lamented that it was now all up with the salvation of Israel, but a *bath kol* (voice) said to him:
>> "It is not so. He will remain in the great sea for four hundred years, and eighty years in the rising smoke of the children of Korah, eighty years under the gates of Rome, and the rest of the time he will wander round in the great cities until the end of the days comes."

---

[74] Ibid., par. 713.

This story describes a Messiah who, though born in Bethlehem, is wafted by divine intervention into the Beyond (sea = unconscious). (pars. 167f.)

This legend has many similarities to the sun-woman text in Revelation, but there is absolutely no reason to believe that they influenced one another. They are totally autochthonous parallels, but in each case the birth occurs at a time of grave external danger and the child is taken into protection. In one case, he is taken up to be with God in heaven; in the other, he is taken into the sea where he will remain for a stipulated period of time. Parallel images such as these that crop up at approximately the same time, indicate that an underlying archetype is activated; it is like a bulb or a root that throws up shoots. When the shoots come up, they are not exactly the same, but similar. The similarities indicate that they derive from the same root. The story of the nativity of Christ is another shoot from the same root. Again the Messiah is born into an environment of grave danger; Herod is out to kill him. Danger surrounds the new-born Self because the established conscious dominant, the conscious authority accepted by the ego, is gravely threatened by the birth of the Self; it senses that its authority will be overruled.[75]

The birth and fate of the Messiah lead Jung into a linked theme, that of the two Messiahs, which he presents in paragraph 168:

> Cabalistic tradition speaks of two Messiahs, the Messiah ben Joseph (or ben Ephraim) and the Messiah ben David [the Messiah as son of Joseph or of David]. They were compared to Moses and Aaron, also to two roes, and this on the authority of the Song of Solomon 4:5 . . . . Messiah ben Joseph is, according to Deuteronomy 32:17, the "first-born of his bullock," and Messiah ben David rides on an ass. Messiah ben Joseph is the first, Messiah ben David the second. Messiah ben Joseph must die in order to "atone with his blood for the children of Yahweh." He will fall in the fight against Gog and Magog, and Armilus will kill him. Armilus is the Anti-Messiah, whom Satan begot on a block of marble. He will be killed by Messiah ben David in his turn. Afterwards, ben David will fetch the new Jerusalem down from heaven and bring ben Joseph back to life. This ben Joseph plays a strange role in later tradition. Tabari, the commentator on the Koran, mentions that the Antichrist will be a king of the Jews, and . . . [another says that the] Messiah ben Joseph actually is the Antichrist. So he is not only characterized as the suffering Messiah in contrast to the victorious one, but is ultimately thought of as his antagonist.

In this paragraph, Jung condenses a great deal of legendary material into very compact form. Let us consider at more length what is implied by this "double Messiah."

The ben Joseph Messiah suggests one with a personal father whereas the ben David Messiah suggests one with an archetypal father; David as the great histor-

---

75 I discuss this theme in more detail in *The Christian Archetype*, chap. 3.

ical king would carry more of the archetypal factor. This idea of two distinct Messiah figures is developed quite explicitly in the Old Testament, where there are a number of texts that all Jewish and Christian scholars agree refer to the Messiah. In the two following examples, one refers to what is called the ben David Messiah, and the other to the ben Joseph Messiah. It is the difference between the royal, victorious, ruling Messiah and the meek, suffering Messiah. An example of the royal Messiah can be found in Psalm II, which is identified as a Messianic psalm:

> Why this uproar among the nations? Why this impotent muttering of pagans—kings on earth rising in revolt, princes plotting against Yahweh and his Anointed ["his Anointed" means Messiah]. "Now let us break their fetters! Now let us throw off their yoke!"
>
> The One whose throne is in heaven sits laughing, Yahweh derides them. Then angrily he addresses them, in a rage he strikes them with panic, "This is my king [that is, his Messiah], installed by me on Zion, my holy mountain."
>
> Let me proclaim Yahweh's decree; he has told me, "You are my son, today I have become your father. Ask and I will give you the nations for your heritage, the ends of the earth for your domain. With iron scepter you will break them, shatter them like potter's ware."
>
> So now, you kings, learn wisdom, earthly rulers, be warned: serve Yahweh, fear him . . . or he will be angry and you will perish. (1:12, JB)

This pictures the regal, ruling, victorious Messiah. There is a very different picture in some of the "suffering servant" passages in Isaiah, which are also universally recognized as Messiah texts:

> As the crowds were appalled on seeing him—so disfigured did he look that he seemed no longer human—so will the crowds be astonished at him, and kings stand speechless before him; for they shall see something never told and witness something never heard before: "Who could believe what we have heard, and to whom has the power of Yahweh been revealed?" Like a sapling he grew up in front of us, like a root in arid ground. Without beauty, without majesty (we saw him), no looks to attract our eyes; a thing despised and rejected by men, a man of sorrows and familiar with suffering, a man to make people screen their faces; he was despised and we took no account of him.
>
> And yet ours were the sufferings he bore, ours the sorrows he carried. But we, we thought of him as someone punished, struck by God, and brought low. Yet he was pierced through for our faults, crushed for our sins. On him lies a punishment that brings us peace, and through his wounds we are healed. (Isa. 52:14-53:5, JB)

Both of these passages refer to the Messiah, but they are totally different. They represent two aspects of the ego's experience of the Self. The one aspect is an imperious authority, one who must be obeyed, and the other is a dispenser of suffering who also shares in the suffering. It is as though Yahweh and Job were united in a single person.

In the course of the individuation process, these two figures are encountered by the ego and to some extent there is an identification with each of them, but it is important that the identification be as little as possible; the figures symbolize the kind of experience that the ego needs to accept while not being possessed by it. There are times when the ego must submit to the imperious authority and there are times when it must be a living expression of it. Similarly, there are times when the ego experiences the redeeming effect of the suffering Self, so to speak, and there are other times when the ego is obliged itself to experience the suffering which then promotes the redeeming aspect of consciousness. The two versions of the Self experience, the active and the receptive, are pictured in these Biblical texts. It is notable that Jung chose as a motto for part one of *Psychology and Alchemy* a passage from one of the suffering servant texts of Isaiah: "The bruised reed he shall not break, and the smoking flax ["flickering wick" would be a better translation] he shall not quench." (42:3, DV)[76]

Returning to fish symbolism, Jung refers to the Book of Tobit in paragraph 174, where he condenses that tale of the healing fish into a couple of sentences. The story is so relevant to the analytic process that it needs to be expanded. The Book of Tobit is one of the books of the Apocrypha. You will not find it in Protestant or Jewish Bibles, but in Catholic Bibles which take their contents from the Septuagint, the Greek Old Testament. The story is the analytic fish story par excellence.

Old man Tobit lived in Nineveh. He was blind and persecuted and neglected, and prayed to die. On that same day, the young woman Sarah, daughter of Raguel who lived in a city in Media, was also contemplating suicide because she had had seven marriages and each time on the wedding night the demon Asmodeus had killed her new husband. These two figures at different levels—the blind old man and the young woman whose demon kills her husbands, were both wishing for death.

In the course of Tobit's prayer he remembered that he had once deposited ten talents of silver, a very sizable sum, with a man in Media. He called his son Tobias to him and said, "I have a deposit of silver in Media and I want you to go and claim it." So Tobias set out with a fellow traveler who turned out to be the angel Raphael. On the first night they camped at the Tigris River bank, and a great fish leapt out and threatened to swallow Tobias's foot. Raphael told him to catch the fish and extract the heart, the gall and the liver from it. There was a furious encounter and Tobias caught the fish and made the extractions, set those parts aside, and ate the rest of the fish.

When they arrived in Media, Tobias recovered the deposited silver, and also met Sarah. He courted her and they married. But then came the wedding night.

---

[76] CW 12, p. 1.

Raphael instructed Tobias on the value of the extracted fish material, telling him to take the liver and heart and burn them; the smoke would drive away the evil demon. And so it happened. The couple returned to Nineveh, where the father's sight was restored by applying the fish's gall to his eyes. At this point the angel Raphael revealed himself for what he was, and flew away.

This story can be recalled whenever a fish dream appears, and there are a lot of fish dreams if one is alert for them. In the story, the original state is one of blindness and despair. One can take Tobit as the ego and Sarah as the anima, or one can reverse this and see Sarah as the ego and Tobit and Tobias as animus figures. Either way, there is a twofold despair—conscious and unconscious. Tobit's prayer sets things in motion because he recalls the deposit of money and sends Tobias out to get it; so the journey gets started, with the helpful angel appearing as the guide.

Then comes the central event of the story in which the fish leaps up and threatens Tobias. It is potentially a curative fish, but it appears at first as threatening. The fish is a kind of lower version of Raphael, one might say. Then there is the struggle with the fish, and the question of who is going to catch whom. Tobias manages to catch the fish and extract its curative qualities, and then everything else follows as a consequence. Tobias meets the anima and the marriage can be successfully consummated because of the curative parts of the fish. A rich quantity of libido is extracted from the unconscious and brought back to consciousness, and simultaneously Tobit's blindness is cured.

The central event of the story is the encounter with the fish, which is what the majority of this book *Aion* is about. As is already evident, and will become increasingly clear as the fish material accumulates, the image of the fish basically has two meanings. It is an image of the cold-blooded, undifferentiated, primordial, infantile psyche, the original concupiscence. The other side of its meaning, in its identification with Christ and the whole aeon, is as a symbol of the Self. So it is the highest and lowest simultaneously, and this corresponds to the fact that when it first appears to Tobias it is a threat until it has been dealt with, and then it becomes a most valuable curative remedy.

Dealing with the fish really has three steps. First is the catching of the fish. Second is the extraction of its healing virtues. Third is applying the remedy in the living situation. One can call those three steps capture, extraction and transformation, and this I consider to be the essence of the whole analytical process.

An example of such an image comes from a dream of my own. Very early in my personal analysis, I had what I take to be my initial dream. In the dream a golden fish was jumping up through the floor and I was trying to catch it. The process of catching it was rather complicated, but I finally succeeded. The next task was to extract its blood. I got it out of the fish and into a beaker. I was boiling the blood, which was supposed to keep it permanently fluid if the process succeeded. The danger was that the blood might clot before the process was finished. An older man, whom I identified as a spokesman for tradition, told me the method would never work, the blood was sure to clot. However, I did not think so. I thought I had a good chance of succeeding and kept on boiling the blood. You can see that three steps are involved in the dream: catching, extracting and transformation. The dream is an individual variant of the Book of Tobit. Many examples of this image are to be found.

Another important theme of this chapter, one which is also fundamental to analytic practice, is the motif of the destruction of the God-image. Jung writes:

> As the highest value and supreme dominant in the psychic hierarchy, the God-image is immediately related to, or identical with, the self, and everything that happens to the God-image has an effect on the latter. Any uncertainty about the God-image causes a profound uneasiness in the self, for which reason the question is generally ignored because of its painfulness. But that does not mean that it remains unasked in the unconscious. What is more, it is answered by views and beliefs like materialism, atheism, and similar substitutes, which spread like epidemics. They crop up wherever and whenever one waits in vain for the legitimate answer. The *ersatz* product represses the real question into the unconscious and destroys the continuity of historical tradition which is the hallmark of civilization. The result is bewilderment and confusion. Christianity has insisted on God's goodness as a loving Father and has done its best to rob evil of substance. The early Christian prophecy concerning the Antichrist, and certain ideas in late Jewish theology, could have suggested to us that the Christian answer to the problem of Job omits to mention the corollary, the sinister reality of which is now being demonstrated before our eyes by the splitting of our world: *the destruction of the God-image is followed by the annulment of the human personality.* (par. 170)

This is the malady of our time—the destruction of the God-image. The more one reflects on it, and the more experience one accumulates, the more one realizes that the great sociological and individual symptoms of our time—crime, alcoholism, drug addiction, child abuse, a state of general disorientation—are all symptoms of the same fact, the destruction of the God-image.

Jung's statement points to the ultimate task of Jungian analysis, which is the reconstruction of the God-image in the individual. This is what the fish story accomplishes, too. They refer to the same thing. As we realize this, we begin to understand how this difficult material which Jung assembles in *Aion* is really profoundly relevant to our analytic work.

13

Paragraphs 177-192

The Historical Significance of the Fish (cont.)

The Eucharist or the host, the sacred food distributed in the ritual of the Mass, is considered to be the transubstantiated body of Christ. It is the literal flesh of Christ that is eaten in the Mass. Jung opens a new subject as he discusses the monster Leviathan, which is also described as eucharistic food:

> In Jewish tradition . . . the *pharmakon athanasias* [the medicine of immortality] is the flesh of Leviathan, the "Messianic fish" . . . . The Talmud Sanhedrin says that the Messiah "will not come until a fish is sought for an invalid and cannot be procured." According to the Apocalypse of Baruch, Behemoth as well as Leviathan is a eucharistic food. (par. 178)

Behemoth and Leviathan are mentioned together in only one place in the Bible. A few verses will remind us of what they are. Yahweh has just made his entrance before Job, and in the course of describing how grand he is in comparison to how small and miserable Job is, Yahweh produces these great monsters as exhibits. He says:

> Behold now, behemoth, which I made as well as thee; he eateth grass as an ox. Lo now, his strength is in his loins, and his force is in the muscles of his belly. He moveth his tail like a cedar. . . . He is the chief of the ways of God. (Job 40:15-19, ASV)

Then he turns to Leviathan:

> Canst thou draw out leviathan with a fish-hook? Or press down his tongue with a cord? . . . Will he make a covenant with thee? . . . That thou shouldst take him for a servant? . . . Wilt thou play with him as with a bird? . . . Behold, the hope of him is in vain. (Job 41:1-9, ASV)

These theriomorphic aspects of Yahweh are shown in the well-known picture by William Blake (figure 14, page 96), who perceived Behemoth as a mammal, a grass eater, and Leviathan as a monster of the depths.

Jung's statement that Leviathan is eucharistic food leads to an important image in Jewish legend, the messianic banquet. Raphael Patai's *The Messiah Texts* brings this material together in a wonderful way, so that we do not have to go searching through all the obscure literature. The legends describe the messianic banquet that will take place when the Messiah comes; the devout or elect will be invited to the banquet with him:

> [The legend says] God created a male and a female Leviathan, and had they copulated . . . [their offspring] would have destroyed the whole world. What did the

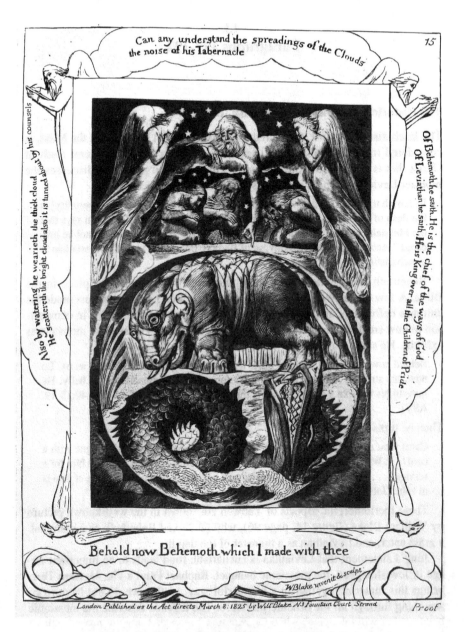

Figure 14. William Blake's Behemoth and Leviathan.
Yahweh reveals to Job his monstrous aspects, Behemoth and Leviathan.

Holy One, blessed be He, do? He castrated the male and killed the female and preserved her in salt for the pious in the Future to Come. And also the Behemoth . . . what did . . . He do? He castrated the male and cooled the female and preserved her for the pious in the Future to Come. . . . In that hour the Holy One, blessed be He, will set tables and slaughter Behemoth and Leviathan . . . and prepare a great banquet for the pious. And He will seat each one of them according to his honor, and say to them: "Do you want to drink apple wine, or pomegranate wine, or grape wine?" And the pious will say, "The choice is Yours . . . " And the Holy One, blessed be He, will bring them wine that was preserved in its grapes since the six days of creation. . . . And each pious man will see His Glory, and each of them will point with his finger and say, "This is God, our God for ever and ever!" And they will eat and drink and rejoice, until the Holy One, blessed be He, commands that the cup of benediction be filled.[77]

The cup of benediction is a kind of great toast of blessing that is to be made; Jung refers to it, saying: "The Jewish 'chalice of benediction' was sometimes decorated with pictures of fishes, for fishes were the food of the blessed in Paradise." (par. 178)

Leviathan represents the primordial infantile psyche which the legend tells us will be assimilated at the time of the coming of the Messiah, at the time of the conscious realization of the Self. You might say that this is a grander version of the image of Tobias eating the great fish that leapt out at him. This legendary idea can be understood in two ways. The legend puts it that when the Messiah comes, the Leviathan will be served up as eucharistic food. That is, when the Self comes, then the primordial infantile psyche will be assimilated. The other way of putting it is that when the primordial psyche is assimilated, then the Messiah will come. I think the latter is psychologically more accurate; it does not involve such magical thinking. The Messiah would represent the Self as consciously realized.

The messianic banquet is the underlying image of the Catholic Mass, in which its symbolism is acted out. Unfortunately, the ritual does not bring about the permanent psychological transformation that consciousness does. I consider the messianic banquet to be a grand image of the whole enterprise of the development of consciousness by collective humanity. I see it as symbolizing the collective effort of our species to create consciousness by confronting and assimilating the primordial psyche which it is born into. In the process of that operation, the primitive God-image is progressively transformed.

My personal image is that we have a huge banquet table around which all humanity sits. On the table lies the vast hulk of Leviathan, waiting to be eaten. Here and there, in little spots, it will have been cooked, but most of it is completely raw. If the individuals who have cooked those little spots eat some of the

---

[77] *The Messiah Texts,* pp. 236ff.

cooked stuff, they will be able to integrate it. But the vast majority of people will be eating the raw slices, and they will just fall into identification with the primordial psyche and live it out; there won't be any consciousness. But through the few who continue to cook their little pieces and eat them, very, very slowly Leviathan is being assimilated and transformed.

In considering ancient examples of fish symbolism, Jung refers to two Jewish apocalypses. Apocalypses are end-of-the-aeon literature. At the end of the last aeon, a number of apocalypses popped up, clustered right around the beginning of our era. One is the Book of Enoch, written about 100 B.C., and two others were written in the last quarter of the first century (75 to 100 A.D.), right after the fall of Jerusalem. The city's demise provoked a number of apocalypses and was the personal dimension for the expression of the archetypal image.

Edgar Hennecke gives a nice summary of the nature of apocalyptic thinking, which he considers to have four major features.[78] One is that it expresses the doctrine of two ages: the current age which is ending, and the age that is about to come. The two ages might also be thought of as time on the one hand, eternity on the other. Of course, the age in which one lives is the decadent, bad age; the age to come is the good one. This ties in with the second feature, pessimism for the present age and hope for the future one. So apocalyptic thinking is a combination of pessimism and hope; short-range pessimism and long-range hope.

Thirdly, this thinking emphasizes the concepts of universalism and of individualism. History is seen as a whole and the world and mankind are thought of as a unity, so that narrow nationalisms are transcended. At the same time, the emphasis is on what goes on between the individual and God, not between a collective and God, and not on the individual as a member of a collective, but on the individual as such, face-to-face with the divine process.

The fourth item Hennecke mentions is determinism, saying that apocalyptic thinking considers that the course of events has been predetermined by God and therefore can, more or less, be calculated. This determinism is equivalent to the activation and the living out of an archetypal pattern. To the extent that an archetype governs the course of events either in an individual's life, or in the life of the collective, the events are determined in a general way; the pattern has already been laid down.

It is interesting to consider, since we are at the end of an aeon, that perhaps apocalyptic literature is showing up again in the modern world. The old-fashioned apocalypses are out of style; they are just a little too primitive in their thinking, but we definitely have end-of-the-aeon literature. Nietzsche's *Thus Spake Zarathustra* is an example, as well as Spengler's *Decline of the West,* and Jung's *Aion,* of course, is a superb example of such literature. Such a work

---

[78] *New Testament Apocrypha,* II, pp. 588ff.

couldn't be written except at the end of an aeon; in the middle of it, you can't see an age in its totality.

The Ambivalence of the Fish Symbol

Jung speaks here of two different apocalypses. The first is the Syrian Apocalypse of Baruch:

> According to the Syrian Apocalypse of Baruch (29:1 ff.), the time preceding the coming of the Messiah falls into twelve parts, and the Messiah will appear in the twelfth. . . . Leviathan will then rise out of the sea. (par. 181)

The Syrian Apocalypse was written by Pharisaic Jews, probably about 75 A.D.; after the destruction of the Temple in 70 A.D.; it contains a dirge over the destruction of Jerusalem. Here, Jerusalem is thought of not only concretely as a city, but as the whole world of believers. There is then a description of the coming judgement, and Baruch tells of twelve woes that are to come to the earth, after which the Messiah will arrive. At this point, Behemoth and Leviathan will appear, and they will be the food for all that are left.

In this apocalypse, there is a vision of a great cloud formed from the sea and floating up into the sky, which contains black waters and white waters and waters of all colors. This cloud emits a series of twelve rivers that descend on the earth. Some of them are rivers of black water, and a few of them are of bright water. Baruch is told that what is being pictured is the entirety of world history from Adam to the Messiah, and these twelve different rivers represent different phases of this history. After the twelfth river the Messiah comes. In *Aion,* Jung draws our attention in passing to a vast multitude of materials, such as the Syrian Apocalypse, but to get to what lies behind those references, one needs to go back to the original texts; then one glimpses the full range of symbolism lying behind what Jung says.

The other apocalypse to which Jung refers is the apocryphal second Esdras:

> Just as in Augustine Christ the fish is "drawn from the deep," so in II Esdras 13:2ff. the "man" came out of the sea like a wind. His appearance was heralded by an eagle and a lion, theriomorphic symbols which greatly affrighted the prophet in the same way that Behemoth inspired chiefly terror in Job. (par. 185)

Jung just drops this reference and moves on, but the text deserves a little more attention. Second Esdras is another apocalypse written at about the same time as the Baruch work. It is impossible to summarize second Esdras because it is composed of a great number of different visions, but the particular vision that Jung refers to is the one in which the prophet-seer sees an eagle with twelve wings and three heads coming up from the sea. The eagle rules over the entire earth. Other wings sprout, some wings fall off; a whole process goes on that is interpreted as an historical sequence. Then a lion comes roaring out of the woods and berates the eagle for its evil, and the eagle is burned.

We are told that the lion represents the Messiah who appears to overcome the evil rulers of the earth, represented by the eagle and its various wings. Then a violent wind stirs the sea, causing the emergence of a man who flies into the clouds of heaven. The voice from his mouth melts everything that hears it, and so is a variation of the rivers of water in the Baruch apocalypse. A multitude of men try to make war against the celestial man, but he stands on a mountain and sends out of his mouth a fiery stream of flaming breath, a storm of sparks which burn up the multitude that is against him. It is all part of an apocalyptic end of the world that is then followed by a last judgement. Finally, as is so often the case with these apocalyptic works, the seer is told to write down his vision and publish it, the same thing told to St. John the Divine in Revelation, which is another classic example of this form of literature.

Tracing the fish symbol from the sea monster Leviathan through other ancient monsters, Jung refers in paragraph 185 to Marduk and Tiamat:

> We are told that Yahweh smote Rahab "by his understanding" *(tebuna)*. Rahab, the sea monster, is cousin german to Tiamat, whom Marduk split asunder by filling her up with Imhullu, the north wind.

Here again, Jung makes a reference and passes on with the assumption that everyone is familiar with it. The following summary of the Marduk story comes from Alexander Heidel's text, *The Babylonian Genesis.* Marduk was the young hero of the gods. The old gods had been tyrannized by the monster Tiamat, so Marduk went to battle with her, denounced her in trenchant terms for her wicked measures, and challenged her to a duel. She became like one in a frenzy who has lost her reason. She accepted the challenge and the two engaged in single combat. Marduk spread out his net and enmeshed her, and when she opened her mouth to devour him, Marduk drove the evil north wind (Imhullu) into Tiamat so that she could not close her lips. Then he shot an arrow through her open mouth and it struck her heart and destroyed her life. Marduk cast down Tiamat's carcass and split her skull with an unsparing club, cut her arteries and caused the north wind to carry her blood southward. Finally he divided the colossal body of Tiamat into two parts to create the universe. With one half of her corpse he formed the sky, and with the other half the earth.

The tale is a variation of the primitive Egyptian creation myth of the separation of the world parents, in which the god Shu came in between them—they were in a state of continuous cohabitation—and lifted the two apart so that one became the sky and the other the earth. This is an image of developing consciousness: whenever consciousness touches an unconscious content, the content is split into opposites. It is a basic theme of creation myths.[79]

---

[79] This theme is discussed further in my *Anatomy of the Psyche,* pp. 183ff.

An example of this particular archetypal image is my own earliest dream, which I am sure occurred before I was a year old. The dream was that I was experiencing, sequentially, smoothness and roughness. Smoothness was heaven and roughness was hell. I did not have any words, just experiential conditions, but they were contrasted with each other. The dream is an example of how, even so early in life, the opposites are being separated. The young emerging ego starts to make distinctions between what it likes and does not like.

This idea of the emergence of the opposites continues in Jung's discussion of the double nature of the fish. The majority of chapter nine of *Aion* concerns this subject. Jung tells us that according to certain early texts, the original sea monster was split into two. Some texts speak of two Leviathans; later the doubling is expressed in the pairing of Behemoth and Leviathan. Jung puts it another way in paragraph 183, in the idea that the original deity split Leviathan off from himself or split a monster off from himself, so that the opposition was then between God and the monster. But then the monster split into two and the opposition was no longer between God and the monster, but between the two monsters. Then there were the two fish, a good fish and a bad fish. This is a variation of the same archetypal image which Jung speaks of later, of the two sons of God, Christ and Satan. The image of the two fishes is the prototype for the two sons: Christ the good fish and Satan the bad fish. The symbol is an example of how the Self differentiates under the influence of consciousness. This can also be seen as a doubling of the shadow which Jung speaks of in paragraph 185:

> This split corresponds to the doubling of the shadow often met with in dreams, where the two halves appear as different or even as antagonistic figures. This happens when the conscious ego-personality does not contain all the contents and components that it could contain.

Still another consideration is that this kind of image in dreams indicates that awareness of the opposites is coming into consciousness. An unconscious content often appears in doubled form in dreams at such a time; it is split like Tiamat. What can happen is that one half of the form is accepted and added to consciousness, the half one likes; the half that one does not like is repressed again.

Also relevant here is the double, paradoxical nature of the fish. After presenting some of the evidence on this, Jung goes on to say:

> The ambivalent attitude towards the fish is an indication of its double nature. It is unclean and an emblem of hatred on the one hand, but on the other it is an object of veneration. (par. 187)

An interesting reference to the despicable aspect of the fish appears in note 61, at the end of paragraph 178: "Compare the *esthie pinaon* in the Pectorios inscription." Jung does not translate those Greek words in the *Aion* text. When we turn back to page 89 we read in note 71 to paragraph 146 Jung's quote from the

Pectorios inscription: "Eat . . . holding the fish in the hands. Nourish now with the fish, I yearn, Lord Saviour," which has an uncertain reading. Jung states that the probable reading is *pinaon* instead of *peinaon* and he goes to the trouble to refer to that note again, in the footnote to paragraph 147. This piqued my interest because with practically all Greek terms Jung adds an English interpretation, but he did not this time. The reason is that he is sneaking in some secret wisdom. You see, "eat *pinaon*" means eat the dirtying thing, eat the filthy thing. Considering that he is talking about eucharistic food, that is pretty shocking. So Jung does not translate the term from the Greek.

This same paradoxical wisdom is alluded to in paragraph 185:

> Just as in Augustine Christ the fish is "drawn from the deep" . . . . The fish drawn from the deep has a secret connection with Leviathan: he is the bait with which Leviathan is lured and caught. This fish is probably a duplication of the great fish and stands for its pneumatic aspect. It is evident that Leviathan has such an aspect because he, like the Ichthys, is eucharistic food.

Jung is saying that symbolically speaking, Leviathan equals Christ. They are symbolically equivalent, so that when one eats Christ's flesh in the eucharistic meal, one is eating Leviathan. Conversely, when one assimilates a bit of Leviathan, the primitive infantile psyche, one is also partaking of the sacred Eucharist.

The symbolism of the north has been discussed previously, but Jung returns to it again in this chapter and reminds us with further material of the double, paradoxical quality of the north. Like the paradoxical fish, the north combines the opposites. It is the place God comes from, the source of Ezekiel's supreme vision, and it is also the place where Set and the devil reside. I think the basic reason for this is that the cosmic axis is rooted at the north star, and it is the center of the universe; the center of the great cosmic mandala is located there. Figure 15 gives a visual image of this. It is a time-lapse photograph of the northern sky. What can be seen there is what Francis Thompson calls the "wheeling systems." He speaks of "where the wheeling systems darken."[80]

The figure shows how it looks if you focus right in on the pole directly. This is where God resides, in the center of that picture. Even though the ancients did not have time-lapse photography, their unconscious would have perceived this image of concentric circles in the sky.

---

[80] "In No Strange Land," line 9, in Louis Untermeyer, ed., *Modern American Poetry and Modern British Poetry.*

Figure 15. Time-lapse Photo of the Northern Sky.
The photograph shows star trails around the Pole star, image of the cosmic center.

14
Paragraphs 193-212

The Fish in Alchemy

A major subject in *Aion* is the image of the fish in alchemy. Jung tracks down fish symbolism through the last 2,000 years and locates the fish symbol as it first shows up in alchemical writings. The initial reference is to a jelly-fish:

> There is in the sea a round fish, lacking bones and cortex, [an alternative translation for cortex would be scales or shell] and having in itself a fatness, a wondrous virtue, which, if it is cooked on a slow fire until its fatness and moisture entirely disappear . . . is saturated with sea-water until it begins to shine. (par. 195)

Jung continues, quoting another treatise:

> When the *citrinitas (xanthosis,* "yellowing") appears, "there is formed the *collyrium* [eyewash] of the philosophers." If they wash their eyes with it, they will easily understand the secrets of the philosophy. (par. 195)

This is reminiscent of the Book of Tobit, where the gall extracted from the fish is the eyewash for the old man's blindness. The round fish cooked on a low fire, which begins to shine, leads Jung into Pliny and to the ancient idea of the *stella marina,* the star of the sea:

> This fish was said to be hot and burning . . . . [and of] so fiery a nature that when you rub it with a stick, you can straightaway use the stick as a torch. . . . This animal . . . generates so much heat that it not only sets fire to everything it touches but also cooks its own food. Hence it signifies the . . . inextinguishable power of true love. (par. 197)

Jung goes on to speak of how the roundness of the jelly-fish and its radial arrangement from a central hub are especially important facts for its symbolism. Figure 16 shows how it looks from the top, from the side and from underneath. It is a living mandala. Jung presents a striking image of the earth as a great jelly-fish. He refers to an alchemist's statement that "In the Pole is found the heart of Mercurius, 'which is the true fire wherein its Lord has his rest.' " (par. 206)

Jung then explains how the earth's east-west meridian and the north-south meridian form a cross, a quaternity, which characterizes the earth's pole: from the pole, the four directions radiate. Thus it is that the northern hemisphere resembles the round body of the *hydromedusa,* the jelly-fish, whose spherical surface is divided by four, or multiples of four, radials, and which therefore looks like a globe seen from the pole. This description indicates a particular connection on Jung's part to the jelly-fish image. We learn in the very next paragraph

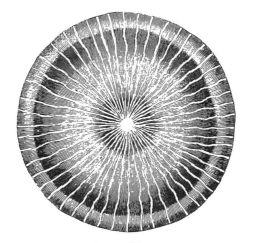

Top View

Side View

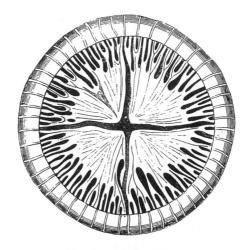

Underside View

Figure 16. The Jelly-fish—a Living Mandala.

that the connection arises from an important dream that Jung had as a young man, although he does not acknowledge here that it is his own dream. In *Memories, Dreams, Reflections* he does say that the dream is his.

> He dreamt that he was walking in a wood. Gradually this grew more and more lonely and wild, and finally he realized that he was in a primeval forest. The trees were so high and the foliage so thick that it was almost dark on the ground. All trace of a path had long since disappeared, but, driven on by a vague sense of expectation and curiosity, he pressed forward and soon came to a circular pool measuring ten to twelve feet across. It was a spring, and the crystal-clear water looked almost black in the dark shadows of the trees. In the middle of the pool there floated a pearly organism, about eighteen inches in diameter, that emitted a faint light. It was a jelly-fish. (par. 208)

It is interesting to notice that in *Memories, Dreams, Reflections* Jung describes the experience more emotionally:

> [In a wood] threaded with watercourses, and in the darkest place I saw a circular pool, surrounded by dense undergrowth. Half immersed in the water lay the strangest and most wonderful creature: a round animal, shimmering in opalescent hues, and consisting of innumerable little cells, or of organs shaped like tentacles. It was a giant radiolarian, measuring about three feet across. [Here the radiolarian is one meter, and in *Aion* it is fifty centimeters. This is an indication that this symbolic fish image is so alive it can't even hold a single size; it shifts.] It seemed to me indescribably wonderful that this magnificent creature should be lying there undisturbed, in the hidden place, in the clear, deep water. It aroused in me an intense desire for knowledge, so that I awoke with a beating heart. . . . [It decided me] overwhelmingly in favor of science, and removed all my doubts.[81]

How was it that this dream led Jung to his vocational orientation? He was in a state of vocational confusion at the time. One idea expressed in his autobiographical account is that this image of a natural organism led him to the idea of studying natural science—*Naturwissenschaft* is the word Jung used. Another idea is that the jelly-fish as a living mandala is a kind of organic pole star, and when a person encounters his own living pole star, it orients him; then he knows where he is, where he is going, what he is supposed to do. I think that both of these ways of seeing the dream are relevant.

The fiery star of the sea, the fish that was so hot it cooked itself, leads into the theme of fire symbolism. Jung cites various texts describing the fire of the star fish and speaking of it in oppositional, antinomial terms. For example, Picinellus is quoted by Jung as saying:

> "This fish . . . glows forever in the midst of the waters, and whatsoever it touches grows hot and bursts into flames." This glow is a fire—the fire of the Holy Ghost

---

[81] *Memories, Dreams, Reflections*, p. 85.

. . . . and refers also to the fiery tongues of the Pentecostal miracle. [This reminds Picinellus of the action of divine grace] . . . which sets on fire the hearts that are drowned in a "sea of sins." For the same reason the fish means charity and divine love. (par. 198)

Jung indicates that this burning star fish is connected with profane love, not just divine love, and can actually represent the fire of hell:

This fish . . . burns but gives no light. [St. Basil says:] "Then conceive in your mind a deep pit, impenetrable darkness, fire that has no brightness, having all fire's power of burning, but without any light. . . . Such a conception describes the fire of hell." This fire is "concupiscentia," the "scintilla voluptatis" (spark of lechery). (par. 199)

Here we have the same fiery fish described on the one hand as representing divine love and divine grace, and on the other hand as the fire of hell and the spark of lechery. Jung notes how curious it is that diametrically opposite interpretations of the same symbol can be given without disturbing the interpreters. This double aspect of the fiery fish corresponds to the double character of the fish which was discussed previously. Another text further illustrates this doubleness:

Take fire or unslaked lime, which the Philosophers say grows on trees. In this fire God himself glows in divine love . . . . and without this fire can the art never be brought to perfection. It is also the fire of the Philosophers . . . . It is also the noblest fire which God created upon earth, for it has a thousand virtues. To these things the teacher replies that God has bestowed upon it such virtue and efficacy . . . that with this fire is mingled the Godhead itself. And this fire purifies, as purgatory does in the lower regions. (par. 200)

So it is both divine loving fire and purgatorial fire at the same time. The reason Jung gives these images such emphasis is that they are the way that the psyche describes itself. This is the nature of libido: it is simultaneously sacred, divine fire, divine love, and at the same time, purgatorial hell fire. On the one hand libido energy manifests as primitive desirousness that consumes when it manifests in its primeval intensity, unconsciously. On the other hand, in its conscious, differentiated form it manifests as transpersonal love, the highest function of the human psyche. Transpersonal love is the capacity to posit the existence of, to perceive, and to live one's life out of objective transpersonal value. It is valuing at the highest, most conscious level. Animals share the lower level of this with us. They can value a good meal, and we can too. But that is not objective love; that is the lower form, *concupiscentia.*

In this context (par. 200, note 20), Jung refers to the vision of Arisleus.[82] The gist of that story is that Arisleus, an alchemical philosopher, descends to the bot-

---

[82] See also *Psychology and Alchemy,* CW 12, pars. 435ff. and 449f.

tom of the sea with some companions to rescue the king of the sea who is in trouble down there. Arisleus runs into some trouble himself, some incest trouble. The result is that he and his companions are imprisoned in a glass house, in other words in an alchemical vessel, and subjected to intense heat. This is why Jung states that "this recalls the vision of Arisleus"; intense fire or heat in the sea corresponds to the hot fiery fish in the sea. That intense heat that Arisleus and his companions experienced had a transformative effect and favorable outcome, but they had to endure the purgatorial fire of it.

According to one text, fire has a quaternary nature:

> According to Blaise de Vigenère, the fire has not two but four aspects: the intelligible, which is all light; the heavenly, partaking of heat and light; the elemental, pertaining to the lower world and compounded of light, heat, and glow *(ardor);* and finally the infernal, opposed to the intelligible, glowing and burning without any light. Here again we encounter the quaternity which the ancients associated with fire, as we saw from the Egyptian conception of Set and the four sons of Horus, and from Ezekiel's vision of the fiery region to the north. It is not at all likely that Vigenère was thinking of Ezekiel in this connection. (par. 203)

Jung adds, in an important footnote to this paragraph:

> The quaternary symbols that appear simultaneously in dreams always point, so far as I can see, to totality or the self. Fire means passion, affects, desires, and the emotional driving-forces of human nature in general, that is, everything which is understood by the term "libido." When the alchemists attribute a quaternary nature to the fire, this amounts to saying that the self is the source of energy.

This powerful statement is slipped in very quietly, without any fanfare. Consider what it means; it has very sizable implications, and is very important in practical analytic work. For instance, at the beginning of an analysis, when one is gathering the anamnesis, the life story of the analysand, we are most interested in knowing about those aspects that have libido intensity, either positive or negative, because those spots of intensity will be indications of where the Self is touching the ego's developmental process. The same thing is true in analyzing the events of everyday life. Intense desires or reactions of all kinds are crucial, whether they be positive, creative and constructive, or devilish and dangerous. Either way, they are from the Self and are the things to which we need to pay most attention. This is one reason why Jung lavishes so much attention on the symbolism of fire and the fiery fish: it is an image of the most important content of the psyche.

Another aspect of fire symbolism from another text is mentioned in paragraph 210:

> Picinellus feels that his *stella maris,* "this fish which burns in the midst of the water but gives no light," besides meaning the Holy Ghost, love, grace, and religion, also symbolizes something in man, namely his *tongue,* speech, and powers of ex-

pression, for it is in these faculties that all psychic life is manifest. He is evidently thinking of an instinctive, unreflecting psychic activity, because at this point he cites James 3:6, "And the tongue is a fire, a world of iniquity among our members, defiling the whole body, setting on fire the wheel of birth, and set on fire by hell."

Jung mentions the fact that this text is akin to Buddhist ideas, which brings to mind a piece of symbolism to consider when one is dealing with the imagery of fire. It is the Buddha's "Fire Sermon." Nothing gives a better quick lesson in the nature of Buddhism than this "Fire Sermon." These are some passages from it:

> All things, O priests, are on fire. And what, O priests, are all these things which are on fire? The eye, O priests, is on fire; forms are on fire; eye-consciousness is on fire; impressions received by the eye are on fire; and whatever sensation, pleasant or unpleasant, or indifferent, originates in dependence on impressions received by the eye that also is on fire. . . . With the fire of passion, say I, with the fire of hatred, with the fire of infatuation; with birth, old age, death, sorrow, lamentation, misery, grief, and despair are they on fire. The ear is on fire; sounds are on fire; . . . the nose is on fire; odors are on fire; . . . the tongue is on fire; tastes are on fire; . . . things tangible are on fire; . . . the mind is on fire; . . . mind-consciousness is on fire; . . . And with what are these on fire? With the fire of passion, with the fire of hatred, with the fire of infatuation; with birth, old age, death, sorrow. . . .
> Perceiving this, O priests, the learned and noble disciple conceives an aversion for the eye, conceives an aversion for forms, conceives an aversion for eye-consciousness, conceives an aversion for the impressions received by the eye; . . . aversion for the ear, . . . aversion for the tongue, . . . aversion for the mind. . . . And in conceiving [these aversions, the disciple] becomes divested of passion, and by the absence of passion he becomes free.[83]

That puts it pretty literally. It is a radical example of how to formulate and constellate a spiritual counter-pole against the infernal aspect of primal fire, primal libido.

The symbolism of fire and the symbolism of the wheel are united in the text from James 3:6 that Jung quotes: "And the tongue is a fire, a world of iniquity among our members, defiling the whole body, setting on fire the wheel of birth, and set on fire by hell." It is interesting to note the differences in Biblical translations. What is translated here "the wheel of birth", is translated elsewhere as the "course of nature," "the cycle of nature," "the whole wheel of creation," "wheel of our existence," and "the course of life."

We can understand this image of the wheel of birth or the wheel of creation as referring to the original Self, the original state of wholeness to which the ego is unconsciously bound. When the process of individuation is constellated, it is required that the ego become conscious and disidentify from the Self. To encourage the ego to do that, this unconscious ego-Self identity, which is a very

---

83 E.A. Burtt, ed., *The Teachings of the Compassionate Buddha,* pp. 96f.

pleasant state of being during infancy and childhood, becomes a fiery torture. The great myth of Ixion is an example of that. Ixion attempted to seduce Hera, but his partner turned out to be only a cloud Hera, and he was then punished by being bound to a fiery, revolving wheel. Many Greek vase paintings show the underworld and Ixion bound to his fiery wheel. It is an image of the torture of being unconsciously identified with the Self when individuation has been activated and is required of you.

There is another interesting reference to this negative wheel in the Orphic gold tablets described in Jane Harrison's book *Prolegomena to a Study of Greek Religion.* The ancient Orphics had the notion, similar to that of the Egyptians, that the deceased person had to answer certain questions successfully in the afterworld in order to get to the state of bliss. So the Orphics buried gold tablets in the tomb of the deceased, with directions inscribed on them as to how to answer the questions. Gold does not deteriorate, so modern archaeologists have dug up the tablets and now we can read them. The deceased are told that they will come to a gatekeeper who will ask them certain questions, and the image of the wheel is one of the things that is supposed to be spoken of. The deceased are to identify themselves, announce who they are and what they have accomplished. Then, according to the tablets, the deceased is supposed to say to the gatekeeper:

> I have flown out of the sorrowful weary Wheel.
> I have passed with eager feet to the Circle desired.
> I have entered into the bosom of Despoina, Queen of the Underworld [that is, Persephone]. . . .
> Happy and Blessed One, thou shalt be God instead of mortal.[84]

The instruction ends with the remarkable statement, "A kid, I have fallen into milk." It is as though once one gets past the gatekeeper, the ocean of milk is the image of heavenly bliss. But first, one has to announce, "I have flown out of the sorrowful weary wheel." This sorrowful, weary wheel corresponds to what was called *heimarmene,* the wheel of one's own horoscope to which one is bound.

As long as one is unconsciously identified with original totality, one is bound to one's archetypal destiny, the sorrowful, weary wheel. To fly out of bondage to that wheel would mean psychologically to become conscious of the wheel of one's wholeness. Then, one chooses one's archetypal destiny willingly. It is no longer unconscious bondage. It is no longer Ixion's fiery torture wheel. The image of bondage to the wheel shows up in all these different cultural contexts, because it corresponds to a basic archetypal reality.

---

[84] *Prolegomena,* p. 585.

15
Paragraphs 213-235

The Fish in Alchemy (cont.)

Jung continues his discussion of the fish symbol in alchemy with a consideration of the cinedian fish and the cinedian stone. "Cinedian" comes from the Greek word *kineo,* meaning to set in motion. Alternative definitions would be to originate or to be the author of. The root *kineo* is the basis of the word kinetic and the word cinema for moving pictures. Regarding the cinedian fish, Jung says:

> A round and transparent fish of a peculiar sort, without "cortices," is described in the *Cyranides:* the "cinedian fish" lives in the sea on the shores of Syria, Palestine, and Libya, is six fingers long, and is a "pisciculus rotundus" [a round little fish]. It has two stones in its head and another one in the third vertebra of the tail . . . . This stone is especially potent and is used as a love-potion . . . . "This stone is twin or twofold: the one is opaque and black, but the other though black is brilliant and shining like a mirror." This is the stone which many seek, without finding it: for it is the dragon's stone. . . .
>
> . . . This stone was known to Pliny and also to the medieval alchemists, who named it *draconites* . . . . It was reputed to be a precious stone, which could be obtained by cutting off the head of a sleeping dragon. (pars. 213f.)

Jung then refers to Ruland's *Lexicon of Alchemy* on the subject of draconites, the dragon's stone. This stone in the cinedian fish is an equivalent of the stone in the head of the dragon or the serpent. Ruland says:

> Draconites is a Precious Stone . . . to be found in the brain of serpents, but unless it is removed while they are alive, it will never become a precious stone, by the inbred malice of the animal who, conscious of death approaching, destroys the virtue of the stone. Therefore the head is removed from dragons while asleep, and thus the gem is secured. . . . The color of the Draconite is white; it drives away all poisonous animals and cures envenomed bites. . . . Our own Chelydrus and watersnake sometimes have gems in their heads, as I myself have seen.[85]

This cinedian fish that contains in its brain and in its backbone these remarkable stones, is shown by its very name to have a moving function corresponding to the motor function of the celestial pole, which was discussed previously. The cinedian fish is the mover, the originator, and this image reminds us of Jung's very pregnant statement that the Self is the source of energy. (par. 203, note 35) The cinedian fish is a motor fish, the fish that motivates; this is one of the aspects of the symbolism of the Self. And it is not only a fish, it is also a stone, and

---

[85] *A Lexicon of Alchemy,* p. 128.

not only a stone, but a double stone. Jung discusses this in paragraphs 215-216:

> The cinedian stone has a double nature, though. as the text shows, it is not at all clear. One might almost conjecture that its double nature consisted originally in a white and a black variety, and that a copyist, puzzled by the contradiction, inserted "niger quidem" (though black). But Ruland distinctly emphasizes that "the color of the Draconite is white." . . .
>
> In view of all this, the double nature of the cinedian stone might signify the polarity and union of opposites, which is just what gives the *lapis philosophorum* its peculiar significance as a uniting symbol.

Jung then goes on to give a psychological interpretation of what this fish-stone or draconite stone would indicate psychologically:

> Our draconite, too, is endowed with extraordinary powers . . . which make it eminently suitable as the "ligature of Aphrodite," i.e., love-magic. Magic exercises a *compulsion* that asserts itself against the conscious mind and will of the victim; that is to say, a strange will arises in him and proves stronger than his ego. The only comparable effect capable of psychological verification is that exerted by unconscious contents, which by their compelling power demonstrate their affinity with or dependence on man's totality, that is, the self and its "karmic" functions.

This quiet little statement of Jung's has considerable psychological implication. Translated into clinical terms, Jung is saying that every neurotic symptom, every compulsion, every addiction, every primitive affect that cannot be controlled by the ego—all these aspects of psychological symptomatology derive their power and effectiveness from the Self. This is very important for practical analysis because the symptom, the primitive affect, the compulsive drive, that unconscious content which has the ego in its grip—that is the dragon, that is the serpent, or the cinedian fish with the motive power. But at the heart of it, contained within it, is the precious stone of the Self. This is what needs to be extracted by the analytic process from the symptom, from the primitive, compulsive experience. The stone can be extracted from the dragon's head, or from the fish's head, becoming then a precious gem.

There is a variation of this idea in the theme of the poisonous toad with a precious jewel in its head. This image is enshrined in Shakespeare's *As You Like It* in these lines: "Sweet are the uses of adversity; / Which, like the toad, ugly and venomous, / Wears yet a precious jewel in his head."[86] This passage is relevant when one is dealing with a psychological difficulty; it suggests the idea that the adversity one is encountering has a sweet use if one can extract the precious jewel that is embedded in it.

Another noteworthy fish is the *Echeneis remora.* As Jung tells us, this is an actual fish, but it has ancient legendary attributes. According to legend, this fish,

---

[86] II, i, 12-14.

if it attaches itself to a ship by its sucker, has the power of stopping the ship in its course, bringing it to a standstill. This ability is revealed in its etymology: the word *Echeneis* derives from two Greek roots: from the verb *eco,* to hold, and *naus,* meaning ship. So the word means "the ship holder." The word *remora* has as its root the word *mora,* which means delay. You will recognize this root in the word moratorium, which is a delay of some kind of obligation such as a payment. Jung quotes a seventeenth-century text regarding this:

> That little fish the *Echeneis,* which has no blood or spiny bones, and is shut up in that deep mid region of the great universal sea. This little fish is extremely small, alone, and unique in its shape, but the sea is great and vast, and hence it is impossible for those to catch it who do not know in what part of the world it dwells . . . . Yet none the less, when we speak somewhat in confidence in the ear of a trusted friend, we teach him that hidden secret of the wise, how he can naturally, speedily, and easily catch the little fish called Remora, which is able to hold back the proud vessels of the great Ocean sea (that is the spirit of the world). Those who are not sons of the art are altogether ignorant and know not those precious treasures. . . . [Thus] it is needful that I instruct you concerning the magnet of the wise, which has the power of attracting the little fish called Echeneis or Remora. (par. 218)

Jung interprets this material in paragraph 219:

> We learn . . . that the fish is found . . . in the centre of the ocean. But the ocean is the "spirit of the world." . . . . [This] is a somewhat unusual term, because the expression more commonly used was the "anima mundi." The world-soul or, in this case, the world-spirit is a projection of the unconscious . . . . This idea is nothing more than an analogy of the animating principle in man which inspires his thoughts and acts of cognition. "Soul" and "spirit," or psyche as such, is in itself totally unconscious. If it is assumed to be somewhere "outside," it cannot be anything except a projection of the unconscious. . . . At any rate, we know that in alchemy "our sea" is a symbol for the unconscious in general . . . . The extremely small fish that dwells in the centre of the universal sea nevertheless has the power to stop the largest ships.

This fish which is so difficult to catch because it is so small in the vast sea can be caught by the "magnet of the wise," which Jung then speaks of:

> There would be no hope whatever of catching this insignificant creature if a "magnet of the wise" did not exist in the conscious subject. This "magnet" is obviously something a master can teach to his pupil; it is the "theoria," the one solid possession from which the adept can proceed. For the *prima materia* always remains to be found, and the only thing that helps him is the "cunning secret of the wise," a theory that can be communicated. (par. 219)

Jung uses the original word *theoria* to draw our attention to the fact that he is not referring to the modern use of the term theory; the original usage meant a beholding, a contemplation. It was more or less equivalent to a revelatory image.

So this magnet of the wise which Jung equates with the *theoria* of the alchemical adept, and which can be transmitted, would correspond psychologically to the analytic procedure and the understanding of the psyche on which that procedure is based. Here and in subsequent chapters, Jung makes a great deal of the fact that this secret, this *theoria,* this doctrine can be taught. However, it can't be taught in collective settings. It can't be taught in classes or books. It can only be taught in individual analysis where the objective reality of one person can be addressed in its individual uniqueness. Jung continues:

> What is it, then, that one adept whispers into the ear of another, fearfully looking around lest any betray them, or even guess their secret? Nothing less than this: that through this teaching the One and All, the Greatest in the guise of the Smallest, God himself in his everlasting fires, may be caught like a fish in the deep sea. Further, that he may be "drawn from the deep" by a eucharistic act of integration (called *teoqualo,* "God-eating," by the Aztecs), and incorporated in the human body. (par. 222)

This is the "secret" that is taught in the analytic process, that in the course of dealing with one's smallest, most despicable, most apparently insignificant psychic matters, one discovers the God-image and makes a connection to it.

Jung finds further associated material in a Cathar text. As mentioned earlier, the Cathari were a neo-Manichean sect which emerged around 1000 A.D. and believed that the material world was evil; that man was an alien and a sojourner in this evil world; and that man's purpose was to free his spirit, which was by nature good, and restore it to communion with God. For the "perfect ones," sexual intercourse was forbidden and severe ascetic renunciation of the world was expected. Jung quotes a text, an alleged revelation, that was described by a member of the Cathars. This material is derived from histories of the Inquisition; the inquisitors extracted it from the heretic. It is evident from the amount of attention Jung gives this text that he considers it quite important psychologically:

> It concerns an alleged revelation which Christ's favorite disciple John was vouchsafed as he "rested in the Lord's bosom." John wished to know what Satan's state was before his fall, and the Lord answered: "He was in such splendour that he ruled the powers of heaven." He wanted to be like God, and to this end he descended through the elements of air and water, and found that the earth was covered with water. Penetrating beneath the surface of the earth, "he found two fishes lying upon the waters, and they were like oxen yoked for ploughing, holding the whole earth by command of the invisible Father from sunset to sunrise [or, from West to East]. And when he went down, he found hanging clouds which covered the broad sea . . . . And when he went down, he found set apart therefrom his 'Osob,' which is a kind of fire." On account of the flames he could not descend any further, so he went back to heaven and announced to the angels that he was going to set up his throne on the clouds and be like the All-highest. He then treated the angels as the unjust steward treated his master's debtors, whereupon he and the

angels were cast out of heaven by God. But God took pity on him and allowed him and his angels to do what they liked for a week. During this time Satan, using Genesis 1 as a model, created the world and mankind. (par. 225)

This text brings up an important image for the Christian aeon, that of the fall of Satan from heaven. We know from Job that in Old Testament times, Satan could still come and go from heaven; he was a guest. The first part of the book of Job takes place in that situation, as Satan is visiting heaven and Yahweh and Satan are in conversation. But in Luke 10:18, Christ announces that he has seen Satan, as lightning, fall from heaven. What Christ saw was evidently a future event, for according to Revelation 12:7-9, Satan was going to fall from heaven at the end of the aeon. Revelation 12:12-13 says:

> Woe for the earth, and for the sea: because the devil is gone down unto you, having great wrath, knowing that he hath but a short time. And when the dragon saw that he was cast down to the earth, he persecuted the woman that brought forth the man child. (ASV)

This event in Revelation belongs to the end of the Christian aeon, even though Christ had an image of it as described in Luke, and even though this Cathar text projects it back prior to creation. It is as though the image is a creation image, but it is one that is particularly applicable to the ending of the Christian aeon. It is interesting that the image of the fall of Satan from heaven should come up in the same scriptures that announce the incarnation of God in Christ, because the incarnation is also a fall from heaven; it is a fall of the good side of God, the good son, from heaven into flesh. Simultaneously with that event, we hear of the prospect of Satan, the bad son of God, who also is going to fall out of heaven and start rampaging around the earth.

Milton also used this image. He lived in the seventeenth century, about a hundred years after our 1500 mark, well into the last quarter of the Christian aeon, and he picked up this idea of Lucifer's rebellion and fall from heaven. I discuss this image in *Anatomy of the Psyche* as an example of *coagulatio* symbolism, in which an entity that previously had existed only spiritually, not concretely, falls and descends to earth, thereby becoming incarnated.[87]

This Lucifer who rebels against God, and gets kicked out of heaven thereby, can be seen as a symbolic description of an initial preconscious act that lays the foundation for the ego. It is an image of primordial ego development. Lucifer is the archetype of the ego, and Prometheus is another version of that same archetype. That is the fundamental basis of this Cathar text, but Jung doesn't give much attention here to the fall-from-heaven aspect of the image; he emphasizes some of its other aspects, for instance the important term *osob,* an old Bulgarian word which Jung says could be translated as "that which is peculiar to him."

---

[87] *Anatomy,* p. 88.

(par. 227) It means something uniquely pertaining to the individual personality. That fits the idea that this image has to do with ego development. By making that rebellious, dramatic gesture that results in the fall, the ego manifests.

Jung then gives an interpretation of the Cathar text as a whole:

Expressed psychologically, . . . the two fishes which the devil found on the primeval waters would signify the newly arisen world of consciousness.

The comparison of the fishes with a yoke of oxen ploughing merits special attention. Oxen stand for the motive power of the plough. [This reminds us of the cinedian fish, the motivating fish.] . . . Since olden times the plough has stood for man's mastery over the earth: wherever man plows, he has wrested a patch of soil from the primal state and put it to his own use. That is to say: the fishes will rule this world and subdue it by working astrologically through man and molding his consciousness. (pars. 230-231)

Jung also notes that the ploughing begins in the west and moves toward the east, indicating in alchemical terms that "the alchemical work starts with the descent into darkness *(nigredo),* i.e., the unconscious." (par. 231) Only at the end of it, one arrives at the east and the newborn sun.

I might add to this comment that the two fishes that Satan discovers when he falls from heaven would correspond also to the opposites the individual ego encounters when it comes into existence. We do not encounter many dreams which literally refer to Satan falling from heaven, but we do encounter a lot of dreams about airplanes crashing. It is the same theme.

Jung continues the theme of the double fish with a discussion of Lambspringk's fish symbol:

That Catharist ideas found their way into alchemy is not altogether surprising. I have not, however, come across any texts which would prove that the Catharist fish symbol was assimilated into the alchemical tradition and so could be held responsible for Lambspringk's fish symbol, signifying the arcane substance and its inner antinomy. Lambspringk's symbol appeared not much earlier than the end of the sixteenth century and represented a revitalization of the archetype. It shows two reversed fishes swimming in the sea—*nostro mari* [our sea]—by which was meant the *aqua permanens* or arcane substance. They are designated "spiritus et anima," and . . . they indicate the double nature of Mercurius. (par. 234)

Figure 17 is from the *Book of Lambspringk,* an alchemical treatise composed of fifteen engravings, accompanied by brief commentaries associated with each picture. The introductory picture is of two fishes in the sea. It summarizes the meaning of the whole text. The commentary accompanying it reads as follows:

The Sages will tell you
That two fishes are in our sea
Without any flesh or bones.
Let them be cooked in their own water;
Then they also will become a vast sea,

The vastness of which no man can describe.
Moreover, the Sages say
That the two fishes are only one, not two;
They are two, and nevertheless they are one,
Body, Spirit, and Soul.
Now, I tell you most truly,
Cook these three together,
That there may be a very large sea.
Cook the sulphur well with the sulphur,
And hold your tongue about it:
Conceal your knowledge to your own advantage,
And you shall be free from poverty.
Only let your discovery remain a close secret.[88]

The admonition to "keep this secret"—don't reveal it to the unworthy—is a theme that crops up again and again in alchemical texts. I think that as psychologists we have to understand the theme of secrecy a little differently. The psychological secret is really perfectly safe. It can't be revealed to the unworthy because it is not that easy to communicate. It can only grow up from inside, and therefore the numinous secret is communicable only to someone who has already had the experience of it.

This corresponds to the alchemical idea that you can't make the Philosophers' Stone unless you already have a little bit of it. I think that the reference to "the secret" in this first Lambspringk picture implies that a crucial part of the secret is the nature of the opposites, as this is a picture of the opposites. The whole of *Aion* is a kind of circumambulation of "the secret" Lambspringk intended to convey through his picture of the two opposed fishes.

Figure 17.
Two Fishes in the Sea.

---

88 A.E. Waite, ed., *The Hermetic Museum,* p. 276.

16
Paragraphs 236-246

The Big Fish Dream

The next major exemplification of the fish theme comes in the "Big Fish dream," which Jung relates in paragraph 236:

> I came to the bank of a broad, flowing river. I couldn't see much at first, only wa-
> ter, earth, and rock. I threw the pages with my notes on them into the water, with
> the feeling that I was giving something back to the river. Immediately afterwards I
> had a fishing-rod in my hand. I sat down on a rock and started fishing. Still I saw
> nothing but water, earth, and rock. Suddenly a big fish bit. He had a silver belly
> and a golden back. As I drew him to land, the whole landscape became alive: the
> rock emerged like the primeval foundation of the earth, grass and flowers sprang
> up, and the bushes expanded into a great forest. A gust of wind blew and set every-
> thing in motion. Then, suddenly, I heard behind me the voice of Mr. X [an older
> man whom she knew only from photographs and from hearsay, but who seems to
> have been some kind of authority for her]. He said, quietly but distinctly: "The pa-
> tient ones in the innermost realm are given the fish, the food of the deep." At this
> moment a circle ran round me, part of it touching the water. Then I heard the voice
> again: "The brave ones in the second realm may be given victory, for there the
> battle is fought." Immediately another circle ran round me, this time touching the
> other bank. At the same time I saw into the distance and a colorful landscape was
> revealed. The sun rose over the horizon. I heard the voice, speaking as if out of the
> distance: "The third and the fourth realms come, similarly enlarged, out of the
> other two. But the fourth realm"—and here the voice paused for a moment, as if
> deliberating—"the fourth realm joins on to the first. It is the highest and the lowest
> at once, for the highest and the lowest come together. They are at bottom one."
> Here the dreamer awoke with a roaring in her ears.

Jung tells us that this dream sums up, in condensed form, the whole symbolism of the individuation process. It can be very useful for amplification whenever one encounters a fish dream. The river can be understood as the water of
the unconscious, and also as the river of life.

The dream, which is shown graphically in Figure 18, can be divided into four
steps. In the first step the dreamer says, "I threw the pages with my notes on
them, into the water." This is an image of the sacrificial action of paying attention to the unconscious, of working on one's dreams, scrutinizing one's complexes, doing active imagination and offering those efforts to the waters out of
which the dreams and the complexes come. This kind of work is psychological
fishing; the dream indicates that fact because as soon as she throws her notes

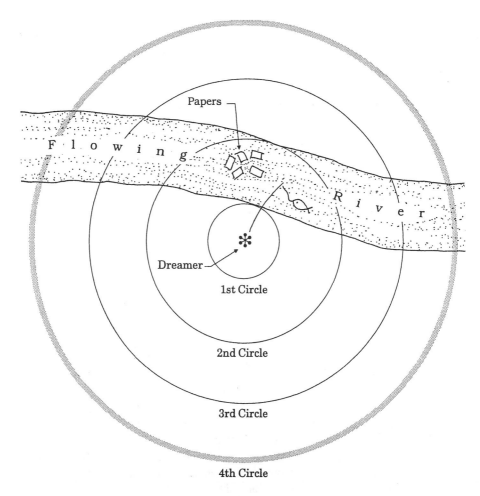

Figure 18. The "Big Fish" dream.
The dreamer (at center) seeks and catches a fish, symbolically a content of the unconscious, after which appears a series of circles representing levels of increasing integration.

into the water she has a fishing rod in her hand. This first step, paying attention to the unconscious, sets all the subsequent sequences into operation.

The second step: with the fishing rod in her hand she catches a fish that has a silver belly and a golden back. This corresponds to Tobias catching the fish on his way to find Sarah, the fish that would cure Sarah of her demonic possession, and cure Tobias's father of blindness. This particular fish has a silver belly and a golden back, so it is a *coniunctio* of Sol and Luna; it signifies the mystery of the opposites and their reconciliation. It is as though in this dream the dreamer has caught both of the Lambspringk fishes at once. This fish is a union of those two.

When the dreamer has caught the *coniunctio* fish, the third step unfolds. The fish now reveals its numinous nature; a theophany occurs. The whole landscape becomes alive. The rocks emerge like the primeval foundation of the earth; flowers and vegetation spring up, a gust of wind sets everything in motion. This is an image of the original creation; the foundation of the conscious personality represented by the rock is being laid down. The life impulse starts the flowering of plants, and the wind of the spirit sets things moving.

Then comes the fourth step, the phenomenon of the authoritative voice. This event occurs occasionally in dreams, and should always be taken with the greatest respect. The voice of the Self is speaking; it is as though there has been a shift now from the natural level of development to the human level. Not only do the wind, earth, and flowers manifest, but now a human entity appears that can communicate on the level of Logos. It makes a pronouncement of transpersonal wisdom. The first statement is that "the patient ones in the innermost realm are given the fish, the food of the deep." The "patient ones" would be, I think, those who are able to make a relation to the unconscious. It does indeed require patience to establish such a connection. When the connection is established, a feeding process occurs. The food of the deep becomes available to the ego.

The second announcement is that "the brave ones in the second realm may be given victory, for there the battle is fought," and the second circle is drawn. Jung suggests that this circle occupied by the "brave ones" might refer to the enduring of a conflict, perhaps between the conscious ego and the shadow. It is certainly true that it takes psychological courage to integrate the shadow, to withdraw our shadow projections. What is required is renunciation for once and for all of the immature device of blaming others for what happens to oneself.

The third circle is not described specifically in the dream. It might correspond to the conscious encounter with the animus or anima. This would be a logically consistent possibility, at any rate. The fourth realm is described as joining onto the first; the highest and the lowest come together—they are at bottom, one. This fourth circle would correspond to an encounter with the Self, with the totality of the psyche. The way it is described recalls the Axiom of Maria—one becomes two, two becomes three, and out of the third comes the one as the fourth.

The Alchemical Interpretation of the Fish

Jung now begins to address the question of how the miraculous fish is to be caught, and returns to the Echeneis/Remora text. After describing the little fish and its qualities, the text speaks of catching it,

> that I may declare to you the clear light of our unique material, or our virgin soil, and teach you in what wise you may acquire the supreme art of the sons of wisdom, it is needful that I instruct you concerning the magnet of the wise, which has the power of attracting the little fish called Echeneis or Remora from out the centre and depth of the sea. (par. 218)

Jung discusses this text, which in effect deals with how to catch the Self:

> The Echeneis exercises an attraction on ships that could best be compared with the influence of a magnet on iron. The attraction, so the historical tradition says, emanates from the fish and brings the vessel, whether powered by sail or oarsmen, to a standstill. I mention this seemingly unimportant feature because, as we shall see, in the alchemical view the attraction no longer proceeds from the fish but from a magnet which man possesses and which exerts the attraction that was once the mysterious property of the fish. . . . It is therefore a remarkable innovation when the alchemists set out to manipulate an instrument that would exert the same powers as the Echeneis, but on the Echeneis itself. This reversal of direction is important for the psychology of alchemy because it offers a parallel to the adept's claim to be able to produce the *filius macrocosmi,* the equivalent of Christ—*Deo concedente*—through his art. (par. 239)

Jung writes here about something corresponding to the work of the analyst who presumes by his technique or procedure to be able to draw the Self from out of the unconscious of the patient. That is the goal of the Jungian analytic process—to constellate the Self in a patient. The Self is what centers, consolidates, and heals, so all of our efforts are devoted to that goal.

This capacity to attract the Self is symbolized in the text by magnetism. The fish itself is a magnet, and the alchemists by their wisdom, their experimental knowledge and what they learn that is passed on from their teachers, acquire the magnetism of the fish from the fish itself, and turn it into an instrument which is then used to draw out the fish. This is the basic image. As Jung says, it was a remarkable innovation when the alchemists set out to manipulate an instrument that would exert the same powers as the Echeneis; the psychological equivalent of it is a remarkable innovation also.

Jung goes on to say that this "magnet of the wise," which could be taught, was the knowledge of how to find the *prima materia.* (par. 240) This then leads into a discussion of the alchemical term "magnesia," one of the many names for the *prima materia.* "Magnesia" is linked to the term magnet, first of all phonetically, and perhaps also etymologically—there is some uncertainty about that. The term magnesia derives from a district in ancient Greece where there were magnesium deposits. According to the Oxford English Dictionary, the magnesium stone is the designation of two different minerals. One is the lode stone; this is the magnet, the original primitive magnet. The other is a stone shining like silver, perhaps talc.

It is not clear which of these two senses gave rise to the alchemical use of the term magnesia. I think that as with most doubled items in symbolism, one can understand both as being valid, the magnetic aspect of the magnesia and also the brilliant white luster. Most of us probably know magnesia chiefly from milk of magnesia of childhood, but the metal magnesium is a silvery, shining metal similar to aluminum. So we arrive at the psychological idea that the *prima materia,* of which magnesia is one of the names, and which is a primitive manifestation of the Self, has an innate luster and has innate magnetic qualities.

The symbolism of magnetism comes up in the modern history of psychotherapy in the work of Franz Anton Mesmer, who has a good claim to be the discoverer of the unconscious, although he did not use that term. Jung says about him that the original references to the unconscious can be traced back to the time of the French Revolution, and the first signs of it can be found in Mesmer.[89]

Mesmer lived from 1734 to 1815; his life paralleled Goethe's, though he was fifteen years older. He was an Austrian physician who was influenced by Paracelsus and developed an idea which he called "animal magnetism." He was evidently a very charismatic man. He was gripped by the magnet archetype, and the basic principles of his ideas of "animal magnetism" were, as he developed them, that there is a subtle, physical fluid that fills the universe and forms a connecting medium between man, the earth, the heavenly bodies, and between man and man. We now call that fluid the collective unconscious.

Mesmer talked of disease as the uneven distribution of this fluid in the human body, and said that recovery occurs when balance is reestablished. By various magnetic techniques this fluid can be channeled, stored and transmitted from one place to another and from person to person. In his very earliest experiments he would have his patient drink water with powdered iron in it, and then he would pass a magnet along the body so that the iron would go to the right place.

He refined that technique, abandoning the literal magnet and powdered iron, but he thought of himself as a living magnet and would do both individual and group therapy. His individual therapy was not too much different from what we do today. He would sit directly in front of the patient, very close, holding the patient's hands and pressing the patient's thumbs into his own hands, looking fixedly into her eyes. I say "her" because I imagine that the magnetism became activated better that way. Then Mesmer would make passes over the body at places that were relevant. That was his individual method. His group method

---

[89] See "The Role of the Unconscious," *Civilization in Transition,* CW 10, par. 21.

was to have the patients sit around a circular tank of water holding iron rods that emerged from the tank. The patients would be joined to each other by a rope, so that they were all linked up, while holding their own individual iron bar. Mesmer would enter and make various movements to circulate the magnetic fluid and this would generate the effects.

So what he was dealing with were quite powerful individual and collective transferences which he described in terms of "animal magnetism," but the image of the magnet was basic and lies at the root of psychotherapy. Jung says:

> In the "Duodecim tractatus" the magnet appears as the symbol of the *aqua roris nostri* (water of our dew), "whose mother is the midpoint of the heavenly and earthly Sun and Moon." This water, the famed *aqua permanens,* is apostrophized by an anonymous author . . . .
>
> The underlying thought here is the idea of the doctrine, the "aqua doctrinae." (pars. 243f.)

This text equates the magnet to water. Jung then says that this particular water which corresponds to the magnet of the wise, is equivalent to the idea of the *aqua doctrinae.* That is a term which Jung takes from Origen and speaks about in several other places.[90] For Origen, the symbolism of water meant the *aqua doctrinae,* the water of doctrine. For instance, after the death of Christ on the cross, his side pierced with a lance (John 19), water came out which was interpreted as *aqua doctrinae.* Again, in Exodus 17:6, Yahweh instructs Moses to strike a rock and water will flow from it for the people to drink. That water was also interpreted as the *aqua doctrinae.*

Jung describes this *aqua doctrinae* in "The Psychology of the Transference." Referring to the seventh picture in the *Rosarium* series, in which the dead, united body is ready to be subjected to dew from heaven, washed by water, he says:

> Here we seem to have a hint about the treatment required: faced with the disorientation of the patient, the doctor must hold fast to his own orientation; that is, he must know what the patient's condition means, he must understand what is of value in the dreams, and do so moreover with the help of that *aqua doctrinae* which alone is appropriate to the nature of the unconscious. In other words, he must approach his task with views and ideas capable of grasping unconscious symbolism. Intellectual or supposedly scientific theories are not adequate to the nature of the unconscious, because they make use of a terminology which has not the slightest affinity with its pregnant symbolism. The waters must be drawn together and held fast by the one water. . . . The kind of approach that makes this possible must therefore be plastic and symbolical, and itself the outcome of personal experience with unconscious contents. It should not stray too far in the direction of abstract intellectualism; hence we are best advised to remain within the framework of

---

90 See *Mysterium Coniunctionis,* CW 14, par. 372, and "The Psychology of the Transference," *The Practice of Psychotherapy,* CW 16, par. 478.

traditional mythology, which has already proved comprehensive enough for all practical purposes. This does not preclude the satisfaction of theoretical requirements, but these should be reserved for the private use of the doctor.[91]

I think that is a very important passage, because in my experience we all tend to cling to abstract theoretical formulations because they are the easiest. They don't require wholeness of response, which is very difficult. I think that this also applies to interpretations which refer back to childhood experience. It is relatively easy to point out that a current life experience, a current manifestation of a complex, derives from its earlier version. We have the theory that enables us to understand that very well. While such interpretations are partially true, the trouble is that they don't heal. They don't transform the original experience. They point it out, but one is still stuck with the original experience. They satisfy the head, but the heart says, "So what?"

What we need at such a time is the *aqua doctrinae,* the relevant amplifying image that has the power to transform the complex or the original traumatic experience, by enlarging the conscious attitude, by setting the original experience in a larger context that releases the ego from bondage to the original trauma. This is how I understand the *aqua doctrinae.*

Paragraph 246, short but difficult, is also related to the analytic enterprise:

> Obviously a distinction must be made between two categories of symbols: first, those which refer to the extrapsychic chemical substance or its metaphysical equivalent, e.g., *serpens mercurialis, spiritus, anima mundi, veritas, sapientia,* etc.; second, those denoting the chemical preparations produced by the adept, such as solvents *(aqua, acetum, lac virginis)* or their "philosophical" equivalent, the *theoria* or *scientia,* which, when it is "right," has miraculous effects on matter.

One has to read this several times to get straight what the basic categories are. The first is the natural, original substances; the second is the preparations compounded by the alchemists. What is emphasized here is the crucial importance of the conscious human enterprise in dealing with the unconscious.

This leads us into the difference that Jung emphasizes between the religious and the alchemical attitudes. Jung goes into this in *Psychology and Alchemy,* distinguishing the Christian from the alchemical formulation—the whole question of who is being redeemed by whom:

> Now, all these myth-pictures [in the alchemical treatises] represent a drama of the human psyche on the further side of consciousness, showing *man as both the one to be redeemed and the redeemer.* The first formulation is Christian, the second alchemical. In the first case man attributes the need of redemption to himself and leaves the work of redemption, the actual *opus [athlon],* to the autonomous divine figure; in the latter case man takes upon himself the duty of carrying out the re-

---

[91] *The Practice of Psychotherapy,* CW 16, par. 478.

deeming *opus,* and attributes the state of suffering and consequent need of redemption to the *anima mundi* imprisoned in matter.[92]

Jung puts this more clearly in a later passage:

> For the alchemist, the one primarily in need of redemption is not man, but the deity who is lost and sleeping in matter. . . . His attention is not directed to his own salvation through God's grace, but to the liberation of God from the darkness of matter. By applying himself to this miraculous work he benefits from its salutary effect, but only incidentally.[93]

This is an elaboration of what it means to make the distinction between the basic natural substances on the one hand, and the preparations compounded by the alchemists on the other, because the preparations do the job. They correspond to the magnet that the alchemist holds in his hand to draw forth the fish from the deep—all very provocative and suggestive imagery concerning the nature of the analytic task.

---

[92] *Psychology and Alchemy,* CW 12, par. 414.
[93] Ibid., par. 420.

17

Paragraphs 247-266

The Writings of Gerhard Dorn

Jung now moves into material from the alchemist Gerhard Dorn. Dorn was a very important figure for Jung; he quotes from him extensively in *Aion,* and devoted an entire chapter of *Mysterium Coniunctionis* to an extended commentary on his work. He also shows up in *Alchemical Studies.*[94]

We do not know very much about Dorn's life, or the actual dates of his birth and death, but approximate working dates are 1520 to 1590. In Marie-Louise von Franz's published commentary on a text of Dorn's, she also makes a few remarks about his life:

> [We know that] he was a physician, a general practitioner, that he was an adherent and passionate pupil and defender of his master, Paracelsus. He also advanced pharmacology to a certain extent . . . . One of his . . . pharmacological contributions was the discovery that if certain chemical medicines were . . . distilled, they then had a . . . more heightened effect.[95]

Dorn was one of the few alchemists at the end of the sixteenth century who realized that alchemical symbolism and tradition implied a religious problem; this is one of the reasons Jung found him so significant. In contrast to many others, he tried to engage the problem of the conflict between the alchemical approach and the religious approach. Dorn was an avid Platonist, and every now and then lapsed into polemic against Aristotle, demonstrating his considerable introversion.

Continuing his discussion of the contrast between natural substances and prepared compounds, Jung quotes an alchemical text and then comments on it:

> "The centre of this magnet contains a hidden salt [a salt would be a prepared compound], a menstruum for calcining the philosophical gold. This prepared salt forms their Mercury, with which they perform the magistery of the Sages in white and in red. It becomes an ore of heavenly fire, which acts as a ferment for their stone." In his [Dorn's] view, therefore, the secret of the magnet's effect lies in a salt . . . hidden in the magnet and prepared by the adept—on the one hand, a product of his art; on the other, already present in nature. (par. 247)

Jung continues on this subject, invoking Dorn:

> A similar state of affairs can be found in Dorn's writings. In his case it is not a

---

[94] See "The Philosophical Tree," CW 13, pars. 375ff.
[95] *Alchemical Active Imagination,* pp. 17f.

question of the *sal sapientiae* [the salt of wisdom], but the "veritas," which for him is hidden in natural things and at the same time is obviously a "moral" concept. This truth is the "medicine, improving and transforming that which *is no longer* into that which it *was before* its corruption, and that which *is not* into that which it *ought to be.*" It is a "metaphysical substance," hidden not only in things, but in the human body . . . "a certain metaphysical substance known to very few, which needeth no medicament, being itself an incorrupt medicament." Therefore "it is the study of the Chemists to liberate that unsensual truth from its fetters in things of sense." (par. 248)

On that same theme Dorn is quoted as saying:

> There is a certain truth *[veritas]* in natural things which is not seen with the outward eye, but is perceived by the mind alone, and of this the Philosophers have had experience, and have ascertained that its virtue is such that it performs miracles. (par. 246, note 32)

> The true doctrine, in Collesson's words, is the magnet whereby the "centre of truth" is liberated from bodies and whereby the bodies are transformed. "The Philosophers, through a kind of divine inspiration, knew that this virtue and heavenly vigour can be freed from its fetters; not by its contrary . . . but by its like." (par. 248)

This means that this "stuff," this magical hidden stuff, called by Dorn *veritas,* is equated with the Echeneis/Remora fish of the previous text, on the one hand, and with the magnet or *aqua doctrinae,* which attracts and catches the Remora fish, on the other hand. We are pursuing this same symbolism under a new image. Later in the chapter there are further remarks on the subject of *veritas:*

> Nevertheless, he [Dorn] succeeded in explaining the magnetic attraction between the imagined symbol—the "theoria"—and the "centre" hidden in matter, or in the interior of the earth or in the North Pole, as the identity of two extremes. That is why the theoria and the arcanum in matter are both called "truth." This truth "shines" in us but it is not of us: it "is to be sought not in us, but in the image of God which is in us." (par. 264)

In paragraph 265, Jung says, "Dorn goes even further and allows the predicate of *being* to this truth, and to this truth alone." In other words, nothing exists except that one thing: "The only thing that truly exists for him is the transcendental self, which is identical with God." This pronouncement, that *veritas* alone has being, means nothing less than that the Self is the root or origin of all that exists. In psychological terminology, it means that the Self is the root and source of all our experience.

Now, having laid out some of these texts, we can consider this archetypal image, *veritas,* which gripped Dorn so powerfully. We translate the word into English as "truth," but the concept has a long historical background and has had a very powerful symbolic impact. In ancient Egypt, it was represented by the

Goddess Maat. It was she who presided at the weighing of souls in the afterlife. Her feather was put in one balance pan and the heart of the deceased was put in the other, and if they didn't balance, the heart was thrown to the monster which was waiting to devour it. The soul of the deceased was measured on the basis of "truth" as the ultimate criterion.

In ancient Greece, the term for truth was *aletheia,* which is interesting because it is a negative term. The *a* is a privative prefix which signifies "absence of," and what is absent is *lethe,* the water of forgetfulness, which is what one drinks when one comes into conscious existence. When the soul is born it drinks *lethe* so that it forgets its prenatal life. For the ancient Greek, truth was *aletheia,* meaning the absence of forgetfulness or the presence of memory. Plato uses this term *aletheia* to distinguish the eternal world of forms from the phenomenal world of appearance; *aletheia* refers to the world of forms. The world of appearances is only a copy or an imitation of that eternal world; *aletheia* is the original. Thus Plato could say in *Timaeus:* "As being is to becoming, so is truth *[aletheia]* to belief."[96] Belief is a kind of copy of truth, not the real thing.

In Hebrew, the word comparable to *aletheia* is *enath* and it is often used in the Old Testament to indicate the nature of Yahweh. For instance, in Psalms 19:9 we read: "The judgements of Yahweh are true, . . . more desirable than gold." (JB) In the New Testament, Christ uses this term to refer to something of supreme importance. For instance, in John 8:32, he says "You will learn the truth *[aletheia* in Greek, *veritas* in Latin] and the truth will make you free." (JB) In John 16:13, Christ tells his disciples that he must die, but after his death he will send the Paraclete, the comforter. He says that when the comforter comes, this "Spirit of truth . . . will lead you to the complete truth." (JB)

So the coming Paraclete is described as the spirit of truth. This corresponds to a reference Jung makes in paragraph 249:

> The doctrine—the "magnet"—is at the same time the mysterious "truth" of which the doctrine speaks. The doctrine enters the consciousness of the adept as a gift of the Holy Ghost.

The Holy Ghost or the holy spirit is a synonym for the Paraclete. So the spirit of truth and the Holy Ghost are symbolic equivalents. When Christ was being examined before Pilate, he said: "I came into the world for this: to bear witness to the truth *[veritas, aletheia];* and all who are on the side of truth listen to my voice." (John 18:37f., JB) Then Pilate, in typical secular response, replied cynically: *"Quid es Veritas?"* [What is truth?] So as you see, this word *veritas* has a lengthy history, and, as Dorn told us, has such a virtue that it performs miracles.

This *veritas* corresponds psychologically to latent consciousness hidden in the unconscious. If we apply this symbolism to the analytic process, we can say

---

[96] *Timaeus,* 29C.

that *veritas* corresponds to the latent consciousness hidden in the unconscious of the patient. It is the consciousness that accompanies the imagery of the Self, of wholeness, and it can be drawn forth as a magnet attracts iron, with the help of the analyst's interpretations and responses, and the consciousness the analyst brings to bear on the psychology of the patient. Another way of putting it would be to say that the analyst's personal relation to the Self functions like a magnet which constellates and draws forth or activates the Self in the patient, bringing it into manifestation. Thus *veritas,* which has the ability to perform miracles, is made manifest.

Another set of associations emerges in paragraph 251, where Jung says: "The alchemist . . . knew definitely that as part of the whole he had an image of the whole in himself, of the 'firmament' or 'Olympus,' as Paracelsus calls it." Jung appends, in note 43: "[This was] an idea that reached its full development 200 years later in Leibniz' monadology."

You see how Jung uses the total cultural history of mankind to illustrate the psyche. He draws on everything; Leibniz is just another example. Let us consider Leibniz briefly. His dates are 1646 to 1716. In Leibniz' theory of monadology, the universe is composed of a vast number of elementary units called monads. Will Durant says about this idea:

> We shall understand the monads better if we think of them "in imitation of the notion that we have of souls." As each soul is "a simple, separate Person," a solitary ego [alone against the world] fighting its way by its own internal will against everything outside it, so each monad is essentially alone, a separate, independent center of force. . . . Every monad [is] unique; in the entire cosmos there are no two beings completely alike . . . each monad feels however confusedly and unconsciously, [that it constitutes] the whole universe; in this way it is a mirror more or less obscurely reflecting and representing the world. And as no individual mind can really look into another mind, so no single monad can see into another.[97]

The monad has no window. Although the monads are called windowless, they are not at all cut off from the world because, as another commentator puts it, each living thing is a perpetual living mirror of the universe. We seem to live in many different worlds, but these are in truth nothing but aspects of a single universe viewed from the special point of view of each monad. Being joined this way, we are not really independent. Everyone feels the effect of all that takes place in the universe. Each created monad thus represents the whole universe within itself. One can see here a philosophical precursor of the empirical discovery of the Self.

Returning to Dorn, Jung takes up the idea of objective self-knowledge. This is related to Leibniz' idea that each of the separated monads sees the universe as

---

[97] *The Age of Louis XIV,* p. 670.

an objective reality, outside of itself. Similarly, the ego can regard the psyche objectively. Jung says:

> This objective knowledge of the self is what the author [Dorn] means when he says: "No one can know himself unless he knows *what,* and not *who,* he is, on what he depends, or whose he is [or: to whom or what he belongs] and for what end he was made." The distinction between "quis" and "quid" [who and what] is crucial: whereas "quis" has an unmistakably personal aspect and refers to the ego, "quid" is neuter, predicating nothing except an object which is not endowed even with personality. Not the subjective ego-consciousness of the psyche is meant, but the psyche itself as the unknown, unprejudiced object that still has to be investigated. (par. 252)

This is an important reference for Jung. He goes into it in even more detail in *Mysterium Coniunctionis.*[98] A remark about experiment is also relevant to this:

> The production of the arcane substance, the "generatio Mercurii," is possible only for one who has full knowledge of the doctrine; but "we cannot be resolved of any doubt except by experiment, and there is no better way to make it than on ourselves." (par. 250)

These two ideas are related because the experimental attitude is part of a so-called objective attitude; one cannot experiment with an entity unless one takes an objective attitude toward it. But then we must ask what it means to have an objective attitude about oneself. Actually, that is the whole effort of the analytic process. However, to have any hope for success, in a certain way one has to start with it too; there has to be a latent, potential, objective attitude toward oneself, or one can never get started toward objectivity, remaining hopelessly one of those fish in the fish pond. One can't take an objective attitude toward water as long as one is a fish swimming around in it. The ability to take an objective attitude toward the psyche, to see one's own psychology as an objective, living process, is evidence that consciousness is present. Jung puts the importance of this very strongly in paragraph 255:

> The final factors at work in us are nothing other than those talents which "a certain nobleman" entrusted to his "servants," that they might trade with them. (Luke 19:12ff.) It does not require much imagination to see what this involvement in the ways of the world means in the moral sense. Only an infantile person can pretend that evil is not at work everywhere, and the more unconscious he is, the more the devil drives him. It is just because of this inner connection with the black side of things that it is so incredibly easy for the mass man to commit the most appalling crimes without thinking. Only ruthless self-knowledge on the widest scale, which sees good and evil in correct perspective and can weigh up the motives of human action, offers some guarantee that the end-result will not turn out too badly.

---

98 See CW 14, pars. 362ff.

The operative phrase there is "ruthless self-knowledge." Ruthless self-knowledge is totally impossible unless it is objective. This is so regarding the awareness of evil, which is what Jung is talking about in this paragraph, because if one perceives evil in the psyche subjectively rather than objectively, it is instantly demoralizing. The ego identifies personally with the evil it perceives, and then there is no more ruthlessness—the ego has become so laden down with guilt that it can't function any longer as a perceiver.

In order to have ruthless self-knowledge, in order to perceive the full existence of darkness in the psyche, one has to perceive the individual psyche as an object rather than as a subject, in other words to perceive the psyche as not the ego. One has to see clearly that although the ego is doing the perceiving, the whole of the psyche is an objective entity, and that whole is not made by the ego, but is only discovered by it. It is discovered by experiment, the same way that the alchemists and later science discovered the nature of the outer world. We do not create ourselves. We are created. That means that what we discover in the individual psyche is what has been created, not what we have made. What we are in our totality is not our subjective responsibility. What we do with it in reality is our responsibility, but not what we find there. That ability to take a radically objective attitude toward the nature of the individual psyche is indispensable to any significant consciousness.

Jung expands on this issue in his comments on a text describing the Philosophers' Stone:

"This stone is below thee, as to obedience; above thee, as to dominion; therefore from thee, as to knowledge; about thee, as to equals." The passage is somewhat obscure. Nevertheless, it can be elicited that the stone stands in an undoubted psychic relationship to man: the adept can expect obedience from it, but on the other hand the stone exercises dominion over him. Since the stone is a matter of "knowledge" or science, it springs from man. But it is outside him, in his surroundings, among his "equals," i.e. those of like mind. This description fits the paradoxical situation of the self, as its symbolism shows. It is the smallest of the small, easily overlooked and pushed aside. Indeed, it is in need of help and must be perceived, protected, and as it were built up by the conscious mind, just as if it did not exist at all and were called into being only through man's care and devotion. As against this, we know from experience that it had long been there and is older than the ego, and that it is actually the *spiritus rector* of our fate. . . .

. . . "This stone is something which is fixed more in thee [than elsewhere], created of God, and thou art its ore, and it is extracted from thee, and wheresoever thou art it remains inseparably with thee. . . . The stone . . . is [dug] out of man, and thou art its ore, namely by working; and from thee it is extracted . . . for without thee it cannot be fulfilled, and without it canst thou not live." (pars. 257f.)

This puts everything in a nutshell: "without thee, it cannot be fulfilled, and without it canst thou not live." That is a concise description of the nature of the relationship between the ego and the Self. Without the ego the Self cannot be brought into conscious realization. And without a living connection to it, conscious realization, the ego cannot live, because the Self is the source of its being. Jung comments in paragraph 259:

> We learn from [this text] that the stone is implanted in man by God, that the laborant is its *prima materia,* that the extraction corresponds to the so-called *divisio* or *separatio* of the alchemical procedure, and that through his knowledge of the stone man remains inseparably bound to the self. The procedure here described could easily be understood as the realization of an unconscious content. Fixation in the Mercurius of the wise would then correspond to the traditional Hermetic knowledge, since Mercurius symbolizes the Nous; through this knowledge the self, as a content of the unconscious, is made conscious and "fixed" in the mind. For without the existence of conscious concepts apperception is, as we know, impossible. . . . That is why it is so extremely important to tell children fairy-tales and legends, and to inculcate religious ideas (dogmas) into grown-ups, because these things are instrumental symbols with whose help unconscious contents can be canalized into consciousness, interpreted, and integrated. Failing this, their energy flows off into conscious contents which normally are not much emphasized, and intensifies them to pathological proportions. We then get apparently groundless phobias and obsessions—crazes, idiosyncrasies, hypochondriac ideas, and intellectual perversions suitably camouflaged in social, religious, or political garb.

The idea here is that the archetypes of the unconscious, in order to have their effects transmitted to the ego, need bridges by which to reach consciousness. These bridges are supplied by religious and mythological images and ideas that already exist as an accepted part of consciousness. This is why Jung considers knowledge of myths and religious dogma to be so important. Those images function as bridges that allow the effects of the archetypes entry, so to speak, into consciousness. If the conscious ego is lacking such ideas, then these archetypal energies flow into containers that are too small for them.

Jung gives an example of this in his 1937 Terry Lectures at Yale University. Jung describes a patient who was gripped by the compulsive idea that he had cancer of the intestines. Although he went through exhaustive medical examinations and was repeatedly assured that there was no physical problem, it made no difference. He was convinced that he had cancer, or if he did not have cancer, he might get it, which amounted to the same thing. Jung then talks about this particular case as an example, and says:

> What, then, shall we say to our patient with the imaginary cancer? I would tell him: "Yes, my friend, you are really suffering from a cancer-like thing, you really do harbor in yourself a deadly evil. However, it will not kill your body, because it is imaginary. But it will eventually kill your soul. It has already spoilt and even poisoned your human relations and your personal happiness and it will go on growing until it has swallowed your whole psychic existence. . . .

It is obvious to our patient that he is not the author of his morbid imagination, although his theoretical turn of mind will certainly suggest that he is the owner and maker of his own imaginings. If a man is suffering from a real cancer, he never believes himself to be responsible for such an evil . . . . But when it comes to the psyche we instantly feel a kind of responsibility, as if we were the makers of our psychic conditions.[99]

Jung continues on this subject a little later:

It is, to my mind, a fatal mistake to regard the human psyche as a purely personal affair and to explain it exclusively from a personal point of view. Such a mode of explanation is only applicable to the individual in his ordinary everyday occupations and relationships. If, however, some slight trouble occurs, perhaps in the form of an unforeseen and somewhat unusual event, instantly instinctual forces are called up, forces which appear to be wholly unexpected, new, and strange. . . . [The archetypal emerges. Collective forces rush up.]

. . . As a matter fact, we are constantly living on the edge of a volcano . . . .

. . . Our cancer case shows clearly how impotent man's reason and intellect are against the most palpable nonsense. I always advise my patients to take such obvious but invincible nonsense as the manifestation of a power and a meaning they have not yet understood. . . . Our patient is confronted with a power of will and suggestion more than equal to anything his consciousness can put against it. In this precarious situation it would be bad strategy to convince him that in some incomprehensible way he is at the back of his own symptom, secretly inventing and supporting it. Such a suggestion would instantly paralyse his fighting spirit, and he would get demoralized. It is far better for him to understand that his complex is an autonomous power directed against his conscious personality.[100]

In other words, God. The patient's cancer phobia is a manifestation of the inner God-image, an autonomous power that transcends the capacity of the ego. This illustrates Jung's remarks on how archetypal energies, if they do not have adequate bridges into consciousness, flow into containers that are too small for them.

---

[99] "Psychology and Religion," *Psychology and Religion,* CW 11, pars. 19f.
[100] Ibid., pars. 24ff.

18
Paragraphs 267-286

The Psychology of Christian Alchemical Symbolism

Jung moves next into a broad historical context:

> [We are] witnessing today the curious spectacle of two parallel world-views neither of which knows, or wishes to know, anything about the other. . . .
>
> . . . In the course of the eighteenth century, there arose that notorious rift between faith and knowledge. Faith lacked experience and science missed out the soul. Instead, science believed fervently in absolute objectivity and assiduously overlooked the fundamental difficulty that the real vehicle and begetter of all knowledge is the *psyche,* the very thing that scientists knew the least about for the longest time. (pars. 267f.)

The two world-views are the world of faith—concretistic, parochial religious faith, in which each person's faith is considered the only true one, and secularized, rationalistic, soulless science. With the eyes for it, one can see this conflict everywhere in the outer world. But, as Jung says in paragraph 280, a conflict between opposites can never be resolved on their own level; they can only be reconciled by finding a third position on a new level. Jungian psychology provides a third position which is capable of reconciling these two world-views.

Not only is the collective psyche split in this fashion; the same split occurs in great numbers of individuals. Of course, there are a great many people who identify with one or the other of these opposing views, but there are also a good number who carry both viewpoints within them, keeping them in compartments. In part of their lives they function out of one of the viewpoints, and in the other part, out of the other. Since the two parts never connect with each other, these individuals never experience any conflict. But if the analyst tries to bring these two hermetically sealed compartments together, there is an explosion and the most violent resistance.

A related issue which often comes up in analytic practice is that of how to deal with individuals who are largely identified with one or the other of these two standpoints. Those identified with the secular, rationalistic attitude very often need to be introduced to mythological and religious imagery; their dreams will suggest this. On the other hand, those who are identified with a traditional, concretistic faith often have to be introduced to Voltaire (or his equivalent), to the rationalist who analyzed away religious faith. I use Voltaire's name particularly because on the landing of the stairs leading to Jung's study where he did his analytic work there was a statue of Voltaire. Jung told an interviewer that he had the statue there to remind him of his shadow.

Concerning the conflict of world-views and its resolution, Jung comments:

> The problems which the integration of the unconscious sets modern doctors and psychologists can only be solved along the lines traced out by history, and the upshot will be a new assimilation of the traditional myth. This, however, presupposes the continuity of historical development. Naturally the present tendency to destroy all tradition or render it unconscious could interrupt the normal process of development for several hundred years and substitute an interlude of barbarism. (par. 282)

I take this remark to be a prediction. The tendency to destroy all tradition is already so far advanced in our collective operations and in our educational systems, that it seems as if history is certain to run its course in just this fashion.

Turning to one side of the split between religious faith and rationalistic science, Jung refers to the Christian creed:

> Our Christian doctrine is a highly differentiated symbol that expresses the transcendent psychic—the God-image and its properties, to speak with Dorn. The Creed is a "symbolum." This comprises practically everything of importance that can be ascertained about the manifestations of the psyche in the field of inner experience, but it does not include Nature, at least not in any recognizable form. Consequently, at every period of Christianity there have been subsidiary currents or undercurrents that have sought to investigate the empirical aspect of Nature not only from the outside but also from the inside.
>
> Although dogma, like mythology in general, expresses the quintessence of inner experience and thus formulates the operative principles of the objective psyche, i.e., the collective unconscious, it does so by making use of a language and outlook that have become alien to our present way of thinking. The word "dogma" has even acquired a somewhat unpleasant sound and frequently serves merely to emphasize the rigidity of a prejudice. For most people living in the West, it has lost its meaning as a symbol for a virtually unknowable and yet "actual"—i.e., operative—fact. (pars. 270f.)

Let us take a look at what the Christian dogma actually is, at what has been the operative myth for the aeon now ending. If we go back to the early part of the aeon, we find simple versions of the creed that give a picture of the basic dogma. Here is a variation of the Nicene Creed, taken from Jung's essay "A Psychological Approach to the Dogma of the Trinity":

> We believe in one God the Father Almighty, Maker of heaven and earth, and of all things visible and invisible. And in one Lord Jesus Christ, the only begotten Son of God, begotten of his Father before all worlds, God of God, Light of Light, very God of very God, begotten, not made, being of one substance with the Father, by whom all things were made; who for us men and for our salvation came down from heaven and was made flesh by the Holy Ghost and the Virgin Mary and became man, and was crucified for us under Pontius Pilate, suffered and was buried, and on the third day rose again according to the Scriptures, and ascended into

heaven, and sitteth on the right hand of God the Father, whence he shall come again in glory to judge the quick and the dead, and whose kingdom shall have no end. And [we believe] in the Holy Ghost, the Lord and Giver of life, who proceedeth from the Father [and from the Son], who with the Father and the Son together is worshipped and glorified, who spake through the prophets. And [we believe] in one holy Catholic and Apostolic Church. We acknowledge one baptism for the remission of sins. And we await the resurrection of the dead and the life of the world to come.[101]

That is it, all in one concise package. If that body of images were an absolute conviction so that one could live out of it with certainty, one's life would be all set; one would be contained. This religious creed can now be understood as a symbolic expression of psychic reality: it is an expression of the process of individuation. The creed tells us first of all that there is a God-image that is the creator and origin of everything. Then it tells us that one aspect of that God-image descended to earth incarnated in a man, in other words, manifested in the ego. The Self on its own initiative incarnated in an ego, with redemptive intentions, intentions to rescue that ego. The redemption would mean, psychologically, to bring to the ego a sense of meaning. This aspect of the Self then re-ascended to where it had come from, indicating that incarnation was not a perpetual event but a temporary one, but there will be a second coming, a second manifestation of the ego's encounter with the Self. That second manifestation will be a different kind of experience; it will be a last-judgment experience. This will then be followed by a general resurrection, a resolution of all repressed complexes and the establishment of the eternal kingdom, in other words, the establishment of the eternal dimension of the psyche, a transition from the temporal experience of existence to something transpersonal and atemporal.[102]

Jung's text again takes up the split between the two belief systems in modern man and the need for continuity of belief systems, including a discussion of anamnesis. You will recall that this theme has come up before. It is worth reiterating because it is such an important theme in practical analysis:

> When a living organism is cut off from its roots, it loses the connections with the foundations of its existence and must necessarily perish. When that happens, anamnesis of the origins is a matter of life and death.
>
> Myths and fairytales give expression to unconscious processes, and their retelling causes these processes to come alive again [so that they promote the anamnesis process] . . . .
>
> . . . The healing and renewing properties of this symbolical water—whether it be *tao,* the baptismal water, or the elixir—point to the therapeutic character of the mythological background from which this idea comes. (pars. 279ff.)

---

101 *Psychology and Religion,* CW 11, par. 217.
102 This is elaborated in more detail in my book *The Christian Archetype.*

That is an important phrase, ". . . the therapeutic character of the mythological background." That is part of the anamnesis experience. In his earlier reference to anamnesis, Jung says:

> This is in exact agreement with the empirical findings of psychology, that there is an ever-present archetype of wholeness, which may easily disappear from the purview of consciousness or may never be perceived at all until a consciousness illuminated by conversion recognizes it in the figure of Christ. As a result of this "anamnesis" the original state of oneness with the God-image is restored. It brings about an integration, a bridging of the split in the personality. (par. 73)

Analysis to a very large extent is an anamnesis—a remembering of what has gone before. There are two dimensions to the analytic anamnesis: the personal and the collective or archetypal one. First the person deliberately recalls his or her personal past, which opens up the personal unconscious. Then if the patient is meant to proceed deeper, the dreams lead beyond the personal unconscious into the collective dimension of the anamnesis, which involves an archetypal, historical remembering: first of all of the family, the ancestral background, tribe, nation, then the archetypal level of humanity as a whole. Finally one gets to his or her origins from the universe itself.[103]

The collective anamnesis corresponds to the Platonic idea of anamnesis, which is usually translated as "recollection." As Plato says in the *Phaedo:*

> If . . . we acquired our knowledge before our birth and lost it at the moment of birth, but afterward by the exercise of our senses upon sensible objects, recover the knowledge which we had once before, I suppose that what we call learning will be the recovery of our own knowledge, and surely we should be right in calling this recollection.[104]

Plato is saying that all cognition is recognition, all knowing is remembering knowledge we once had. This is not literally true, but it is psychologically true in terms of the exploration of the unconscious in both its personal and its archetypal layers. We were once in touch with both those layers. We "knew" it all once before, but then we forgot it. In the course of developing consciousness, even if we are not neurotic, there is a split between the ego and the unconscious, a split from one's roots. If we can remember where we came from, can go through that process of anamnesis, then we can recover our lost wholeness.

---

[103] I want to emphasize how important I think it is that every analysis begin with a careful, systematic scrutiny of the individual history. I think one should uniformly, at the beginning of each analysis, ask the prospective analysand to write a personal biography with emphasis on those aspects of the life history that have the most libido charge, positively and negatively, and then go through this biography in some detail, subjecting it to the analytic dialogue so that the review becomes part of the living experience of the analysis.

[104] *Phaedo,* 75E-76. *Anamnesis* is the Greek word translated here as recollection.

Jung considers further the need for continuity of cultural development, citing the example of the Apostle Paul in Athens:

> If Paul were alive today, and should undertake to reach the ear of intelligent Londoners in Hyde Park, he could no longer content himself with quotations from Greek literature and a smattering of Jewish history. (par. 275)

He would have to extend himself farther afield in order to engage the split modern mind.

Paul's visit to Athens took place at the beginning of this aeon. He was in the process of introducing a new world-view to the ancient world. Something analogous is taking place now at the beginning of the new aeon. Jungian psychology has the task of introducing a new world-view and so the experience of Paul in Athens, to which Jung alludes in several places in his works, is relevant as a kind of traditional pattern of this recurrent issue. When Paul was in Athens, he gave a speech before the council of the Areopagus, starting out:

> Men of Athens, I have seen for myself how extremely scrupulous you are in all religious matters, because I noticed, as I strolled around admiring your sacred monuments, that you had an altar inscribed: To An Unknown God. Well, the God whom I proclaim is in fact the one whom you already worship without knowing it. (Acts 17:23, JB)

Paul slipped right into the established standpoint. Further on in this speech, Paul quoted a Greek poet as saying "We are all his [God's] children," and made use of this too. This image of Paul preaching to the Athenians is a traditional form indicating how to proceed with the introduction of a new level of consciousness. It must be done by relating the new insights to the accepted ideas of the past. Jung puts it very clearly in *Mysterium Coniunctionis:*

> Any renewal not deeply rooted in the best spiritual tradition is ephemeral; but the dominant that grows from historical roots acts like a living being within the ego-bound man. He does not possess it, it possesses him.[105]

Reflecting on this remark you will realize that Jung is here describing his own *modus operandi.* This is the basic principle of Jung's books, which is why they are so full of amplification and traditional imagery presented and seen in a new way, in the light of depth psychology. Jung uses Paul's method in talking to the Athenians, but in a much more sophisticated way.

Jungian psychology today is in a position analogous to that of Christianity two thousand years ago. It must relate itself to the traditional imagery it is destined to replace. Alchemical symbolism is particularly useful in this, because it provides a bridge between the traditional Christian dogmatic images and the modern scientific mind—one reason Jung found it so helpful.

---

[105] CW 14, par. 521.

19
Paragraphs 287-305

Gnostic Symbols of the Self

Now Jung turns from alchemical symbolism to Gnostic imagery of the Self. For data on the Gnostics, Jung relies very heavily on Hippolytus's work, *The Refutation of All Heresies.* Hippolytus, whom we discussed in chapter eight, was a Presbyter at Rome, and lived from approximately 170 to 236 A.D. He wrote a very comprehensive attack on the Gnostic heresies, and in the course of attacking them he described their doctrines very fully, indicating that they had a certain fascination for him in spite of himself. We are fortunate to have available an English translation of Hippolytus's treatise in its entirety.[106]

Jung continues here to examine the symbolism of the magnet, moving on from the earlier alchemical material on the Echeneis remora fish and the magnetic effect that it exerted on ships, and on the magnetic effect of a certain kind of doctrine in catching the fish. He identifies three texts in Hippolytus's work that speak of the magnet. The first is the Paradise Quaternio text. It is summarized in paragraph 288. This text is quite important in the rest of *Aion;* later on Jung uses the imagery of the Paradise Quaternio for other purposes. The text here is from *The Ante-Nicene Fathers,* a lengthier version than Jung gives us. Hippolytus says:

> [The Gnostics assert that] Edem [Eden] is the brain . . . they suppose that man, as far as [he is a] head only, is Paradise. . . . [And that a] "river, which proceeds out of Edem," i.e. from the brain, "is divided into four heads, and that the name of the first river is called Phison; . . ." [this is] the eye, which by its honor (among the rest of the bodily organs), . . . furnishes testimony to what is spoken . . . The name of the second river is Gihon: . . . [which] is hearing . . . And the name of the third [river] is Tigris. . . . this is smelling . . . But the fourth river is Euphrates [which is] the mouth, through which are the passage outwards of prayer, and the passage inwards of nourishment. (The mouth) makes glad, and nurtures and fashions the Spiritual, Perfect Man. This [the Gnostics say] is "the water that is above the firmament," concerning which . . . the Savior has declared, "If thou knewest who it is that asks, thou wouldst have asked from Him, and He would have given you to drink living, bubbling water." Into this water, he says, every nature enters, choosing its own substances; and its peculiar quality comes to each nature from this water, more than iron does to the magnet.[107]

---

[106] See Roberts and Donaldson, *The Ante-Nicene Fathers,* vol. 5.
[107] Ibid., pp. 57f.

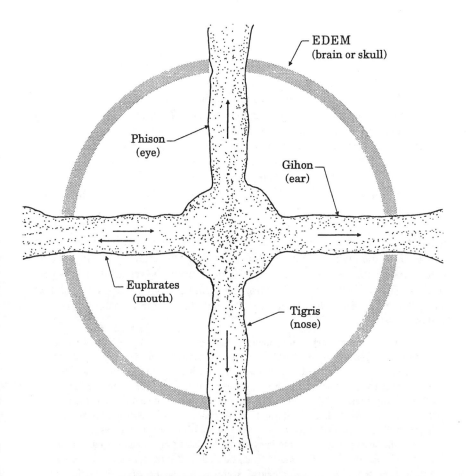

Figure 19. The Paradise Quaternio Text.
The Gnostic text equates Paradise with the human head or brain, and the four
rivers which arose in Paradise with the four orifices of the head: eye, ear, nose
and mouth. The waters have the power to make one whole.

So with this first Gnostic text, we return again to the magnet. This material is pictured in figure 19, showing the brain which has at its center the source of the four rivers. They divide and one river comes out of the eye, another out of the ear, another out of the nose, and the fourth river out of the mouth. This is a kind of active imagination image with the skull or the brain, the "round thing" in man. As Jung tells us in paragraph 288, the first three rivers are similar, but the fourth, the Euphrates, the mouth, is of a special nature because things move both ways in the mouth: food goes in and prayer comes out. The fourth one is special, corresponding to the psychological fact that the fourth function brings totality up with it, and therefore is of a singular nature. As the image indicates, Euphrates the mouth promotes a two-way dialogue with the Self or the Godhead—nourishment goes in, to the ego, and nourishment goes out to God via prayers.

Furthermore, this Euphrates water is described as the water above the firmament, which is referred to in the first chapter of Genesis, where it is said that God made the firmament and divided the waters which were under the firmament from the waters which were above the firmament. The firmament is the heavenly vault, and the Euphrates water corresponds to celestial water which exists beyond the heavenly limit. It is also referred to as Christ's living water, mentioned in the Book of John, in which Jesus meets the Samaritan woman at a well and says to her: "If you only knew what God is offering / and who it is that is saying to you: / Give me a drink, / you would have been the one to ask, / and he would have given you living water." (4:10, JB) Here Christ is identifying himself as the living water that the Gnostics equate with the Euphrates and also with the water above the firmament. Jung remarks about this water:

> As the reference to John 4:10 shows, the wonderful water of the Euphrates has the property of the *aqua doctrinae,* which perfects every nature in its individuality and thus makes man whole too. It does this by giving him a kind of magnetic power by which he can attract and integrate that which belongs to him. (par. 289)

This corresponds to the fact that when one is in touch with the Self, the libido connection that is generated has the effect of locating the scattered fragments of one's identity that reside in the world. In reading and in daily encounters with people and events in the world, one can identify what belongs to oneself by noticing one's reactions. One values what belongs to oneself, one has an "ah ha" experience—oh, that's something significant! Reading and going through the world with that awareness, one can constantly pick up things that belong to oneself, which corresponds to what Jung says about this water. It gives one a kind of magnetic power by which one can attract and integrate pieces of one's identity.

Once I came across a dream of this water, after a session with a patient in which I found myself being particularly "brilliant" in making amplifications of the dream we were discussing. I don't take credit for such brilliance; it is projected into me and I just act it out; it comes from the unconscious of the patient.

But nonetheless, after such a session of rich amplification, the patient dreamt that a stream of crystal-clear water was coming out of the mouth of the analyst. That is the river Euphrates water.

The second Gnostic text, the "Signs of the Father," is summarized by Jung in paragraph 290. Here is a fuller version:

> According to [the Gnostics,] the universe is [composed of] Father, Son (and) Matter. . . . Intermediate between the Matter and the Father sits the Son, the Word, the Serpent. . . . At one time he is turned towards the Father . . . at another time . . . [he is] turned towards Matter. . . . the son, by a power that belongs to himself, transfers the signs of the Father *[patrikoi charakteres]* from the Father into Matter. . . . if any one of those (beings) [down in the darkness of Matter] will have strength to perceive that he is a paternal mark [the sign of the Father], . . . [that] he is of the same substance . . . with the Father in heaven, [then he] returns thither. [This only happens if he has the doctrine.] . . . No one, then, . . . can be saved or return (into heaven) without the Son, and the Son is the Serpent. For as he brought down from above the signs of the Father, so again he carries up from thence those [signs] roused from a dormant condition and rendered . . . substantial. . . . .And he transfers (those marks) to those who close the eyelid, as the naphtha drawing the fire in every direction towards itself; nay rather, as the magnet (attracting) the iron.[108]

The idea, represented here in figure 20, is that the son/serpent carries the signs of the father down from heaven into matter, where man resides. The man who has the right doctrine recognizes that he has the signs of the father. Another way of putting it is that when one has the right doctrine, the sign of the father that is brought down is transferred to him. Once transferred, it is rendered substantial, is materialized, incarnated, and then is transferred back to the serpent and is carried back to heaven again in embodied form. This is the idea behind the "Signs of the Father" text. Jung says about it:

> Here the magnetic attraction does not come from the doctrine or the water but from the "Son," who is symbolized by the serpent, as in John 3:14. ["And as Moses lifted up the serpent in the wilderness, even so must the Son of man be lifted up."] Christ is the magnet that draws to itself those parts or substances in man that are of divine origin, the signs of the Father, and carries them back to their heavenly birthplace. The serpent is an equivalent of the fish. (par. 291)

Since we are dealing here with the image of the snake, we should note Jung's remarks about snake symbolism. This is an excellent summary of the symbolism of the snake which is such a common dream image:

> [The serpent] appears spontaneously or comes as a surprise; it fascinates; its glance is staring, fixed, unrelated; its blood cold, and it is a stranger to man: it crawls over the sleeper, he finds it in a shoe or in his pocket. It expresses his fear of everything

---

[108] Ibid., p. 63.

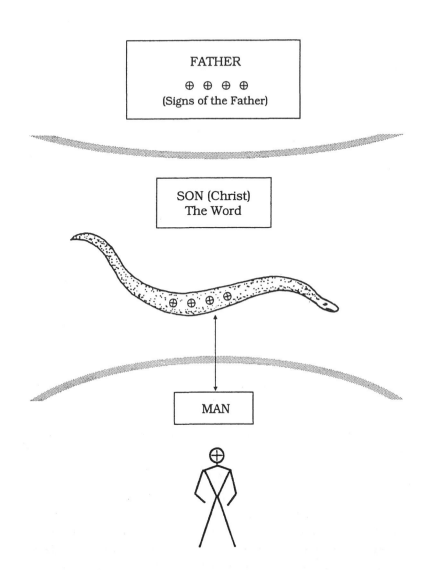

Figure 20. The "Signs of the Father" Text.
The Gnostic text describes how Christ as a serpent (center) brings the divine qualities of God (the "Signs of the Father") from heaven down into the world of matter,
and draws out the parts of man that are of divine origin,
then carries them back to heaven.

inhuman and his awe of the sublime, of what is beyond human ken. It is the lowest (devil) and the highest (son of God, Logos, Nous, Agathodaimon). The snake's presence is frightening, one finds it in unexpected places at unexpected moments. Like the fish, it represents and personifies the dark and unfathomable, the watery deep, the forest, the night, the cave. When a primitive says "snake," he means an experience of something extrahuman. (par. 293)

It is well to remember these remarks whenever one encounters a snake dream because such an image almost always generates a highly ambiguous, highly charged atmosphere indicating the activation of the unconscious at quite a primordial level, and signifies the prospect of an important step in individuation. On one hand the snake threatens to bite and poison the dreamer; on the other hand it is the bringer of the signs of the father, that is, the marks of wholeness. So a snake dream always conveys the double idea of a danger or something ominous, and a revelation.

The third Gnostic text, the Ray of Light, is summarized by Jung in paragraph 292. Here is a somewhat fuller form:

The Sethians affirm that the theory concerning composition and mixture is constituted according to the following method: The luminous ray from above is intermingled, and . . . blended in the dark waters beneath; and (both of these) become united, and are formed into one compound mass . . . [But then it is possible to separate the different ingredients of that compound mass.] For each of the things that have been commingled is separated . . . [and with that separation, then the different substances] hurry toward their own peculiar (substances), as iron towards the magnet . . . . In like manner, the *ray* of light which has been commingled with the water, having obtained from discipline and instruction its own proper locality, hastens towards the Logos that comes from above.[109]

To summarize this passage, the ray of light comes down from the light region above and gets all mixed up in the dark waters. But then the Logos descends as a dividing sword and this has the effect of separating the mingled mixture, and the rays of light which have been all mixed up in the dark waters separate themselves and are attracted, like iron filings, to the Logos, to their proper place. The scriptural reference is to Matthew 10:34-36, to which the Gnostics give a totally different interpretation from that of conventional historians. Christ is speaking:

Think not that I come to send peace on the earth; I came not to send peace, but a sword. For I came to set a man at variance against his father, and the daughter against her mother, and the daughter-in-law against her mother-in-law, and a man's foes shall be they of his own household. (ASV)

The Gnostics interpret the "sword aspect" of Christ as the Logos, which has the effect of separating the rays which had been mixed up in the darkness. This

---

[109] Ibid., p. 68.

image of rays descending corresponds to the Gnostic idea of Sophia falling into the embrace of darkness, and having to be rescued. Concerning the ray of light, Jung says:

> Here the magnetic attraction comes from the Logos [the sword]. This denotes a thought or idea that has been formulated and articulated, hence a content and a product of consciousness. Consequently the Logos is very like the *aqua doctrinae,* but whereas the Logos has the advantage of being an autonomous personality, the latter [the *aqua]* is merely a passive object of human action. (par. 293)

To summarize these three texts which have different images for the same magnetic agent:

1) The Paradise Quaternio text has the image of the water of the Euphrates, the water which for every nature attracts that which is proper to it.

2) The Signs of the Father text has the serpent image which attracts those who carry the signs of the father;

3) The Ray of Light text has the Logos as a dividing sword image which attracts the light from the dark mixture.

About these three symbols, Jung comments:

> [The first agent] is an inanimate and in itself passive substance, *water.* It is drawn from the depths of the well, handled by human hands, and used according to man's needs. It signifies the visible doctrine, the *aqua doctrinae* . . . . [In the second case] the agent is an animate, autonomous being, the *serpent.* . . . [In the third case] the agent is the *Logos,* a philosophical idea and abstraction of the bodily and personal son of God on the one hand, and on the other the dynamic power of thoughts and words.
>
> It is clear that these three symbols seek to describe the unknowable essence of the incarnate God. But it is equally clear that they are hypostatized to a high degree. (pars. 293f.)

Remembering this threefold sequence—water, serpent, sword—as variations of the symbol of the magnet will allow the appearance of any one of them to call the others to mind. The result will be that some of that living water may flow out of one's mouth on the right occasion.

From these Gnostic texts, Jung draws together common threads which go to make up the idea of the unconscious God. He quotes several sources to illustrate the idea and sums up in paragraph 303. This is an important idea for the late Jung, and it is a revolutionary contribution.

> These utterances on the nature of the Deity express transformations of the God-image which run parallel with changes in human consciousness, though one would be at a loss to say which is the cause of the other. The God-image is not something *invented,* it is an *experience* that comes upon man spontaneously—as anyone can see for himself unless he is blinded to the truth by theories and prejudices. The unconscious God-image can therefore alter the state of consciousness, just as the latter

can modify the God-image once it has become conscious. This, obviously, has nothing to do with the "prime truth," the unknown God—at least, nothing that could be verified. Psychologically, however, the idea of God's ignorance *[agnosia]* or of the unconscious God *[anennoetos theos]*, is of the utmost importance, because it identifies the Deity with the numinosity of the unconscious.

I think the outstanding statement here, practically speaking, is that the unconscious God-image can alter the state of consciousness, just as the latter (the state of consciousness, the ego) can modify the God-image once it has become conscious. This exemplifies the symbolism of the Euphrates river mouth, which moves in both directions. The unconscious God-image, when it is activated, has an intense effect on the ego, and the danger is that the ego will become possessed and identified with it and then function as a kind of primitive Yahweh. That is one possibility. The other is that if the ego is able to meet the onslaught of the unconscious God-image with sufficient conscious awareness, the God-image itself is transformed.

In "Answer to Job" Jung makes a number of additional remarks about the unconscious God; in the baldest possible terms he states the following:

> The naive assumption that the creator of the world is a conscious being must be regarded as a disastrous prejudice which later gave rise to the most incredible dislocations of logic. For example, the nonsensical doctrine of the *privatio boni* would never have been necessary had one not had to assume in advance that it is impossible for the consciousness of a good God to produce evil deeds. Divine unconsciousness and lack of reflection, on the other hand, enable us to form a conception of God which puts his actions beyond moral judgment and allows no conflict to arise between goodness and beastliness.[110]

The whole idea of the unconscious God leads Jung into the thought of Meister Eckhart, with whom Jung had a very intimate connection. Eckhart lived from approximately 1260 to 1328, the same time as Dante. In a letter, Jung refers to Eckhart as one of the ten "pillar[s] of the bridge of the spirit which spans the morass of world history."[111] One out of ten. (The ten are: Gilgamesh, *I Ching, Upanishads,* Lao-tzu, Heraclitus, The Gospel of John, the Letters of Paul, Meister Eckhart, Dante and Goethe's *Faust.)*

Regarding Eckhart, Jung says:

> Meister Eckhart's theology knows a "Godhead" of which no qualities, except unity and being, can be predicated; it "is becoming," it is not yet Lord of itself, and it represents an absolute coincidence of opposites . . . . Union of opposites is equivalent to unconsciousness, so far as human logic goes, for consciousness presupposes a differentiation into subject and object and a relation between them. Where there

---

110 *Psychology and Religion,* CW 11, par. 600, note 13.
111 *Letters,* vol. 1, p. 89. See also Jung's essay on Eckhart in *Psychological Types,* CW 6, pars. 407-433.

is no "other," or it does not yet exist, all possibility of consciousness ceases. Only the Father, the God "welling" out of the Godhead, "notices himself," becomes "beknown to himself," and "confronts himself as a Person." . . . As the Godhead is essentially unconscious, so too is the man who lives in God. (par. 301)

This is a striking idea. The text, however, requires a little explanation. Eckhart distinguished between Godhead and God. What he calls the Godhead is what we would call the unconscious, original Self, the original unconscious All, so to speak. When the ego is immersed in it, identified with it, the ego does not exist as a separate entity, and God does not really exist either. God, on the other hand, as a term used by Eckhart, is a consequence of consciousness; it is born in the human soul. This is the basic theme of Eckhart's teaching—that God is born in the human soul, in a process parallel to the nativity of Christ. He does not exist, really, until he is born there. This is the idea that Jung found so appealing, that God requires conscious man in order to come into existence. Eckhart was the first one to state this clearly; he was a depth psychologist manqué.

Gnostic Symbols of the Self (cont.)

Jung continues the Gnostic material by laying out some of the Gnostic symbols for the universal "Ground" or the divine substance:

> The most important of these images is the figure of the demiurge. The Gnostics have a vast number of symbols for the source or origin, the center of being, the Creator, and the divine substance hidden in the creature. Lest the reader be confused by this wealth of images, he should always remember that each new image is simply another aspect of the divine mystery immanent in all creatures. My list of Gnostic symbols is no more than an amplification of a single transcendental idea, which is so comprehensive and so difficult to visualize in itself that a great many different expressions are required in order to bring out its various aspects. (par. 306)

The basic idea in Gnosticism was that a heavenly stuff fell out of, or descended from, or was lured out of heaven into matter, into the dark realm. This heavenly substance then gave rise to the world and to light; it brought about creation because it was living stuff. A number of different terms or images were applied to the divine substance. It was often called the Primordial Man, the First Man, the Anthropos (which is the Greek word for "man"). Sometimes it was called *nous,* or light. One common term for the heavenly stuff was Sophia, the Divine Wisdom. Jung summarizes this latter image, speaking of

> Sophia . . . who "sinks into the lower regions" . . . She was forcibly held captive by the lower powers . . . . She corresponds to the much later alchemical idea of the "soul in fetters" . . . . "The soul once turned towards matter, fell in love with it, and, burning with desire to experience bodily pleasures, was no longer willing to tear herself away from it. So was the world born." . . . In *Pistis Sophia* . . . she is the daughter of Barbelo. Deluded by the false light of the demon Authades, she falls into imprisonment in chaos. (par. 307, note 33)

A section from that passage in *Pistis Sophia* gives the feeling of this symbolic image which is so important psychologically:

> It came to pass . . . that she [Sophia] looked below and . . . thought to herself: I will . . . take the light [from that region] and fashion for myself light-aeons . . . This then thinking, she went forth from her own region [and went below]. . . . [And she] came into the regions of the chaos and drew nigh to that lion-faced light-power [which is also called the Self-willed; that is the translation of the term "Authades". All his emanations] surrounded her, and the great lion-faced . . . power devoured

. . . Sophia, and cleaned out her light and devoured it, and her matter was thrust into the chaos. . . . That is Yaldabaoth, of whom I have spoken unto you many times. When this befell, Sophia became very greatly exhausted, and that lion-faced . . . power set to work to take away from Sophia all her light-powers, and . . . surrounded Sophia . . . and pressed her sore. And Pistis Sophia cried out most exceedingly, she cried to the Light of lights above . . . and uttered this repentance saying thus: "Oh, Light of lights in whom I have had faith from the beginning, hearken now, O Light, unto my repentance. Save me, O Light, for evil thoughts have entered into me."[112]

Sophia has been caught. Her light has been taken over by the lion-faced self-willed power. It is a provocative image, an image of ego development. Any kind of fall from heaven that brings heavenly light stuff down into the lower world, corresponds to a fall into ego manifestation, which is what the expression "self-willed" points to. An example of this image occurred in a dream:

I descend to the basement of a whorehouse run by a brutal man. I discover a bruised and battered young woman who nevertheless had a glowing beauty. I kiss her and awaken her. I am overcome momentarily with a sense of compassion for her, for me, for the pathos of the human condition. The tough owner stands at the top of the staircase.[113]

This image encapsulates in a single synoptic form the basic task of the whole analytic process: to descend into the unconscious and to rescue or redeem the soul-image that is imprisoned there.

Jung next takes up the theme of the Naassenes and the serpent Naas, which was their image of the divine substance in all creatures, comparable to the Anthropos or to Sophia:

The Naassenes themselves considered Naas, the serpent, to be their central deity, and they explained it as the "moist substance," in agreement with Thales of Miletus, who said water was the prime substance on which all life depended. Similarly, all living things depend on the Naas; "it contains within itself, like the horn of the one-horned bull, the beauty of all things." It "pervades everything, like the water that flows out of Eden and divides into four sources *[archas]."* (par. 311)

In a fuller version of this text Hippolytus discusses the Naassenes who take that name because their deity is Naas, which means serpent:

They do not worship any other object but Naas . . . [and therefore they are called the Naassenes]. But Naas is the serpent from whom, i.e., from the word Naas, (the Naassene) says, are all that under heaven are denominated temples (Naous). . . . [The Naassene] states that to him alone—that is, Naas—is dedicated every shrine and every initiatory rite, and every mystery; and in general, that a religious cere-

---

112 G.R.S. Mead, trans., *Pistis Sophia,* pp. 36f.
113 See my book, *The Living Psyche: A Jungian Analysis in Pictures,* p. 91.

mony could not be discovered under heaven, in which a temple (Naos) has no existence; and in the temple itself is Naas, from whom it has received its denomination [its name] of temple (Naos). [The word for serpent is Naas, and the word for a temple is Naos. By an etymological trick typical of the writers of antiquity, they are stating here that the word for temple is derived from the word for serpent.] . . . And these [Gnostics] affirm that the serpent is a moist substance, just as Thales . . . the Milesian (spoke of water as an originating principle), and that nothing of existing things, immortal or mortal, animate or inanimate, could consist at all without him. And that all things are subject unto him, and that he is good, and that he has all things in himself, as in the horn of the one-horned bull . . . [or, according to the Authorized Version of the Bible, the horn of the unicorn] so as that he imparts beauty and bloom to all things that exist according to their own nature and peculiarity, as if passing through all, just as ("the river) proceeding forth from Edem, and dividing itself into four heads."[114]

Then follows, in *The Ante-Nicene Fathers,* the Paradise Quaternio text concerning the Garden of Eden and the four rivers that flowed out of it. The Gnostics equate the serpent Naas with the water of the Garden of Eden rivers and with the original water that is at the root of all things according to Thales the philosopher, and with the temple, Naos. This serpent is a continuation of the serpent discussed previously as the serpent that comes down from heaven carrying the signs of the father. This serpent is the living water that permeates and originates all things. It is the numinous presence that inhabits every temple.

Here is an idea, remarkable for 2,000 years ago, that there is an entity prior to all the separate religious denominations, the separate temples set up for different deities. There is a primordial stuff that is the essence of divinity which inhabits all of those temples regardless of the particular deity that the temple is consecrated to. In other words, this is a truly psychological generalization, a symbolic announcement of the numinosum that lies behind all religious phenomena. This conception is a significant accomplishment, and it helps to explain why Gnosticism was so interesting to Jung and is so relevant to depth psychology.

In paragraph 313, a long tightly-packed paragraph, Jung condenses a lengthy Gnostic description of the original man or Anthropos, which equates him with Adam and with the images of the original man as he shows up in various mythological traditions, and finally leads to the image of the ithyphallic Hermes. Paragraph 313 is interrupted for a digression and then returns to complete its material in paragraphs 325-327. These paragraphs are hard to grasp because they are so condensed. Jung performs a valuable service for us by skimming off the psychological cream of a whole body of material. If read slowly and repeatedly, the message will come through. Parts of paragraph 313 illustrate that this material is perfectly clear if one reads carefully enough:

---

114 Roberts and Donaldson, *The Ante-Nicene Fathers,* vol. 5, p. 57.

For the Naassenes, the universal "Ground" is the Original Man, Adam, and knowledge of him is regarded as the beginning of perfection and the bridge to knowledge of God.

This is clear and corresponds to what we experience when dreams bring up images of the Anthropos, the original man. They do indeed provide a bridge to the knowledge of the transpersonal. They do make a connection to wholeness. Jung goes on:

He [the original man] is male/female [i.e., double, a union of opposites]; from him come "father and mother"; he consists of three parts: the rational *[noeron]* the psychic, and the earthly *[choikon]*. These three "came down together into one man, Jesus."

I think that what lies behind this—the symbolism of the descent of the three-fold entity—is the fact that when the contents of the unconscious come into ego realization, they enter the realm of threeness. The symbolism of threeness belongs to the spatio-temporal world of ego existence; space and time are ego categories. Although it is true that triads are incomplete quaternities, it is also true that when manifestations of original wholeness fall into egohood, into space and time, they take on triadic characteristics, and we see that symbolism of the three here. Jung goes on:

For the Naassenes, says Hippolytus, place the "procreative nature of the Whole in the procreative seed." . . . "This, for them, is the hidden and mystical Logos" . . . likened to the phallus of Osiris. [That was the one part of dismembered Osiris that was never found again.] . . . A further synonym is the ithyphallic Hermes Kyllenios. "For they say Hermes is the Logos."

Hermes Kyllenios refers to an ithyphallic statue of Hermes—Hermes with an erect penis—that existed in the Temple of Hermes on Mount Kyllene. That was the highest mountain in the Peloponnesus, and it was sacred to this god. The Gnostics equated this Hermes with the Logos. The sexual symbolism leads Jung into a digression to another text to which we will return. If one disregards the digression, the account is completed starting in paragraph 325 where Jung picks up the symbolism of Hermes again and talks about some of his attributes: conjurer of spirits, guide of souls, equipped with the golden wand. The phallic imagery of the Hermes statue leads Jung to another text involving sexual imagery, which I call the Christ Coniunctio text. The reference to this text is found in paragraph 314 where Jung writes:

It is related there that Christ took this Mary [not the Virgin Mary] with him on to a mountain, where he produced a woman from his side and began to have intercourse with her. . . . It says that Mary received such a shock that she fell to the ground. Christ then said to her: "Wherefore do you doubt me, O you of little faith?" This was meant as a reference to John 3:12: "If I have told you earthly things and you do not believe, how can you believe if I tell you heavenly things?"

Jung then comments on this text:

This symbolism may well have been based, originally, on some visionary experience, such as happens not uncommonly today during psychological treatment. For the medical psychologist there is nothing very lurid about it. The context itself points the way to the right interpretation. The image expresses a psychologem that can hardly be formulated in rational terms and has, therefore, to make use of a concrete symbol, just as a dream must when a more or less "abstract" thought comes up during the *abaissement du niveau mental* that occurs in sleep. These "shocking" surprises, of which there is certainly no lack in dreams, should always be taken "as-if," even though they clothe themselves in sensual imagery that stops at no scurrility and no obscenity. They are unconcerned with offensiveness because they do not really mean it. It is as if they were stammering in their efforts to express the elusive meaning that grips the dreamer's attention. (par. 315)

This brings up the whole question of how one should understand overtly sexual imagery as it shows up in dreams. I think that in the great majority of cases such dream images have nothing at all to do with concrete sexuality. Rather, they concern *coniunctio* or union symbolism. It is as though the unconscious which generates dreams is rooted in biological nature and therefore expresses ideation in terms of natural images. For example, this dream from a middle-aged woman with emerging creative powers as a poet and scholar:

There is a party at my mother's apartment. A strange and disturbing man, Mr. X, a poet, is the guest of honor. [After several episodes the mother leaves the party.] When she does, there is a kind of universal, spontaneous rejoicing which I also feel, though I don't know what's up. I find out soon enough, though. For almost at once X gathers all the women around him in a semicircle, whereupon he undresses and ejaculates a huge stream of sperm which falls like a fountain on each of us. I'd thought the idea was for us to serve him in this way, but as it turns out that's only part of it. Because as the sperm shower hits us severally, we each experience our own separate and individual orgasms.[115]

Now you can't get more sexual than that, as far as imagery is concerned, but what is referred to is her baptism in her own creative powers emerging from the unconscious. Here is another example from the same patient, in the same general period of time:

I see a young man, naked, glistening with sweat, who catches my attention first by his physical attitude—a combination of the falling motion of a Pietà figure and the energetic release position of the famous Greek Discobolus. . . . He stands out . . . by the fact that he has an enormous phallus in the form of a third, extended leg. The man is in agony with the burden of his erection.[116]

---

115 See my *Anatomy of the Psyche,* p. 63.
116 See my *Ego and Archetype,* p. 70.

She then has intercourse with him and undergoes a reversal of orientation, a kind of revolution. This is an example of the threefoldness of a content of the unconscious entering consciousness: a three-legged man, the third leg being at the same time a great phallus. The point of the dream is not concrete sexuality; sexual imagery is used to refer to something else—the connection to the creative unconscious.

Returning to the idea of God being born in the human soul, touched on earlier in connection with Meister Eckhart, Jung refers to Angelus Silesius:

> Meister Eckhart, using a different formulation, says that "God is born from the soul," and when we come to the *Cherubinic Wanderer* of Angelus Silesius, God and the self coincide absolutely. The times have undergone a profound change: the procreative power no longer proceeds from God, rather is God born from the soul. (par. 321)

Jung refers to Angelus Silesius in several different places. Angelus Silesius was in fact a pen name; his real name was Johannes Scheffler. He was a Polish mystic who lived from 1624 to 1677. He repeats Eckhart's ideas precisely and more extremely. For example:

> God is my centre when I close him in;
> And my circumference when I melt in him.[117]

> I know that without me
> God can no moment live;
> Were I to die, then He
> No longer could survive. . . .

> In me is God a fire
> And I in Him its glow;
> In common is our life,
> Apart we cannot grow.[118]

Jung adds,

> It would be absurd to suppose that such audacious ideas as these and Meister Eckhart's are nothing but figments of conscious speculation. Such thoughts are always profoundly significant historical phenomena, borne along on the unconscious currents of the collective psyche.[119]

These two, Silesius and Eckhart, are forerunners of depth psychology.

Jung also refers in *Aion* to another idea which presaged later psychic developments—Johannes Kepler's idea of the God-image falling into nature. Jung refers to this as

---

117 *Mysterium Coniunctionis,* CW 14, par. 132, note 71.
118 *Psychological Types,* CW 6, par. 432.
119 Ibid., par. 433.

a still crude observation of Nature that was just beginning to assimilate the archetype of man. This attempt continued right up to the seventeenth century, when Johannes Kepler recognized the Trinity as underlying the structure of the universe—in other words, when he assimilated this archetype into the astronomer's picture of the world. (par. 323)

This idea can also be found in a book written jointly by Jung and Wolfgang Pauli, where Pauli quotes Kepler as writing:

> The image of the triune God is in the spherical surface, that is to say, the Father's in the center, the Son's in the outer surface, and the Holy Ghost's in the equality of relation between point and circumference . . . .
>
> [A] straight line [formed by] the movement of a point located in the center [of the sphere] to a single point on the surface, represents the first beginnings of creation, emulating the eternal generation of the Son.[120]

Kepler is thinking about the circular orbit of the planets around the sun. He has the idea that the astronomical image is a representation of the Trinity; the central sun is the Father; the planet is the Son; and the centripetal bond that holds them together is the Holy Ghost. This conception corresponds to what Jung speaks of elsewhere as the projection of the numinosum into matter, which is the basis of modern science. The God-image is now lodged in nature; Kepler's ideas were early expressions of that. Physics, chemistry, biology—the energy that is generated to investigate those sciences—derives from the projection of the God-image into nature; this is the source of the fascination. Jung quotes William James as saying: "Our esteem for facts has not neutralized in us all religiousness. It is itself almost religious. Our scientific temper is devout."[121]

With real scientists, the ones who make the advances, the pursuit of scientific knowledge is a religious enterprise. That is what is so important about science for the modern psyche. The missing God-image that has fallen out of religion, has fallen into nature and into the scientific observation of nature. This is one reason why Jung insists on being absolutely true to the scientific tradition: to the extent that the God-image is still functioning in an authentic way, it is in the temper of modern science.

---

[120] *The Interpretation of Nature and the Psyche,* pp. 159f.
[121] *Pragmatism,* pp. 14f.

Gnostic Symbols of the Self (cont.)

In this chapter, presenting a dense stream of Gnostic imagery, Jung begins his discussion of what he calls the cosmic triad and the Moses Quaternio. This image receives a great deal of attention later in the book. The initial reference is found in paragraph 328, where Jung, in his condensed, synoptic style, describes Hippolytus as saying:

> The Naassenes . . . derived all things from a triad, which consists firstly of the "blessed nature of the blessed Man on high, Adamas," secondly of the mortal nature of the lower man, and thirdly of the "kingless race begotten from above," to which belong "Mariam . . . Jothor . . . Sephora . . . and Moses. . . ." Together these four form a marriage *quaternio.*

This is concentrated text. The cosmic triad consists of three levels. The higher Adam is one level. The fourfold grouping of Mariam, Jothor, Sephora and Moses is a second level. The lower Adam is the third. We have here the common phenomenon of triadic symbolism merging with quaternity symbolism. There is a threefold sequence of the unfolding levels, but what is constructed, at least on the middle level, is a quaternity. Here, as in the other Hippolytus texts, the Gnostics assimilate the imagery of the Hebrew-Christian scriptures and the Greek myths into their own elaborate cosmic fantasy. In this case, the Gnostics take the basic characters from the Book of Exodus and turn them into a Gnostic image.

The four Biblical characters are Mariam, Jothor, Sephora and Moses. Moses, of course, is the man who led the Israelites out of slavery, and his name calls up associations of release from bondage, crossing the Red Sea and reaching the Promised Land. The Gnostics used this imagery a great deal. Jethro (Jothor) was Moses' father-in-law, and also a Midianite priest. Moses had to flee after he murdered the Egyptian slave driver. He escaped into the wilderness where he tended the flocks of Jethro and married Jethro's daughter, Sephora. Jethro suggests wisdom belonging to an alien, non-Israelite culture. Mariam is Moses' sister, and in one text she is referred to as a prophetess. Sephora, Moses' wife, is called in one text the "Ethiopian woman"; she is associated with blackness. This is the Moses Quaternio which will reappear later in the text. Jung proceeds from this quaternio to speak of the triad—the three levels:

> The triad is characterized by various names that may be onomatopoetic: Kaulakau, Saulasau, Zeesar. Kaulakau means the higher Adam, Saulasau the lower, mortal man, and Zeesar is named the "upwards-flowing Jordan." The Jordan was caused

by Jesus to flow up-stream;[122] it is the rising flood and hence, as already mentioned, is the begetter of gods. "This, they say, is the human hermaphrodite in all creatures, whom the ignorant call 'Geryon of the threefold body' [that is, . . . 'flowing from the earth']." (par. 330)

There is a pun here, a play on the Greek words. Geryon was a monster having three bodies, and he was conquered by Heracles in his tenth labor. Heracles had stolen Geryon's cattle and so had to conquer this three-bodied monster. According to the play on words, the term Geryon derives from "Ge-rian" which means "earth flowing." There is further word play, making an analogy between the word Geryon and the word Jordan. Twist Jordan a little, and you get the word "Jo-rian," something else flowing; so Gerian and Jorian are a play on those two kinds of river. The Gnostic texts are full of that kind of fluid, "phony" etymology; what makes it so interesting for us is that now we witness the unconscious behaving the same way in dreams. It likes that kind of playful stuff. It is a shameless punster.

This upward-flowing Jordan is also linked with the cosmogonic Logos, and a quote from the first chapter of John is mentioned, in which Christ is described as the "life that was in him." So that scripture is linked with this particular Gnostic image. One can begin to see the rich network of associations that go to make up these Gnostic texts. And since the Gnostics were functioning just exactly as the unconscious can be seen doing today, Jung speaks of them as, really, the original psychologists. They took the imagery of scripture and myth empirically, not dogmatically, and used it to exemplify their own themes, which are basically psychological themes.

The text proceeds with a number of different images, all of which cluster around the same primordial idea, the idea of the original man, the original creative stuff, the initial totality. Jung summarizes Hippolytus's remarks on this theme in paragraph 331, referring to a particular one of these images, the omen cup: "This Logos or quaternity is 'the cup from which the king, drinking, draws his omens.' "

This is a reference to Genesis 44, in which Joseph's brothers are sent home after their visit to him, and following Joseph's orders the king's cup is deposited in the young brother Benjamin's seed sack. He is set up by Joseph. When the brothers are gone but not far off, Joseph tells his men to follow and search them. Then Joseph asks the brothers why they have stolen his cup. The servants remark that this cup is used by the king to cast his omens. What the Gnostics are saying is that the Logos quaternity corresponds to the cup found in Benjamin's

---

[122] The middle level, the quaternity, has the name "kingless race" and also "upwards-flowing Jordan." The "kingless race" can be understood as referring to individuals who are their own authority, and therefore have no king over them. If you belong to a kingless race, you are your own king.

bag of wheat. It is also the beaker of Anacreon. The Gnostics shift with absolute ease from the Hebrew Bible to Greek sources. The beaker of Anacreon refers to some verses by Anacreon, a Greek poet. His words are: "My tankard tells me / The sort I must become."[123] In other words, the poet knows who he is, what his essential identity or nature is, by his cup. *In vino veritas* is the underlying idea; the cup of Anacreon tells you who you are.

The image of the omen cup then leads Hippolytus on to the wine miracle at Cana which he says, " 'showed forth the kingdom of heaven'; for the kingdom of heaven lies within us, like the wine in the cup." (par. 331) The scripture telling of the wine miracle at Cana, in which Christ turned water into wine for the wedding party (John 2), has now been taken over by this Gnostic text.

The Gnostic text is like a gobbling mouth, digesting all these images that it finds relevant and creating a network of associations. If you look at them closely enough, the moment comes when they begin to speak to you. For a while they just seem like dull, disconnected pieces. But if you put your attention into this network, it comes alive, and you realize that you are looking at the fabric of the living psyche; that is why Jung puts out this material. It is very hard to have that experience from reading *Aion* unless you pour your attention into it in detail. If you do, if you follow up these associations with care and look them up one by one, the moment will come when you will have a unique experience. You will see the living psyche in its shimmering reality.

The references continue. They do not stop with the wine miracle at Cana. In paragraph 331, Jung brings up Christ's references to the Self, in which he says to his disciples: "Can you drink of the cup that I must drink . . . ?" (Mark 10:38, JB) This cup is the cup of Christ's Crucifixion. Then Jung refers to John 6:53: "If you do not eat the flesh of the Son of Man, and drink his blood, you will not have life in you." (JB)

Jung points out that the Gnostic text says Christ "was conscious of the *individual nature* of each of his disciples, and also of the need for each 'to come to his own special nature.' " (par. 331) The idea here is that each person drinks the blood of Christ, but each is nourished by that blood in his own unique way; it nourishes the individual nature. In a passage in Hippolytus that Jung does not quote, the Gnostic explains that what he means is that from one and the same river that waters a certain area, the olive tree draws oil, the grape vine draws wine, and other plants draw what suits them—each according to its own genus.[124] So also is it with individuals: each partakes of the same cup, deriving from it what is uniquely relevant to themselves.

Jung continues in paragraph 332 with the theme of the God who dwells in the

---

123 Quoted in Roberts and Donaldson, *The Ante-Nicene Fathers,* vol. 5, p. 53.
124 Ibid., p. 57.

flood, another image, like the omen cup, for the original totality. He speaks of "Corybas, who was descended from the crown of the head . . . and permeates all things. . . . He is the God who *dwells in the flood.*" Jung need not describe this symbol here as he has already discussed it at some length in "Paracelsus as a Spiritual Phenomenon," where he comments:

> That is the god who dwells in the great flood. In the Psalter he calls and cries out from many waters. [This is a reference to Psalm 29 which says, "The voice of Yahweh over the waters! . . . Yahweh sat enthroned for the flood." So the image of the God dwelling in the flood is extracted from that particular passage in Psalms.] The many waters, they say, are the multitude of mortal men, whence he calls and cries aloud to the uncharacterized Man [the unformed, invisible man]: "Save mine Only-Begotten from the lions."[125]

This last is a reference to Psalms 21:22. There, the idea is that the God who is crying from the waters—the text says the waters are the generations of men—would be the collective image of the Anthropos that is drowning in the collectivity of mass man and that is calling for rescue. In reply to him, the Biblical text declares: "Thou art mine. When thou shalt pass through the waters, I will be with thee, and the rivers shall not cover thee." (Isa. 43:1-2) (At some variance from the Biblical texts, what Hippolytus means by rivers is the moist substance of generation.) All of this illustrates how the various significant scriptural passages are plucked out of their original context and deposited in a new context in the whole Gnostic scheme.

The images of the God who dwells in the flood and the voice calling from the waters have an important alchemical parallel. It is the image of the king drowning in the sea and calling out, asking to be rescued. One of the pictures in Michael Maier's *Atalanta Fugiens* shows the king drowning in the sea, and a passage reads:

> [The king] calls from the depths: Who shall deliver me from the waters and lead me to dry land? Even though this cry be heard of many, yet none takes it upon himself, moved by pity, to seek the king. For who, they say, will plunge into the waters? Who will imperil his life by taking away the peril of another? Only a few believe his lament, and think rather that they hear the crashing and roaring of Scylla and Charybdis. Therefore they remain sitting indolently at home, and give no thought to the kingly treasure, nor to their own salvation.[126]

So here is an image, the God in the sea, that began in one context in the Biblical scriptures, was plucked out of that and used in another context by the Gnostics, and then was picked up by the alchemists and used in still a third setting. And now Jungian psychology takes the image and uses it in still a fourth context

---

[125] *Alchemical Studies,* CW 13, par. 182.
[126] Quoted by Jung in ibid., par. 181.

as referring to the transpersonal Self that resides in the unconscious and needs to be rescued by the ego, which must descend into the flood to redeem it. We can understand it now as the unconscious, abandoned God-image calling for conscious realization.

Still another network of Gnostic material centers on the image of the door or gate, another expression of the original totality. This reference is found in paragraph 333:

> From the center of the "perfect man" flows the ocean (where, as we have said, the god dwells). The "perfect" man is, as Jesus says, the "true door," through which the "perfect" man must go in order to be reborn.

This is picking up a passage from Matthew 7:14f.: "It is a narrow gate and a hard road that leads to life, and only a few find it." (JB) Also related is Christ's statement in John 10:9: "I am the gate . . . ; Anyone who enters through me will be safe: he will go freely in and out and will be sure of finding pasture." (JB)

This gate and door imagery is continued in paragraph 336 of *Aion,* where the reference is to Jacob's dream at Bethel. Jacob dreamed of a heavenly ladder and angels descending and ascending. When he awoke from this dream he said: "How awe-inspiring this place is! This is nothing less than a house of God; this is the gate of heaven!" (Gen. 28:12-18, JB) The Gnostics link this particular image, the gate of heaven that Jacob dreamt of, with Christ's remarks about being the gate. The Gnostics are doing exactly the same thing the Jungian psychologist does. The image is the living entity, and they do not mind tearing it out of its context at all, because what they relate to is the living image itself.

There are many dreams of gates or doors, especially ones that open into strange and new regions. Once aware of these particular images as psychic organisms, one will recognize them and will be able to use this material to amplify them—if nowhere else, in one's own mind. (It is not advisable to dump too much amplification material on people; they can be drowned in it.) But it is very important, when listening to a dream, that these images are resonating in one's own mind. They will affect one's attitude toward the dream, and that larger, ampler attitude communicates itself through the unconscious to the patient.

Jung continues this string of images of the original totality with Hippolytus's text about the Mumia of Paracelsus:

> Hippolytus goes on to say that he is called Papa (Attis) by the Phrygians. . . . This "Papa" is also called *[nekus]* (cadaver), because he is buried in the body like a mummy in a tomb. A similar idea is found in Paracelsus . . . : "Life, verily, is naught but a kind of embalmed mummy, which preserves the mortal body from the mortal worms." The body lives only from the "Mumia," through which the . . . wandering microcosm . . . rules the physical body. [Jung gives various synonyms for this "Mumia," which is also] "the door whence all creatures are created." . . . The Mumia is born together with the body and sustains it . . . .

The Paracelsian Mumia . . . corresponds in every way to the Original Man, who forms the microcosm in the mortal man." (pars. 334f.)

This is a strange and interesting idea, that there is a second body lodged inside our visible body, like a cadaver buried in a tomb. This second body is of a nature different than the visible one; it is like a preserved mummy—it is immortal, an immortal precursor of our mortal temporal existence. The image is similar to the idea of the skeleton in relation to the flesh. Flesh disintegrates very quickly after death, yet the skeleton lasts indefinitely. Paracelsus's idea of the Mumia, and the Gnostic idea of the cadaver buried in the body are similar; both refer to that immortal inner entity that exists, prior to and subsequent to our temporal existence. It is eternal; it is outside of time.

Now Jung turns from the Bible to Greek mythology, with a reference in paragraph 338 to the *Odyssey* tale in which Menelaus, trying to return from Troy, does not know how to get home. He is told that he must catch Proteus, the sea god, who comes up out of the sea with a herd of seals at noon. Menelaus has to hide under a smelly seal skin (Homer makes a good deal out of how it stinks, how disagreeable it is). When Proteus comes up with his herd of seals, Menelaus rushes out and grabs him. Proteus is capable of changing into all kinds of shapes, but Menelaus holds onto him in whatever shape he changes into, until finally Proteus says, "Okay, what do you want of me?" Menelaus says, "I want to know how to get back home to Greece," and Proteus tells him.

This is a wonderful image for psychological purposes, as it expresses very aptly the way one sometimes has to deal with the unconscious. Needing something from the unconscious, one has to hold onto it. A certain kind of active imagination pours such diligent attention into the unconscious that it finally comes through with what one needs to know.

The next image of original totality, in paragraph 340, is that of the point.[127] This Monoïmos quotation, in which the monad is described as the point, evokes the image of the Self as the point, the invisible origin and center of everything. Greek geometry begins with the description of the point: it is nothing but position. It does not have any magnitude. When it moves, it generates a line. And when a line moves, it generates a plane. And when a plane moves, it generates a solid. Then when the solid moves, one has space and time.

And so all our conscious existence, everything we can perceive in spatio-temporal reality, starts out as a point. Euclid's geometry can be thought of as a vast geometrical cosmogony, and it was that symbolic quality that made it so gripping for the ancients, as a study that revealed the nature of the world. And these geometrical images still come up in dreams today.

---

[127] See also above, p. 129, and *Mysterium Coniunctionis,* CW 14, pars. 40ff.

22

Paragraphs 347-365

The Structure and Dynamics of the Self

Recall the subtitle of *Aion:* "Researches into the Phenomenology of the Self"—very scientific. Jung's strict empirical method is demonstrated in this work. The last few chapters of *Aion* are difficult to understand, and one might be tempted to ask if there is not an easier way than Jung's to present the material. But there is a very good reason for his approach. Jung is strictly empirical here, and he presents an objective study of certain imagery of the psyche—specifically, of the archetypal psyche and the archetype of the Self.

In order to investigate the depth psyche, which is what he is doing here, he has to deal with its manifestations much as an archaeologist deals with the buried remains of a lost civilization. He has to dig them out, and then order, classify and present the artifacts, the data gathered by his excavation. This can be done in two places when one is studying the psyche. One can dig in the individual psyche, in which case one examines dreams, fantasies, unconscious symptoms, the phenomena that develop in the course of a depth analysis. This is individual archaeology, so to speak.

The other place one can dig into is the collective psyche, in which case the archaeological data are found in religions, myths and fairy tales, which correspond to collective dreams and fantasies. In Jung's study of alchemy and Gnosticism, he is doing the latter, excavating the collective psyche, digging below its surface phenomena. It is hard work, but it is the only way to explore the psyche if one is going to do it with strict objectivity and not just impose theoretical preconceptions upon it. Imposing a meaning on the data in advance, which makes it understandable and easy to read, is not an empirical procedure. To be properly empirical, one examines the raw data first and then draws conclusions, not the other way around.

The Gnostics are particularly interesting as a source of psychological artifacts because their material illustrates the amplifying process of the unconscious. They take two great roots of the Western psyche, Greek mythology and the Hebrew-Christian scriptures, and assimilate these sources to their own doctrine. Jung makes an important statement on this matter in his essay "The Philosophical Tree." He is writing about the importance of comparative research into symbols, which is just what *Aion* is. This is his methodological statement:

> In consequence of the collective nature of the image it is often impossible to establish its full range of meaning from the associative material of a single individual.

. . . [Thus] the necessity of comparative research into symbols . . . becomes evident
. . . . For this purpose the investigator must turn back to those periods in human history when symbol formation still went on unimpeded, that is, when there was still
no epistemological criticism of the formation of images, and when, in consequence, facts that in themselves were unknown could be expressed in definite visual form. The period of this kind closest to us is that of medieval natural philosophy, which reached its zenith . . . in alchemy and Hermetic philosophy.[128]

One could add that a more remote example of this same kind of material is
found in the fantasy systems of the Gnostics. The crucial piece of Jung's statement is "when there was still no epistemological criticism of the formation of
images." This means a time of a naive attitude which did not distinguish clearly
between subject and object, or between fantasy and outer reality. As soon as
there is some epistemological sophistication, the ability to criticize the process
of "knowing," then one no longer naively projects inner fantasy imagery into the
outer world, for there is some inkling that to do so reveals something of oneself.
There is a shyness, a self-criticism of such behavior. Of course, there are plenty
of people still around who have very little epistemological criticism, but Jung is
talking about the cultural development of the race. The race first began to learn
epistemological criticism around the sixteenth century. The philosophers who
brought it to the fore were Locke, Berkeley and Hume.

Jung returns here to the work of Monoïmos, last heard from in the preceding
chapter in reference to the dot as an image of the original totality. Monoïmos
was a second-century Gnostic whose life is completely unknown except that he
was named "the Arab." The passage from Monoïmos that Jung quotes, which is
repeated from Hippolytus, is quite remarkable psychologically coming from the
second century:

> Seek him from out thyself, and learn who it is that taketh possession of everything
> in thee, saying: *my* god, *my* spirit, *my* understanding, *my* soul, *my* body; and learn
> whence is sorrow and joy, and love and hate, and waking though one would not,
> and sleeping though one would not, and getting angry though one would not, and
> falling in love though one would not. And if thou shouldst closely investigate these
> things, thou wilt find Him in thyself, the One and the Many, like to that little point
> *[kereia]*, for it is in thee that he hath his origin and his deliverance. (par. 347)

A modern psychologist could not put it more succinctly. This tells us that we
should make a discrimination between our own will and the unconscious. The
ability to make that distinction is the crucial discovery in the process of an encounter with the Self. We first have to realize that we are not one, but two; there
is an Other inside. As this dawns on us, we discover at the same time that much
of what we do in our daily life is not our choice at all. We discover ourselves

---

[128] *Alchemical Studies*, CW 13, par. 353.

doing things that we had not intended, not to mention overt slips and accidents and other very crude challenges to our inclination. As we become more and more aware of this twoness, we realize the reality of the Self. This is what Monoïmos states.

Jung sees a parallel in this text to the ideas in the Upanishads, the ancient Hindu scriptures. The word "upanishad" literally means "sitting near, devotedly," which suggests that by sitting near, one receives secret instruction from a teacher and thus divine knowledge is communicated. The Upanishads were written in Sanskrit, and were unavailable to those not knowing that language until approximately 1650 A.D., when they were translated into Persian. They did not reach Western Europe until 1801, when the Persian translation was further translated into Latin.

The influence of the Upanishads was soon apparent. The most notable person to be influenced by the work was Schopenhauer, whose whole philosophy is a kind of Westernized, one-sided elaboration of the Upanishads. Another such person was Ralph Waldo Emerson. Nietzsche was much affected by them, and so was Jung, both directly and through Schopenhauer and Nietzsche. He took the term "Self" from the Upanishads. Jung quotes from them in paragraphs 348 and 349. A slightly expanded form of these same quotations makes them more vivid and gives them more impact:

> At whose behest does the mind think? Who bids the body live? Who makes the tongue speak? Who is that effulgent Being that directs the eye to form and color and the ear to sound?
>
> The Self is ear of the ear, mind of the mind, speech of the speech. He is also breath of the breath, and eye of the eye. . . . Him the eye does not see, nor the tongue express, nor the mind grasp. Him we neither know nor are able to teach. Different is he from the known, and different is he from the unknown. . . . That which is not comprehended by the mind but by which the mind comprehends—know that to be Brahman . . . .
>
> That which is not seen by the eye but by which the eye sees—know that to be Brahman. . . . That which is not heard by the ear, but by which the ear hears—know that to be Brahman.[129]
>
> He who dwells in all beings but is separate from all beings, whom no being knows, whose body all beings are, and who controls all beings from within—he, the Self, is the Inner Ruler, the Immortal.[130]

These words were written no later than 500 B.C. They show how the East, notably India, is far beyond the West in psychological sophistication.

Jung continues on in his many-branched description of the Self and its relationship to consciousness, saying:

---

129 *Kena Upanishad,* trans. Swami Prabhavananda and F. Manchester.
130 *Brihadakanyaka Upanishad,* trans. Swami Prabhavananda and F. Manchester.

The self is a true "complexio oppositorum," though this does not mean that it is anything like as contradictory in itself. It is quite possible that the seeming paradox is nothing but a reflection of the enantiodromian changes of the conscious attitude which can have a favorable or an unfavorable effect on the whole. The same is true of the unconscious in general, for its frightening figures may be called forth by the fear which the conscious mind has of the unconscious. The importance of consciousness should not be underrated; hence it is advisable to relate the contradictory manifestations of the unconscious causally to the conscious attitude, at least in some degree. (par. 355)

Jung refers here to something I want to emphasize by baptizing it with a fancy name, the Reciprocality Principle. The word "reciprocal" is used here as it is used in mathematics. In mathematics, we know that every number is reciprocal. The reciprocal of 2/3 is 3/2. The reciprocal of 5 is 1/5. To find the reciprocal, one has to turn a whole number into a fraction or into a fractional notation at least; in other words, into a double term. Reciprocality can exist only when two terms exist. When one multiplies two reciprocals, the product is always one. I think that is psychologically significant.

The psychological Reciprocality Principle is that the unconscious responds inversely to the conscious ego. The ego's relation to any particular psychological quality or content can be expressed in a fractional term, and then according to the Reciprocality Principle, the unconscious manifestation of that quality will be a reciprocal of the conscious manifestation. For example, let us say we are dealing with the quality of aggressiveness on a scale of ten. At zero, one would be a total victim, a total quivering, knee-shaking, fleeing victim. At the other end of the scale one would be a total aggressor—chasing, attacking. Now let us say that our particular ego is very much in the victim realm, with an aggressiveness fraction of only 2/10. By the Reciprocality Principle then, the unconscious will have an aggressiveness fraction of 10/2.

In other words, if the ego is very much identified with being the victim, the unconscious will have the aggressor constellated in it and will start chasing the ego. The ego, of course, will be running. We all know from observing animals that if one animal runs, a cat for example, a dog will chase it. If the cat stops running and turns around, the dog suddenly stops and the dog might start running. This illustrates how the unconscious can work. The principle holds true not only within the individual, but in the individual's relationship with the environment. If a speaker behaves like a weak, fearful victim at the lectern, it will not be long before the whole audience will be after him.

This is the way the unconscious works and this is the way the transference and countertransference work. So with a patient who is very much identified with the victim role, no matter how mild-mannered and gentle the analyst may think he or she is, the alert analyst will catch him- or herself bullying the patient because that is what is constellated. This principle works with all sorts of other qualities too. Typically, a patient comes to see an analyst because the patient is feeling sick, weak or wounded, and this constellates in the analyst the contrasting powers of health, power and healing. As long as those qualities are carried by the analyst, they won't help the patient at all. The task is to reverse those reciprocal fractions, to know how to hand back to the patient what has been constellated in the analyst. This is not so easy to do, but it is useful to know what is going on at least, and I think the Reciprocality Principle is helpful there. I use this term rather than calling it "reciprocity," which ordinarily carries a connotation of mutuality.

Another aspect of the relationship between conscious and unconscious is referred to by Jung in paragraph 355:

> Between the conscious and the unconscious there is a kind of "uncertainty relationship," because the observer is inseparable from the observed and always disturbs it by the act of observation. In other words, exact observation of the unconscious prejudices observation of the conscious and vice versa.

Jung's term, "uncertainty relationship," refers to the Uncertainty Principle of nuclear physics that was first formulated by Werner Heisenberg. This principle states that the position and velocity of a subatomic object cannot both be precisely measured at the same time, even in theory. Any attempt to measure precisely the velocity of a subatomic particle, such as an electron, knocks it about in an unpredictable way; likewise, observing it upsets its position. If its position is measured, then its velocity is altered. The very act of observation of subatomic particles alters their condition so that exact, objective readings are impossible. More generally, the principle indicates that an observer is drawn into the data being observed and influences it in an unavoidable way.

Precisely the same state of affairs occurs in observation of the unconscious: the unconscious is altered by the process of observation. This means that there is no such thing as an absolutely objective piece of psychological data from the unconscious because, in order to have observed it, the observer has seen it, touched it and brought it back. In the process of doing all this, one has put one's fingerprints on it. The reverse is also true. Both the observer and the observed influence each other. Not only does the ego influence the unconscious when it observes it, but also the unconscious, the Self, modifies the ego that is observing it. There is an eye-of-God aspect to the Self which observes the ego, just as the ego, when it reaches a certain level, can observe and affect the Self.[131] Jung refers to this in his remark about the "uncertainty relationship."

Jung now returns to the Gnostic symbols of the Self, and specifically to the Moses Quaternio (initially considered here in the previous chapter). He reaches

---

131 See my *Mysterium Lectures,* pp. 65ff.

the conclusion that just as there is an upper and a lower Adam in the triad that created the Moses Quaternio, so there must be an upper and a lower quaternio of the four figures in the Moses family. Figures 21 and 22 repeat Jung's diagram of this situation. Jung builds further on this structure as *Aion* proceeds. To recapitulate the Moses or Anthropos Quaternio: first there is the higher Adam, an anthropos figure that splits into four. Those four figures then synthesize or unite in a lower Adam. The four figures of the quaternio are Moses, Jethro, Miriam and Zipporah (Sephora).

Moses kills the slave driver and flees to Midian. He then meets Jethro, his future father-in-law, and marries his daughter Zipporah. The fourth figure is Miriam, Moses' sister. She had saved him in his infancy by hiding him in a basket in the bulrushes to be found by the Pharaoh's daughter. In one scripture, Miriam is called a prophetess, a seer, so that aspect of her characterizes the higher Miriam. But in another passage, she spoke against Moses and was angry with him for marrying Zipporah; she incurred Yahweh's wrath and he turned her white as a leper until he relented.

The angry, vengeful Miriam is the lower Miriam, placed in the Shadow Quaternio shown in figure 22. Zipporah, daughter of Jethro, is called in one text the black Ethiopian. In that shadow quality, she is the negative Zipporah and relegated to the Shadow Quaternio. In other scriptures she is the wise Zipporah and so occupies the Anthropos Quaternio. The same doubleness applies to Jethro, the priest of Midian who therefore has the wisdom that accompanies priestly knowledge, but on the other hand was outside the traditional Israelite realm, the "pagan outsider." In this aspect, he is the lower Jethro. The same thing applies to the two aspects of Moses, the higher Moses and the lower or carnal Moses.

What can be understood so far about the Moses or Anthropos Quaternio is that what is called the lower Adam in the figure is us, the ego, the ordinary empirical ego. The ego occupies a mid position and if it looks in one direction it encounters a light, bright, spiritual quaternity. If it looks in the opposite direction, it encounters a dark, shadowy, dubious quaternity in which, looking all the way through it, the serpent can be seen at the bottom. We are not through with this quaternio yet. It will get more complex.

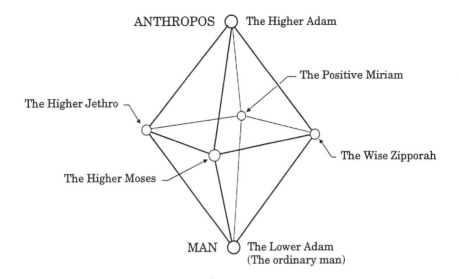

ANTHROPOS ◯ The Higher Adam

— The Positive Miriam

The Higher Jethro

The Wise Zipporah

The Higher Moses

MAN ◯ The Lower Adam
(The ordinary man)

Figure 21. Anthropos Quaternio.
The upper figure represents one of the levels
on which the Self can be manifested. At each
level, an original unity—shown at the top of
the figure—divides into four parts, each ex-
pressive of an aspect of the original totality.
This allows the different qualities to become
more conscious, but since once separated they
are in conflict with each other, they must be
again brought into unity (at the bottom of the
figure).

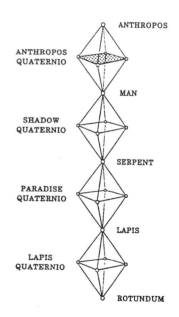

ANTHROPOS

ANTHROPOS
QUATERNIO

MAN

SHADOW
QUATERNIO

SERPENT

PARADISE
QUATERNIO

LAPIS

LAPIS
QUATERNIO

ROTUNDUM

KEY: The Four-Fold *Quaternio*

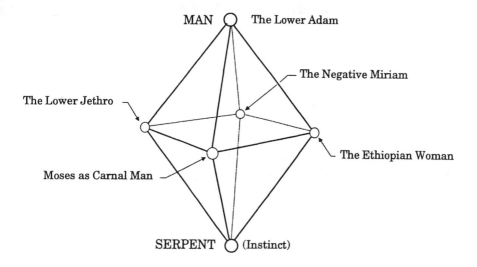

MAN ○ The Lower Adam

— The Negative Miriam

The Lower Jethro

The Ethiopian Woman

Moses as Carnal Man

SERPENT ○ (Instinct)

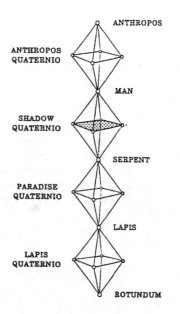

ANTHROPOS

ANTHROPOS
QUATERNIO

MAN

SHADOW
QUATERNIO

SERPENT

PARADISE
QUATERNIO

LAPIS

LAPIS
QUATERNIO

ROTUNDUM

Figure 22. Shadow Quaternio.
The lower Adam represents the ego, which
occupies a mid position between the spiritual
quaternity and the shadow and instinct level.

KEY: The Four-Fold *Quaternio*

23
Paragraphs 366-380

The Structure and Dynamics of the Self (cont.)

Continuing the material on the dark aspects of the Self, which he began by introducing the Shadow Quaternio, Jung takes up a Gnostic image:

> The good, perfect, spiritual God was opposed by an imperfect, vain, ignorant, and incompetent demiurge. There were archontic Powers that gave to mankind a corrupt "chirographum" (handwriting) from which Christ had to redeem them. (par. 366)

In footnote 25, Jung quotes briefly from Colossians. The reference is more understandable given a larger portion of the text. In Colossians 2:10-15 (AV), Paul describes to the members of the congregation their blessed condition, now that they are part of the church:

> And ye are complete in him, which is the head of all principality and power: in whom also ye are circumcised with the circumcision made without hands . . . [you are] buried with him in baptism [that refers to Christ] . . . [and you are also] risen with him through the faith of the operation of God, who hath raised him from the dead. And you, being dead in your sins and the uncircumcision of your flesh, hath he quickened together with him, having forgiven you all trespasses. [He (Christ) has blotted] out the handwriting of ordinances that was against us, which was contrary to us, and took it out of the way, nailing it to his cross; and having spoiled principalities and powers, he made a show of them openly, triumphing over them.

The idea here is that humans have been tainted with the handwriting of the evil archons and Christ redeems them from that negative handwriting. They are redeemed from what are called the "principalities and powers." The word translated as "principalities" is the Greek word *archos*. Another translation of it is "cosmic powers." This handwriting is another example of the "signs of the father" that the serpent brought down, which was discussed in an earlier passage. In this case, however, the handwriting is negative. As the newborn soul descends into incarnation, into its earthly existence, it goes through the planetary spheres. As it goes down, it takes on qualities of the various planetary deities, so that when it arrives on earth it is encumbered with those qualities, with that handwriting, so to speak. Psychologically, this handwriting would refer to our ancestral or archetypal background which has imprinted us with its patterns.

Handwriting also represents one's destiny. An example of that is the handwriting on the wall described during Belshazzar's feast. (Dan. 5:27) Belshazzar desecrated the sacred vessels from the sanctuary by bringing them to his feast and using them for the drinking of wine. Then the handwriting on the wall appeared. No one could read it until Daniel was brought in and determined that it said, "You have been weighed in the balance and found wanting." This was a manifestation of destiny announced from the depths of the unconscious.

Some time ago I came across a short story that had this same theme. The basic image was that a man discovered handwriting appearing on the wall of his clothes closet, but he could not decipher the words. Each day he would check and there would be more words. It became more and more ominous. Eventually it turned out that his wife who was going mad was writing on the wall of the closet, but it is the same archetypal image as that found in the Belshazzar story.

Jung's discussion of the dark aspects of the psyche then turns to the idea of the modern mind's descent into the darkness of matter:

> Modern science has given us an unparalleled knowledge of the "dark" side of matter . . . . and made the very roots of life itself an object of investigation. In this way the human mind has sunk deep into the sublunary world of matter, thus repeating the Gnostic myth of Nous, who, beholding his reflection in the depths below, plunged down and was swallowed in the embrace of Physis. (par. 368)

The Gnostic image of Nous sinking into matter corresponds to the story of the fallen angels as described in the Book of Enoch, an apocryphal work. In this book, at a time just before the flood of Noah:

> It happened after the sons of men had multiplied in those days, that daughters were born to them, elegant and beautiful. And when the angels, the sons of heaven, beheld them, they became enamored of them, saying to each other: Come, let us select for ourselves wives from the progeny of men, and let us beget children. (7:1f.)

The angels fell out of heaven to earth and copulated with human women (who brought forth giants) and taught men the arts and sciences at the same time. They revealed to man the secrets of heaven. As a consequence of this, there arose much godlessness and corruption that brought on the flood. This is the same theme that Jung is referring to, one which is occurring in our own time. I have seen this image of giants generated by fallen angels in modern dreams. In one, an individual walking along the New Jersey Palisades overlooking New York City watches as the city is being invaded by giants, extraterrestrial aliens: "The land has been leveled . . . fireballs were in the sky . . . it was the end of the world . . . A great race of giants had come from outer space."[132] As he watches, the giants scoop people up and eat them. It is the same motif as that described in the Book of Enoch, and that Jung writes about in paragraph 368.

In paragraph 370 Jung returns again to the Shadow Quaternio, saying:

> By "shadow" I mean the inferior personality, the lowest levels of which are indis-

---

132 See my *Creation of Consciousness,* p. 28.

tinguishable from the instinctuality of an animal. This is a view that can be found at a very early date, in the idea of the "excrescent soul" *[prosphues phuche]* of Isidorus.

The Greek term translated as "excrescent soul" derives from the word "prospio" which means "to grow upon" or "to be attached to." The root stem "phaèo," to grow, arises from the same stem as that of the word physis, which is translated as "nature." So the implication is that a certain aspect of the psyche has growths on it, appendages. Jung refers to a quotation from Isidorus, which is to be found in the writings of Clement of Alexandria. A section of that text will illuminate this "excrescent soul":

> The adherents of Basilides are in the habit of calling the passions appendages: saying that these are in essence certain spirits attached to the rational soul, through some original perturbation and confusion; and that, again, other bastard and heterogeneous natures of spirits grow on to them like that of the wolf, the ape, the lion, the goat . . . [These appendages] assimilate the lusts of the soul to the likeness of the animals. . . . Man, according to Basilides, preserves the appearance of a wooden horse, according to the poetic myth, embracing as he does in one body a host of such different spirits.[133]

This idea is very similar to the handwriting symbol, because once again, the newborn soul acquired these appendages or growths upon itself as it descended through the planetary spheres, receiving from each of the planetary archons an appendage of its own nature. Macrobius says about this image:

> By the impulse of the first weight the soul, having started on its downward course from the intersection of the zodiac and the Milky Way [it is on its way down from the upper heaven.] to the successive spheres lying beneath, as it passes through these spheres . . . [it] acquires each of the attributes which it will exercise later. In the sphere of Saturn it obtains reason and understanding, called *logistikon* and *theoretikon;* in Jupiter's sphere, the power to act, called *praktikon;* in Mars' sphere, a bold spirit or *thymikon;* in the sun's sphere, sense-perception and imagination, *aisthetikon* and *phantastikon;* in Venus' sphere, the impulse of passion, *epithymetikon;* in Mercury's sphere, the ability to speak and interpret, *hermeneutikon;* and in the lunar sphere, the function of molding and increasing bodies, *phytikon.*[134]

A poem by Henry Vaughn, "The Importunate Fortune," describes the reverse movement, as the earth-bound soul is cleansing itself of its earthly attachments. It returns upward through the cosmic ladder, giving back all those appendages which the archons had passed on to it on its way down. These are images in which the psyche describes in its own terms, so to speak, the incarnation of the

---

[133] *Stromata,* II, 20, 113, in Roberts and Donaldson, *The Ante-Nicene Fathers,* vol. 2, pp. 371f.
[134] See my *Anatomy of the Psyche,* pp. 134ff.

ego, the way the ego comes into being by appropriating the various archetypal entities. The ego takes fragments of them and incorporates them into its own being, generating that so-called "appendage soul." In the incarnated existence, one lives out of those various archetypal factors unconsciously. Through the individuation process, these archetypal entities with which one has been identified become subject to conscious realization. That process of consciousness separates the ego from its appendages. It corresponds to Vaughn's image of the soul ascending the ladder and handing back to the archontic powers the qualities that had been impressed on it on its way down.[135]

This is quite a beautiful image of psychological development. It is not based on a theory; since it has all arisen through myth, we can understand that the psyche itself is telling us how it undergoes development.

Two quaternios described by Jung have already been examined here, the so-called upper and lower Moses Quaternios. The first was called the Anthropos Quaternio and the second the Shadow Quaternio. The Shadow Quaternio at its lowest term was represented by a serpent. Jung now builds another quaternio below the serpent, which he calls the Paradise Quaternio. It derives from Hippolytus, a quotation discussed previously.[136] Here is the gist of it again:

> [The Gnostics (Naassenes)] assert that Edem is the brain . . . tightly fastened in encircling robes, as if (in) heaven. But they suppose that man, as far as the head only, is Paradise, therefore that "this river which proceeds out of Edem," that is, from the brain, "is divided into four heads, and the name of the first river is called Phison [which refers to the eye] . . . the second river is Gihon . . . [which refers to hearing and the ear]; the third [river] is Tigris [which refers to smelling and the nose]. . . . The fourth river is Euphrates. This they assert, is the mouth through which are the passage outwards of prayer, and the passage inwards of nourishment. [The mouth] makes glad, and nurtures and fashions the Spiritual Perfect Man.[137]

The water of the Euphrates is "the water that is above the firmament," and it is also the water about which Christ was speaking when he said, "If only you knew . . . who it is that is saying to you: 'Give me a drink,' you would have been the one to ask, and he would have given you living water." (John 4:10, JB)

Jung now combines the Moses Quaternio of Gnostic origin with what he calls the Paradise Quaternio, which is pictured in figure 23. In this quaternio the serpent divides into the four rivers of Eden, uniting again in the lapis. Jung comments:

> For the Naassenes Paradise was a quaternity parallel with the Moses quaternio and of similar meaning. Its fourfold nature consisted in the four rivers. . . . The serpent

---

135 This is further discussed in my *Mysterium Lectures,* pp. 154ff.
136 See above, chap. 19, page 139.
137 Roberts and Donaldson, *The Ante-Nicene Fathers,* vol. 5, p. 57.

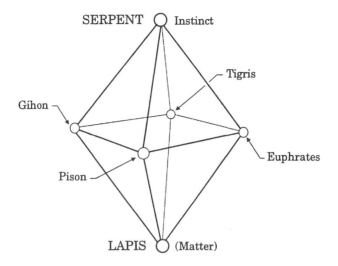

SERPENT ⬭ Instinct

Tigris

Gihon

Pison

Euphrates

LAPIS ⬭ (Matter)

Figure 23. Paradise Quaternio.
The figure represents a third level at which
the Self may manifest. The four rivers
represent the separation of the original
serpent or instinctual level into its components. They reunite as lapis or the original
basic material of the visible world.

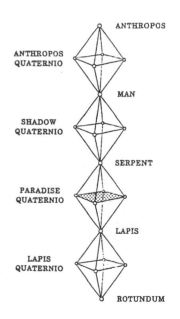

ANTHROPOS

ANTHROPOS
QUATERNIO

MAN

SHADOW
QUATERNIO

SERPENT

PARADISE
QUATERNIO

LAPIS

LAPIS
QUATERNIO

ROTUNDUM

KEY: The Four-Fold *Quaternio*

in Genesis is an illustration of the personified tree-numen. . . . It is the tree's voice, which persuades Eve . . . "to eat of the tree." (par. 372)

The next level is what Jung calls the Lapis Quaternio, pictured in figure 24. This is how Jung moves us from the Paradise to the Lapis Quaternio:

> The snake symbol brings us to the images of Paradise, tree, and earth. This amounts to an evolutionary regression from the animal kingdom back to plants and inorganic nature, epitomized in alchemy by the secret of matter, the *lapis.* (par. 374)

As Jung says, we are involved here with a downward movement from the heavenly anthropos, the upper Moses Quaternio, to the inferior Moses Quaternio, the shadow region, through the serpent, down to the level of nature where the tree and the rivers of the Garden of Eden are manifest—all the way down to brute matter symbolized by rock, just ordinary stone. Here, Jung is talking about the lapis not as the end product of the alchemical opus, but as the *prima materia,* the elemental stony stuff. Jung says that "the lapis was thought of as a unity and therefore often stands for the *prima materia* in general . . . . [representing] a bit of the original chaos." (par. 375)

The alchemical task in dealing with that *prima materia,* that original chaos, was that it had to undergo a *separatio* process. Jung comments:

> In the chaos the elements are not united. . . . They represent . . . an original state of conflict and mutual repulsion. This image serves to illustrate the splitting up or unfolding of the original unity into the multiplicity of the visible world. (par. 375)

This "splitting up" corresponds to the separation of the *prima materia* into the four elements—earth, air, fire and water. In paragraph 376 Jung says, "The constitution of the *lapis* rests on the union of the four elements, which in their turn represent an unfolding of the unknowable inchoate state, or chaos."

So in this lower quaternio, the lapis as the *prima materia* of the alchemical process undergoes differentiation into the Lapis Quaternio (into the four elements). Then those separated elements are reunited into the rotundum. The diagram of the Lapis Quaternio summarizes the alchemical process and also the psychological process. It could also be said that in the Lapis Quaternio there is a sequence of three states: first there is a circle, then a square, then a circle again. The sequence of the original unity (as a circle), followed by the square represented by the four elements, and then by the union of the four elements as an outer circle, is an image of the twofold process of analysis and synthesis, of *separatio* and *coniunctio,* that constitutes the total process of psychological development. Here is a dream that explicitly uses this particular image:

> There are three squares, heating units made of metal coil or neon tubing. They represent my sexual problems. Now they have been disconnected and are being cleaned. There is a new world concept of God, a widening of awareness of the

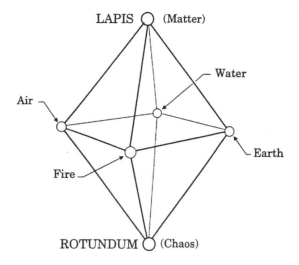

Figure 24. Lapis Quaternio.
The fourth or Lapis Quaternio has at bottom
the unknowable beginning state or chaos, out
of which unfold the four elements, which in
turn unify into the lapis.

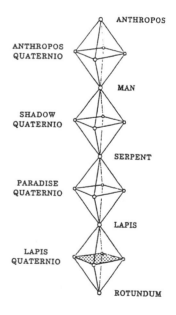

KEY: The Four-Fold *Quaternio*

vastness of the universe. Against the background of eternity a thing as temporal as a sexual problem is inconsequential. The washing is in a sense a ritual washing, a cleansing of the three squares to let them fall into their natural place in the vast overall.

In the dream, my mind played with the visual image of the three squares. It was only natural to draw a circle first inside each, then outside each.[138]

The dream brings up a specific image which describes a state of completion. We start off in a condition of unconscious unity, represented by the first circle. The course of psychological development requires progressive differentiation of that unity, hopefully into four more or less conscious functions. But the functions, as long as they remain separate, are in antagonism with one another. To complete the process, the original unity has to be re-achieved on the level of consciousness, which is represented by the second circle.

Jung's discussion of the lapis leads him to the symbolism of the *vas* or vessel:

This *lapis* symbolism can once more be visualized diagrammatically as a double pyramid. [As can be seen in figure 24, the conclusion of this lapis pyramid is the rotundum.] Zosimos calls the *rotundum* the omega element . . . which probably signifies the head. . . . The *vas* is often synonymous with the *lapis,* so that there is no difference between the vessel and its content. . . . The anonymous author of the scholia to the "Tractatus aureus" also writes about the squaring of the circle and shows a square whose corners are formed by the four elements. In the centre there is a small circle. [It is the same Lapis Quaternio image.] . . . In a later chapter [the author of the scholia] depicts the vessel, "the true philosophical Pelican." (par. 377)

Figure 25 represents this pelican; at first sight it may not seem impressive, but there is a lot condensed in this little diagram. Jung considers the "philosophical pelican" as rather important because he returns to it in *Mysterium Coniunctionis* where he speaks about it at some length.[139] He goes on here to quote the "anonymous author" referred to in paragraph 377 as saying, regarding the pelican image:

A is the inside, as it were the origin and source from which the other letters flow, and likewise the final goal to which all the others flow back, as rivers flow into the ocean or into the great sea. (par. 378)

This pelican image is the same as that of the four rivers of paradise.[140] The head of the four rivers can be seen, and they flow out of eye, ear, nose and mouth, going to make up a mandala—exactly the same as the "philosophical pelican" image which is simply abstracted a little more. In both the four-river and the philosophical pelican images, a fourfold entity flows out of the central

---

[138] See my *Ego and Archetype,* p. 210.
[139] CW 14, pars. 8ff.
[140] See above, chap. 19 and figure 19, page 140.

source, and in effect creates a square. In the pelican the square can be visualized by connecting the letters B, C, D and E with straight lines.

These images are so significant, so worth one's attention and reflection, because they are the elemental images by which the psyche manifests its ground, the nature of its basic unified being. In dreams and in analytic work, one finds infinite variations on this underlying ground plan. This central entity is described as the containing *vas,* the vessel. This brings up the whole complicated vessel symbolism of psychology.

Basically, the vessel represents the vessel of Selfhood in the individual psyche. In ordinary human life, this containing vessel is projected into relationships, into groups, into a church, or into other collective settings. The individual's sense of containment or fulfillment is dependent upon the connection to whatever that collective vessel is. The analytic relationship often serves as an embodiment of that vessel. That is all right as a temporary phenomenon, but it is not permanently satisfactory. Eventually the vessel must somehow find its way back into the individual.

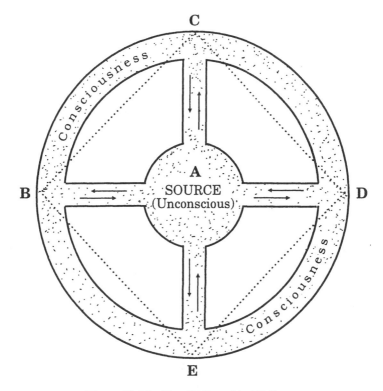

Figure 25. The True Philosophical Pelican.

24
Paragraphs 381-401

The Structure and Dynamics of the Self (cont.)

Chapter 14 of *Aion* continues with the series of quaternity images from the Gnostic texts. We have previously considered four quaternities:

1. The upper Moses or Anthropos Quaternio.
2. The lower Moses or Shadow Quaternio.
3. The Paradise Quaternio involving the four rivers of the Garden of Eden.
4. The Lapis Quaternio, representing the alchemical process whereby the *prima materia* is split into the four elements and then synthesized again into the rotundum.

These four quaternios Jung has elaborated are connected to one another by common images. They fall into a string as indicated in the lower diagram of figure 26. They have as common terms the anthropos, man, the serpent, the lapis and the rotundum. Jung proceeds to turn the chain into a circle by putting the tail of it into the mouth of the first figure. This procedure is reflected in the upper diagram of figure 26, in which the chain of quaternios is turned into a circular or square structure. In doing this, the image of anthropos and rotundum overlap and are considered as the same, so it is now the anthropos/rotundum that starts off the sequence.

Later in the chapter, Jung takes this sequence one step further and turns it into an abstract formula. For the present, let us examine this fourfold quaternio in more detail and see what the various elements represent psychologically.

The four separate entities in the lower drawing of figure 26 represent four different realms or aspects of the psyche, and wholeness can manifest itself in any one of them. When it does, a quaternity pertaining to that realm arises. Certain typical symbolism and imagery is associated with each of these four realms. The anthropos quaternity is associated with spiritual symbolism, the shadow quaternity with animal symbolism (including humans, since we too are animals). The paradise quaternity appears in terms of plant imagery. The lapis quaternity is associated with mineral, inorganic symbolism.

In addition, each of these realms has a triad built into its structure; not only is it a quaternity, but it also contains a triadic or developmental process. So we have a quaternity representing the static aspect of that realm of the psyche, and a triad representing the developmental process whereby that realm unfolds. To summarize briefly each of the four quaternities:

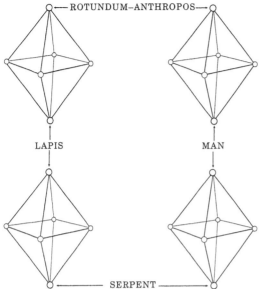

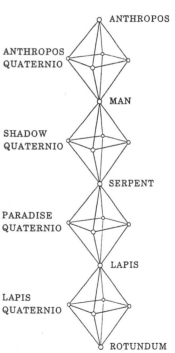

Figure 26. Fourfold Quaternio.
The drawing on the right shows the four
quaternios or aspects of the Self, connected by
their common terms. Descent from the
spiritual level through the chthonic and
vegetative spheres to the level of inorganic
matter results in transformation of an
originally unconscious state into a conscious
one. This is also shown in the figure above,
which pictures the process as a continuous
circle, with the lowest and highest terms, the
beginning and the end states, coinciding.

The anthropos or spiritual quaternity.

The images that represent this aspect of the psyche pertain to the upper regions, the heavens, the celestial, with images of light, so that atmospheric, cosmic phenomena belong here. *Sublimatio* symbolism is particularly at home.[141] An example is Henry Vaughn's poem:

> I saw Eternity the other night
> Like a great Ring of pure and endless light,
> All calm as it was bright,
> And round beneath it, Time in hours, days, years
> Driv'n by the spheres
> Like a vast shadow mov'd, In which the world
> And all her train were hurl'd.[142]

This is a vast picture of heavenly, cosmic imagery with emphasis on light. It is a classic example of the anthropos or spiritual quaternity. Another example would be the vision of the heavenly rose which concludes Dante's *Divine Comedy*. Dante's image is essentially a great rose of light, and another example of the symbolism of the Anthropos Quaternio.

The shadow or animal quaternity.

This represents the lower, dark, carnal realm symbolized by dubious human figures or by animals, including all warm-blooded animals, but also descending on the evolutionary scale to the cold-blooded ones. This realm refers to the chthonic world.

Dreams or images involving dubious human beings or animals in a fourfold or circular structure are examples of this quaternity. A classic example would be the four sons of Horus who were divine guardians buried with the deceased in ancient Egypt. One son had a jackal head, one a falcon head, one a dog head and one a human head. The vision of Ezekiel, which will be discussed later, includes creatures that are very similar symbolically to the four sons of Horus; these creatures each had four faces. One of the faces was that of a lion, one was that of an ox, one was that of an eagle, and one was that of a man. The same symbolism was taken over intact in Christian mandalas involving the four Christian evangelists who are represented as a lion, ox, eagle and man.

Examples of this quaternity can also be found in the dream series in *Psychology and Alchemy*. For instance, in one of the dreams a gibbon is to be reconstructed in a square.[143] In another, animals are being transformed into men, again, in a square.[144]

---

141 See my *Anatomy of the Psyche*, chap. 5.
142 "The World," lines 1-7, in *The Complete Poetry of Henry Vaughn*.
143 CW 12, pars. 164ff.
144 Ibid., par. 183.

The paradise quaternity.

This realm involves vegetable, plant, tree and garden symbolism. It is an image of wholeness set in the plant world. Trees are important in this category. An example is Jung's "Liverpool dream," which had as its central feature a magnolia tree on an island illuminated in perpetual sunshine.[145] In the dream series in *Psychology and Alchemy,* there are dreams of a garden under the sea, of a green plant growing out of a sphere, of a green tree in a circle.[146]

The lapis quaternity.

This involves fourfold structures that are composed of stones, jewels, crystals, or pertain in some way to the inorganic world. A good example is the image of the heavenly Jerusalem found at the end of the Book of Revelation. This heavenly city descends from above, and to the extent that it derives from heaven, it belongs to the anthropos/spiritual quaternity. As it is described, however, it is made up of precious stones:

> [I saw a] great city, the holy Jerusalem, descending . . . and her light was like a stone most precious . . . The wall had twelve gates. The [material of the] wall was jasper, and the city was pure gold, like unto clear glass. The foundations of the wall . . . were garnished with all manner of precious stones [jasper, sapphire, chalcedony, emerald, twelve in all]. (Rev. 21:10-19, AV)

It is a grand image of a fourfold structure made up of inorganic stuff, stone— an example of the lapis quaternity.

These quaternity realms are something to keep in mind, because one encounters dream imagery involving them all the time. Very frequently the quaternities one encounters are not pure at all, but are mixed or overlapping. Indeed, the more differentiated quaternities that have undergone the *circulatio* process will be highly mixed. Each one of these four realms will have an effect on the other. This will be discussed here further in the final chapter, in connection with Jung's abstraction of the quaternios into a formula.

Jung tells us in a letter that this formula is based on Ezekiel's vision.[147] The vision of Ezekiel is the most differentiated expression of the God-image in the entire Old Testament and central to all of Western civilization. Its imagery was picked up in Christian art and mandalas. The same imagery appeared in Jewish mysticism. Gershom Scholem has written about Merkabah mysticism, which means throne or chariot mysticism.[148] Ezekiel's vision is the image of a great throne-chariot. To complete it all, modern depth psychology has taken the same

---

[145] *Memories, Dreams, Reflections,* p. 198.
[146] CW 12, pars. 154, 198, 232.
[147] *Letters,* vol. 2, p. 118.
[148] See *Major Trends in Jewish Mysticism,* pp. 40ff.

image and used it as a foundation for the most differentiated visualization of the Self. This gives some idea of the central importance the Ezekiel vision has for the Western psyche. An abbreviated description of the vision follows. Ezekiel says:

> As I looked, . . . a stormy wind came out of the north, and a great cloud, with . . . fire flashing forth continually . . . . And from the midst of it came the likeness of four living creatures. . . . Each had four faces, and . . . four wings. . . . Under their wings . . . they had human hands. . . . Each had the face of a man in front; . . . the face of a lion on the right side, . . . the face of an ox on the left side, and . . . the face of an eagle at the back. . . . In the midst of the living creatures there was something that looked like burning coals of fire . . . torches moving to and fro . . . .
>
> Now as I looked at the living creatures, I saw a wheel upon the earth beside the living creatures, one for each of the four of them. . . . The appearance [of the wheels] . . . was like the gleaming of a chrysolite . . . . [They could move] in any of their four directions . . . . The four wheels had rims and they had spokes; and their rims were full of eyes . . . And when the living creatures went, the wheels went beside them; and when the living creatures rose from the earth, the wheels rose. . . .
>
> Over the heads of the living creatures there was the likeness of a firmament, shining like crystal . . . . And . . . I heard the sound of their wings like the sound of many waters. . . .
>
> And above the firmament over their heads there was a likeness of a throne . . . like sapphire; [upon it was seated one who had the appearance of a man] . . . . And upward from . . . his loins I saw as it were gleaming bronze . . . and downward from . . . his loins I saw . . . the appearance of fire, and there was brightness round about him. [like the bow which appears in the clouds on a rainy day] Such was the appearance of the likeness of the glory of the Lord. (Ezek. 1: 4-30, RSV)

This is a stupendous vision of the numinosum, highly differentiated into a fourfold quaternity. It is a quaternity of creatures and wheels, but each creature is a subordinate quaternity, just like those in figure 25.

In paragraph 392 of *Aion,* Jung refers to an alchemical picture and then gives in Latin the verses that describe it. Here is an English translation:

> You who imitate the work of nature, must look for four balls
> In which a bright fire is active.
> Let the undermost have reference to Vulcan, let the second show
> Mercury, at the third circle stands Luna:
> The fourth is Apollo, that is also called the fire of nature,
> Let this chain guide your hands in art.

Jung goes on to discuss this symbolism. It refers first of all to the four elements. From above downward, the four elements are earth, water, air and fire and correspond to sun, moon, Mercury and earthly fire, Vulcan. Apollo or sun refers to earth. Careful reading of the text indicates that the grouping is justified and is not arbitrary, though it is surprising.

These four elements are in turn related by Jung to the four states of aggregation of matter: solid, liquid, gas and flame. From the image in the picture we can see that the common denominator of all the elements is fire, in other words, energy. What would this mean psychologically? I understand it to mean that psychic contents are aggregations of psychic energy or libido. This is really no more than saying what modern physics has discovered, that matter and energy are two expressions of the same phenomenon. We now know that matter can be transformed into energy ($E = mc^2$). This image indicates that the same thing applies to the psyche: psychic contents exist by virtue of their energy content.

Also, we can say that their mode of manifestation is determined by the level of the energy's activation. An unconscious content or complex can remain utterly quiescent until it is activated. As long as there is little energy charge, it is earth, so to speak; it is in that most solid of states. But if it is heated up, if it is activated, then it can turn into water or air or fire. This is an idea to reflect upon. Consider that psychic contents are all energy manifestations that appear under different modes, depending on their differing levels of activation.

Jung speaks about the four balls of fire—Apollo, Vulcan, Luna and Mercurius—and says that three of them are straightforward and one is ambivalent; that one is the Mercurius duplex. This is typical imagery in which the three entities are joined by an unusual fourth. Jung says in paragraph 397:

> If we look at this quaternio from the standpoint of the three-dimensionality of space [he is referring to the chart in paragraph 396 on which height, depth, width and time are pictured, in place of Apollo, Vulcan, Luna and Mercurius], then time can be conceived as a fourth dimension. But if we look at it in terms of the three qualities of time—past, present, future—then static space, in which changes of state occur, must be added as a fourth term. In both cases, the fourth represents an incommensurable Other. . . . Thus we measure space by time and time by space.

Jung continues:

> The space-time quaternio is the archetypal *sine qua non* for any apprehension of the physical world—indeed, the very possibility of apprehending it. It is the organizing schema par excellence among the psychic quaternities. (par. 398)

Here Jung is expressing a revolutionary insight which builds a bridge between the psyche and the physical world. It says in effect that our ability to perceive, to function in and relate to the physical world of matter, is an expression of the Self, of the quaternity. It is important to know that this insight is based on an earlier discovery of the philosopher Immanuel Kant, which is vital for an understanding of Jung.

Kant's basic idea is that perception and understanding of the external world are structured according to a priori forms or categories of the mind. When we perceive the external world of objects as we do, laid out in three dimensions of space, and continuous in the sequence we call time, these structures of space and time do not exist in the outer world. They are structures that our mind imposes or projects onto the raw physical sensations in order to make sense out of them. It is the mind that creates the orderly universe of space and time. Kant's discovery was revolutionary for epistemology, the science of knowledge.[149]

In this description of the space-time quaternity, Jung assimilates the Kantian idea to his own discovery of the Self. The implications of this are immense because, for one thing, they reveal that perception of the psyche and perception of the physical world overlap. Each is perceived through the organ of the Self. Jung alludes to something like this in his remark in paragraph 381:

> The quaternity is an organizing schema par excellence, something like the crossed threads in a telescope. It is a system of co-ordinates that is used almost instinctively for dividing up and arranging a chaotic multiplicity, as when we divide up the visible surface of the earth, the course of the year, or a collection of individuals into groups.

What Jung does not specifically state, but what is implied, is that Kant was doing this same thing when he made the discovery that we perceive and order the sensations from the external world by means of the quaternity of the space-time image. This image is one version of the crossed threads in the telescope of our perception.

Jung points out imagery parallel to the joined quaternities from a number of sources, including the Clementine creation myth:

> I would like . . . to mention the peculiar theory of world creation in the Clementine Homilies. In God, pneuma and soma are one. When they separate, pneuma appears as the Son . . . but soma, actual substance *[ousia]* or matter *[ule]* divides into four, corresponding to the four elements. (par. 400)

And out of that, psyche and a number of syzygies or paired opposites appear. Once again, this material is so condensed that it is very difficult to understand. It is elaborated here in figure 27.

This basic image is of some importance to Jung and was mentioned earlier, in paragraph 99. There Jung talked about the Clementine image of God, in which the right hand of God is good and the left hand is evil. Here in paragraph 400, another version of the same image, the unitary God divides into a good son and a bad son. The good son is the right hand, the right arm, so to speak, the pneuma/spirit. The bad son is matter, and this matter further divides into the four elements, out of which then comes the devil. This is just the first pair of opposites. Other opposites which emerge from the unitary God are heaven and earth, day and night, male and female, light and dark, sun and moon, life and death, Adam and Eve. This is quite a close parallel to the Kabbalistic Sefirotic Tree, also an

---

[149] For an introduction to Kant's ideas, see Will Durant, *The Story of Philosophy.*

image of the Deity emanating into a series of opposites.[150]

The Clementine idea is important for Jung because it is an early God-image that explicitly contained the opposites and did not split them apart, even though it was a Christian image expressed in a Christian text. It foreshadowed Jung's conception of the Self as a reconciliation of opposites.

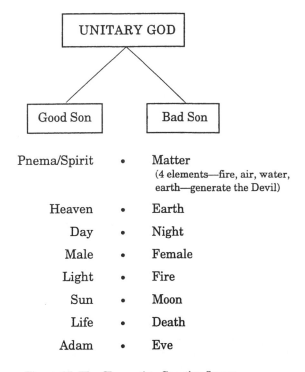

Figure 27. The Clementine Creation Image.
The diagram shows the Clementine creation myth, an early Christian image of God which contained the opposites. At the top of the figure, God unfolds from himself a series of pairs of opposites, starting with the good son or spirit, and the bad son or matter. Matter further divides into the four elements, and their mixing gives rise to the devil. The further paired opposites subsequently also emanate from God.

---

150 See *Mysterium Lectures*, pp. 39ff.

25
Paragraphs 402-429

The Structure and Dynamics of the Self (cont.)

In the last chapter we considered how Jung spoke of the space-time quaternio in two different ways. In one version, the three dimensions of space make up three of the terms and time makes up the fourth. The other way of looking at it was that time has three aspects—past, present and future. The fourth term of the quaternity would be space.

An example of the first version appeared in *The Los Angeles Times* on October 8, 1988. The near-death experience of an English philosopher, Sir Alfred J. Ayer, "a formidable atheist," was discussed in some detail. He told of his experience when for four minutes his heart stopped beating. He said:

> I was confronted by a red light, exceedingly bright and also very painful, even when I turned away from it. I was aware that this light was responsible for the government of the universe. Among its ministers were two creatures who had been put in charge of space. [Charged with seeing that space was kept in working order, the ministers had failed, and space was like a] badly fitting jigsaw puzzle.

Ayer said he recalled feeling that he needed to put aright the suddenly chaotic laws of nature and simultaneously extinguish the painful red light that seemed to be "signaling that space was awry." Remembering that Einstein's general theory of relativity treats space and time as a whole, Ayer said he thought he could cure space by operating upon time. Trying to make contact again with the ministers,

> I hit upon the expedient of walking up and down, waving my watch, in the hope of drawing their attention not to my watch itself, but to the time which it measured. This elicited no response. I became more and more desperate, until the experience suddenly came to an end [and his heart started beating again].

What Ayer encountered in this situation of universal "red alert" was that space was awry, and he realized that what was missing was "the fourth"; this was what he tried to bring to the threefold nature of space: "the fourth"—time. The Ayer story illustrates Jung's idea of the space-time quaternity.

Jung continues here his elaboration of the anthropos, shadow, paradise and lapis quaternio/quaternities. In paragraphs 403 through 407, he speaks of how this sequence manifests in the historical and cultural process of the Christian aeon. He sees the sequence of the four quaternities as corresponding to the historical development of the collective psyche.

The first 500 years, up to 500 A.D., would correspond to the anthropos qua-

186

ternity, the spiritual realm which reflects the collective attitude of that period—pneumatic, spiritual, and not of this world. The period from 500 to 1000 A.D. would correspond to the shadow quaternity, referring to the animal realm, including carnal man. Jung says that this period corresponds to the time when the church became worldly, losing its strictly spiritual approach. It descended, so to speak, into relations with carnal man. (Indeed, some of the Popes themselves did a pretty good job of descending into carnality.)

The years between 1000 and 1500 A.D. would correspond to the paradise quaternity which we have connected with plant symbolism. Jung associates it historically with the emergence and development of alchemy. The period of 1500 to 2000 A.D., Jung associates to the lapis quaternity, referring to the inorganic realm of matter, and to the age of scientific materialism and the deification of matter. Jung's idea is that the whole aeon, so far as the collective psyche is concerned, has been a *circulatio* process through those four quaternities.

In the course of discussing how the fourfold quaternio manifests itself historically, Jung makes an interesting summarizing statement. He says that the modern mind can no longer conceive of a psyche that is oriented exclusively upward, as was the original pneumatic attitude of the church.

> Only through Christ could he [man] actually see this consciousness mediating between God and the world, and by making the person of Christ the object of his devotions he gradually came to acquire Christ's position as mediator. Through the Christ crucified between the two thieves man gradually attained knowledge of his shadow and its duality. This duality had already been anticipated by the double meaning of the serpent. Just as the serpent stands for the power that heals as well as corrupts, so one of the thieves is destined upwards, the other downwards, and so likewise the shadow is on one side regrettable and reprehensible weakness, on the other side healthy instinctivity and the prerequisite for higher consciousness.
>
> Thus the Shadow Quaternio that counterbalances man's position as mediator only falls into place when that position has become sufficiently real for him to feel his consciousness of himself or his own existence more strongly than his dependence on and governance by God. (pars. 402f.)

That statement is packed with import. Jung is referring to the basic idea that the human being exists as a mediator between God and the world. Jung says that this symbolic position was first presented by the image of Christ who was the son of God and descended from above, while at the same time he was incarnated flesh that was man. Thus he served the mediating function between God and the world.

Then Jung expresses the remarkable idea that one becomes that upon which he meditates—man's worship of Christ the mediator functions as a kind of prelude to his assuming that role himself. An additional aspect of this idea is the remark, "Through Christ crucified between two thieves, man gradually attained knowledge of his shadow and its duality." The canonical image of the Crucifixion is that it was actually a triple crucifixion. On either side of Christ a thief was crucified at the same time. One of those thieves, the one on the left, cursed Christ and the other one blessed him. The result was that the one who cursed him descended to hell on his death, and the one who blessed him ascended to heaven. The Crucifixion took place between the opposites and united the two realms heaven and hell by the fact that the two thieves went in different directions. Jung tells us that this image, which was meditated upon in innumerable church services and innumerable artistic representations, had the unconscious effect of preparing us for a conscious knowledge of the shadow and the opposites.

Jung's formula, abstracted from the four joined quaternios, is pictured in paragraph 410, and reproduced here in figure 28. It is an abstract fourfold quaternity which can be thought of either as a static entity or as a circular process of continual clockwise movement running A through D and then repeating itself.

As mentioned previously, this formula is quite similar to the vision of Ezekiel; you will notice in the formula that each of the four quaternities has at each of its four corners representations of itself and of the other three quaternities. This feature corresponds to the vision of Ezekiel in which each of the four living creatures had four faces—an angel, an ox, a lion, and an eagle. But there is a difference between this formula and the Ezekiel vision, because in the vision each creature has a wheel beside it, just as in the formula each quaternity has a letter beside it—but in the vision the wheels are all the same, whereas in the formula the letters are different. So the formula has achieved a higher level of differentiation than that achieved by the vision.

Figure 28 also shows an example of how this formula works and can be applied and imagined in operation. Let us say for example that the four terms—A, B, C, D—refer to the four elements: A = fire, B = air, C = water, D = earth.

Starting at the top, fire undergoes a fourfold differentiation with the original fire dividing into four different kinds of fire, corresponding to the alchemical image of four kinds of fire. (par. 393) Then the process moves on to the next entity, B (air), which undergoes differentiation into four kinds of air. We have the same sequence for water, C, and earth, D.

One could go through this same sequence with the four psychological functions represented as A, B, C and D. Say that A is intuition, B is thinking, C is feeling, D is sensation. Each of the functions would go through a fourfold differentiation in the course of this whole process of *circulatio*. The implication of Jung's formula is that something like this unfolding differentiation does happen in the process of individuation. Jung summarizes this more succinctly in paragraph 410, speaking of the rotation of the mandala:

> When psychic contents are split up into four aspects, it means that they have been subjected to discrimination by the four orienting functions of consciousness. Only

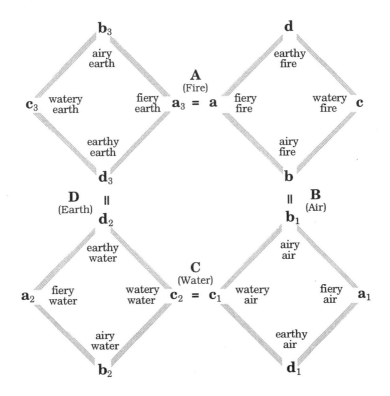

Figure 28. Formula of the Self.
Jung's abstraction of the fourfold quaternity into a general formula is shown here.
An example of the application of this formula to the differentiation of the four
elements is indicated by the terms in parentheses. Moving clockwise from A
through D, aspects of each element are separated.

the production of these four aspects makes a total description possible. The process depicted by our formula changes the originally unconscious totality into a conscious one. The Anthropos A descends from above through his Shadow B into Physis C (= serpent), and, through a kind of crystallization process D (= *lapis)* that reduces chaos to order, rises again to the original state, which in the meantime has been transformed from an unconscious into a conscious one. Consciousness and understanding arise from discrimination.

Jung then presents us with some parallels to this 16-term formula. We are dealing with the symbolism of the number 16, here—four quaternities. For example, let us consider the table with four columns and four rows in paragraph 414, reproduced here as figure 29.

The first column refers to aspects of the alchemical work. The second column refers to the four elements. Each of these four types of alchemical work is associated with one of the elements: water, earth, air and fire. The third column refers to ideas behind these four operations. The fourth column refers to the psychological entities which apply to the four aspects of the alchemical work. The fourth term in this column, the sixteenth in the sequence, is the mysterious one, the ambiguous one, just like the fourth term of a sequence of four. It is the mystery, the goal of all the previous ones. It is the mystery that can't really be named. It is called the "arcanum."

Jung presents the 16-fold schema in a little more detail in *Psychology and Alchemy,*[151] but even there it takes some work to figure out exactly what he means. He presents it here as an example of a 16-fold sequence, as an analogy to the 16-term series of quaternities. In paragraph 416 he also brings in a second parallel, Kircher's quaternity system. He explains Kircher's idea that there are four different levels which are associated with the numbers 1, 10, 100, 1000 and they are analogous to the four quaternities. Kircher identifies number one as corresponding to God, the root of all things; number two as 10, the duality, the spiritual world; number three, 100, the realm of soul and intelligence; number four, 1000, the realm of body and all concrete things.

Here again one sees the same kind of sequence from above downward, which Jung applied to the fourfold quaternity, going from the spiritual realm of the anthropos quaternity down to brute matter in the lapis quaternity. Jung is trying to demonstrate, through these parallels, that the psyche has a tendency to generate fourfold quaternities.

Finally, I want to consider the theme of the aeon of Aquarius. With this theme, I have just left the book *Aion,* because Jung does not mention the aeon of Aquarius. I am mentioning it as a logical consequence of everything that has gone before. Let us return to the frontispiece of *Aion,* where we started. It will be

---

[151] CW 12, pars. 366ff.

4 Levels of the Alchemical Work	Elements Related to the 4 Levels	Concepts Related to the 4 Levels	Psychological Aspects of the 4 Levels
Work on natural things	Water	Ideas about composites or natural things	Sense perception
Work to discriminate the parts of natural things	Earth	Ideas about discriminated things	Intellectual discrimination
Work to discriminate the soul from nature	Air	Concepts of "simple things" (such as Platonic ideas)	Reason
Work by the intellect on nature	Fire	Concepts about simplest things; ether, the quintessence	Arcanum

Figure 29. 16-Term Diagram of Alchemical Processes.
This further example of a 16-fold schema is based on an alchemical text. It shows
parallels between four levels of the alchemical work (first column), the metaphori-
cal images of the four elements (second column), basic concepts used in the work
(third column), and psychological factors (fourth column).

recalled that this is a picture of the Mithraic god Aion, a human figure, winged, with a lion's head, encircled by a great serpent. This image also comes up in Jung's experience of confrontation with the unconscious. It is not in *Memories, Dreams, Reflections* but is to be found in the 1925 seminar account which *Memories* reproduces only partially. Jung describes his encounter with Elijah and Salome and his descent to the unconscious. He met Salome and Elijah and there was also a serpent with them.

> Then a most disagreeable thing happened. Salome became very interested in me, and she assumed that I could cure her blindness. She began to worship me. I said, "Why do you worship me?" She replied, "You are Christ." In spite of my objections she maintained this. I said, "This is madness," and became filled with skeptical resistance. Then I saw the snake approach me. She came close and began to encircle me and press me in her coils. The coils reached up to my heart. I realized as I struggled that I had assumed the attitude of the Crucifixion. In the agony and the struggle, I sweated so profusely that the water flowed down on all sides of me. Then Salome rose, and she could see. While the snake was pressing me, I felt that my face had taken on the face of an animal of prey, a lion or a tiger.[152]

This parallels the image of Aion. Now what does this vision mean? I think that one of the things it means is that Jung is the first representative of the new aeon, and it was his experience to go through the initiation of being identified with the god Aion. Jung is the new Aion, he is the harbinger of the new aeon— what I call and what I think will in the future be called the Jungian aeon. Jung could not have perceived and summarized the content of the aeon of Pisces unless he was already outside it. You cannot see something in its totality, objectively, until you are already out of it. Jung was already in the next aeon, so to speak. Just as Christ was the first person to enter the aeon of Pisces, so Jung is the first to inaugurate the aeon of Aquarius.

This leads us to inquire, at least briefly, what the qualities of the aeon of Aquarius might be; we have been talking about the aeon of Pisces until now.

The term "Aquarius" has three different interpretations that I know of. It is called "water man," "water carrier" and "water pourer." Aquarius is pictured as a human figure carrying a jug of water. Sometimes he is pouring water from the jug and sometimes he is just carrying it. This suggests three different things. First, Aquarius is a human figure, not an animal or fish, suggesting that the aeon of Aquarius is going to be of a human nature, not less. Further, the figure is carrying water rather than being immersed in it like a fish. That suggests that the two aeons will have a totally different relation to the psyche; it is the difference between being a fish immersed and being a carrier and pourer. Third, we have the image of a vessel, an allusion to the symbolism of the alchemical vessel and

---

152 *Analytical Psychology, Notes of the Seminar Given in 1925 by C. G. Jung*, p. 96.

to the capacity to contain the psyche, rather than be contained by it. Instead of being a fish contained in a psychic fish pond, the individual becomes a conscious carrier and dispenser of the psyche.

Both Mark and Luke recount that Christ directed two of his disciples to make preparations for the last supper. He said "Go into the city and you will meet a man carrying a pitcher of water. Follow him." (Mark 14:13; Luke 22:10, JB)

This man leads the disciples to the house in which they are to go to the upper room for the Passover meal or last supper.[153] This is an image of the aeon to come 2,000 years later, visible even at the opening of the aeon of Pisces. It corresponds also to certain symbolic aspects of Christ. Christ was pictured as a water bearer and water dispenser. To the Samaritan woman at the well he said that if she had asked him for a drink, he would have dispensed eternal living water for her. (John 4:10)

Also there is the image of a stream of water flowing from Christ's belly when his side was pierced at the Crucifixion. These images indicate that in a certain sense Christ foreshadowed Aquarius as a water dispenser. But the water he dispensed did not generate more dispensers; it generated fishes rather than water carriers because the church became the water carrier, the fish pond in which the faithful fish could swim. Who discovered water? We know who did not discover it—the fish. We can now say the person who discovered it was Aquarius. Jung discovered water.

If my reading of the symbolism is correct, the aeon of Aquarius will generate individual water carriers. The numinous reality of the psyche will no longer be carried by religious communities—the church, the synagogue or the mosque—but instead it will be carried by conscious individuals. This is the idea Jung puts forward in his notion of a continuing incarnation, the idea that individuals are to become incarnating vessels of the Holy Spirit on an ongoing basis. He developed this idea more fully in the next work he wrote, "Answer to Job." But that is another story.

---

153 I am grateful to Steve Galipeau for drawing my attention to this passage.

Text Corrections and Additions to *Aion*

In paragraph 40, the last sentence on page 20 should read "The more civilized, the more conscious and complicated a man is."

In paragraph 43 on page 23, fifth line, regarding the interpretation of the phrase "to the extent": the original German word is *insofern,* which can probably best be translated within the context as "inasmuch as." That term, as it is used, implies "since."

In paragraph 48 at the top of page 26, the line should read "those who get their decision from an external authority . . ."

On page 27, paragraph 51, the phrase "Eros, dear Socrates, is a mighty daemon," is from Plato's *Symposium,* Sec. 202E.

In paragraph 73 on page 41, the 2nd line from the top: I would suggest, to improve the comprehension of the sentence starting "But it proves harmful . . . ," inserting in parentheses "(the split) proves harmful . . . ."

In paragraph 91 on page 51, the word "appetible" in the fourth line of the quote, is not in general use, but means something that excites the appetites, but is desirable.

In paragraph 98, page 54, near the end of the paragraph, the 1959 edition of *Aion* reads, "The *privatio boni* may therefore be a psychological truth." This was corrected, in the 1968 edition, to, "The *privatio boni* may therefore be a metaphysical truth."

On page 56, note 51 is a reference to *The Pseudo-Clementine Homilies.* The reference is in Roberts and Donaldson, *The Ante-Nicene Fathers,* vol. 8, pp. 339f.

In note 52, the reference in *The Ante-Nicene Fathers* is also in vol. 8, p. 334.

In note 54, p. 57, there is an error; the chapter referenced should be VIII, not VII. Note 54 is referenced in *The Ante-Nicene Fathers,* vol. 8, p. 341.

On page 112 in paragraph 174, note 38, the quote should read: "Like a fish which darts at a baited hook, and does not only lay hold of the bait . . ."

On page 112 in paragraph 174, fourth line from the end, "Tobit" should be replaced by "Tobias."

On page 129 in paragraph 198, *alles Vergängliche is nur ein Gleichnis,* a quotation from the last few lines of *Faust,* part two, means "Everything transitory is but a parable."

On page 139, two lines from the end of paragraph 215, the word "Chronos" should here be spelled "Cronos," because it is not time but Saturn being referred to.

On page 139, note 60, in the English version of Ruland's *Lexicon,* the correct page reference is 128, not 203.

On page 139, in note 67, the *Elenchos* reference should be V, 11.

On page 144, note 81, the origin of the saying referred to is now known to be from The Gospel of Thomas, saying number three, in the Nag Hammadi Library.

Bibliography

For details of alchemical texts cited, see the bibliography in *Aion*

Aeschylus. *Agamemnon.* Trans. H. Weir Smyth. *Aeschylus.* Vol. 2. Loeb Classical Library. Cambridge: Harvard University Press, 1983.

———. *Seven Against Thebes.* Trans. David Grene. *The Complete Greek Tragedies.* Vol. 1. Ed. David Grene and Richmond Lattimore. Chicago: University of Chicago Press, 1959.

Alighieri, Dante Gabriel. *The Divine Comedy.* Trans. Lawrence Grant White. New York: Pantheon Books, 1948.

Augustine, Aurelius. *The City of God.* In *The Works of Aurelius Augustine, Bishop of Hippo.* Vol. 2. Trans. and ed. Marcus Dodds. Edinburgh: T.T. Clark, 1934.

Benedict of Nursia, St. *The Rule of Saint Benedict.* Ed. and trans. Abbot Justin McCann. London: Burns Oates and Washbourne Ltd., 1952.

Budge, E.A. Wallis. *The Book of the Dead.* New York: Dover Publications Inc., 1967.

Burtt, E. A., ed. *The Teachings of the Compassionate Buddha.* New York: Mentor Books, 1955.

Cumont, Franz. *The Mysteries of Mithra.* New York: Dover Publications, Inc. 1956.

Durant, Will. *The Story of Philosophy.* New York: Simon and Schuster, 1953.

Durant, Will and Durant, Ariel . *The Age of Louis XIV.* New York: Simon and Schuster, 1963.

———. *The Age of Napoleon.* New York: Simon and Schuster, 1975.

Edinger, Edward F. *Anatomy of the Psyche: Alchemical Symbolism in Psychotherapy.* La Salle, IL: Open Court, 1985.

———. *The Christian Archetype: A Jungian Commentary on the Life of Christ.* Toronto: Inner City Books, 1987.

———. *The Creation of Consciousness: Jung's Myth for Modern Man.* Toronto: Inner City Books, 1984.

———. *Ego and Archetype: Individuation and the Religious Function of the Psyche.* Boston: Shambhala Publications, 1992.

———. *The Living Psyche: A Jungian Analysis in Pictures.* Wilmette, IL: Chiron Publications, 1990.

———. *The Mysterium Lectures: A Journey through C.G. Jung's Mysterium Coniunctionis.* Toronto: Inner City Books, 1995.

Eliot, T.S. *Four Quartets.* New York: Harcourt, Brace and Company, 1943.

Evans, R. *Jung on Elementary Psychology.* New York: E.P. Dutton and Co., Inc., 1976.

Goodenough, Erwin R. *Jewish Symbols in the Greco-Roman Period.* Vol. 5. New York: Bollingen Foundation, 1956.

Harrison, Jane. *Prolegomena to the Study of Greek Religion.* New York: Meridian Books, 1957.

Harter, Jim, ed. *Animals: Illustrations of Mammals, Birds, Fish, Insects, etc.* Orig. ed. 1419. New York: Dover Publications, Inc., 1979.

Heidel, Alexander. *The Babylonian Genesis.* Chicago: University of Chicago Press, 1963.

Hennecke, Edgar. *New Testament Apocrypha.* Ed. Wilhelm Schneemelcher. Philadelphia: The Westminster Press, 1963.

Homer. *The Iliad.* Vol. 2. Trans. A.T. Murray. Loeb Classical Library. Cambridge: Harvard University Press, 1960.

————. *The Odyssey.* Vol. 1. Trans. A.T. Murray. Loeb Classical Library. Cambridge: Harvard University Press, 1984.

James, William. *Pragmatism.* New York: Longman's, Green and Co., 1909.

Jonas, Hans. *The Gnostic Religion.* Boston: Beacon Press, 1963.

Jung, C.G. *Analytical Psychology, Notes of the Seminar Given in 1925* (Bollingen Series XCIX). Ed. William McGuire. Princeton: Princeton University Press, 1989.

————. *The Collected Works* (Bollingen Series XX). 20 vols. Trans. R.F.C. Hull. Ed. H. Read, M. Fordham, G. Adler, Wm. McGuire. Princeton: Princeton University Press, 1953-1979.

————. *Letters* (Bollingen Series XCV). 2 vols. Trans. R.F.C. Hull. Ed. G. Adler, A. Jaffé. Princeton: Princeton University Press, 1973.

————. *Memories, Dreams, Reflections.* Ed. A. Jaffé. New York: Random House, 1963.

————. *Nietzsche's Zarathustra.* Ed. J.L. Jarrett. Princeton: Princeton University Press, 1988.

Jung, C.G. and Wolfgang Pauli. *The Interpretation of Nature and the Psyche.* New York: Pantheon Books, 1955.

Leoni, Edgar. *Nostradamus and His Prophecies.* New York: Bell Publishing Co., 1982.

Mead, G.R.S., trans. *Pistis Sophia.* London: John W. Watkins, 1947.

Ostrowski-Sachs, Margaret. *From Conversations with C. G. Jung.* Zürich: Juris Druck and Verlag, 1971.

Patai, Raphael. *The Messiah Texts.* Detroit: Wayne State University Press, 1979.

Plato. *Phaedo.* Trans. Hugh Tredennick. In *Plato, Selected Dialogues.* Ed. Edith Hamilton and Huntington Cairns. New York: Bollingen Foundation, 1963.

————. *Timaeus.* Trans. Benjamin Jowett. In *The Dialogues of Plato.* Vol. 2. New York: Random House, 1920.

Plotinus. *Plotinus.* Trans. and ed. A.H. Armstrong. New York: Collier Books, 1962.

Prabhavananda, Swami and Manchester, Frederick, trans. *The Upanishads.* Hollywood, CA: The Vedanta Press, 1983.

Roberts, Alexander and Donaldson, James, eds. *The Ante-Nicene Fathers.* Grand Rapids, MI: William B. Erdmans Publishing Co., 1986.

Ruland, Martin. *A Lexicon of Alchemy*. Trans. A.E. Waite. York Beach, Maine: Samuel Weiser Inc., 1984.

Scholem, Gershom. *Major Trends in Jewish Mysticism*. New York: Schocken Books, 1941.

Schopenhauer, Arthur. *The World as Will and Representation*. Trans. E.F.J. Payne. Indian Hills, CO: The Falcon's Wing Press, 1958.

Thompson, John, ed. *The Book of Enoch*. Trans. Richard Laurence. Thousand Oaks, CA: Artisan Sales, 1980.

Untermeyer, Louis, ed. *Modern American Poetry and Modern British Poetry*. New York: Harcourt, Brace and Company, 1936.

Vaughn, Henry. *The Complete Poetry of Henry Vaughn*. Ed. Freuch Fogle. New York: Doubleday, 1964.

von Franz, Marie-Louise. *Alchemical Active Imagination*. Irving, TX: Spring Publications Inc., 1979.

_____. *The Passion of Perpetua*. Irving, TX: Spring Publications, Inc., 1980.

Waite, A.E., ed. *The Hermetic Museum*. New York: Samuel Weiser Inc., 1974.

Ward, Charles A. *Oracles of Nostradamus*. New York: Random House, Modern Library, 1940.

Index

Authors' works appear under authors' names; Books of the Bible by name;
page numbers in *italics* refer to illustrations